IN AND AROUND
RECORD REPOSITORIES
IN
GREAT BRITAIN
AND IRELAND

Compiled by

Rosemary Church & Jean Cole

Edited by

Avril Cross

Published by

Family Tree Magazine

Second edition 1990.

Published by
Family Tree Magazine
J M Armstrong Publishing
141 Great Whyte
Ramsey
Huntingdon
Cambridgeshire
PE17 1HP
England

First published as *In and Around Record Offices in Great Britain & Ireland* by the Wiltshire Family History Society 1987.

Also by Jean Cole
Tracing Your Family History,
3rd Edition, published by *Family Tree Magazine* 1988

Tracing Your Family Tree (with Michael Armstrong)
Published by Equation 1988

Bid Time Return, a family history play and video (with Beryl Hurley) published by Wiltshire Family History Society 1987.

ISBN 0 9511465 4 8

This book is dedicated to David Church and Reg Cole

Preface

This is a detailed guide to the procedures and facilities of over 200 repositories which hold archives and local history collections. It is hoped that it will be of great value to family, local and other historians in their research.

Our most grateful thanks go to all the archivists and librarians who took the time to complete our questionnaire, and we hope the book will prove to be of assistance to them in their work.

Explanatory Notes

County Record Offices all have similar archives and so we have tried to draw your attention to some of those which may not be generally known. We would suggest that before contemplating research at any repository the user of this book should write for relevant publications, always including a stamped, addressed envelope; self addressed, stamped envelope or International Reply Coupons (otherwise there will be no reply, as funds are very limited).

Opening hours: All repositories close on the country's Public Bank Holidays, often with additional closures.

Children: Archives are irreplaceable and therefore researchers are advised to leave babies, young children and pets at home, as they are not welcomed in repositories.

Disabled: For disabled researchers amenities are varied, depending on the type of building. It is advisable always to write or telephone in advance.

Document Ordering: Some researchers may wish to order records in advance of a visit, so this section indicates whether this is possible, as well as general information on the ordering procedure when at the record repository.

Postal Research: Where no specific charge is made, requests should be kept to a minimum. If photocopies are supplied, cost must be covered as well as postage. In some cases where repositories have a donation box or fund, gifts are always appreciated. Local history libraries welcome any items of local interest for their collections.

Places of Interest: In this section we have tried to include those of particular relevance to family and local historians.

Tourist Offices have been included, as they supply lists of hotels and detailed leaflets on places of local interest.

Identification: Most repositories require identification containing a name and address (other than the reader's ticket) ie driving licence, passport, pension book etc.

Nonconformist, original and copied registers, are at the Public Record Office, Chancery Lane, London, or at County Record Offices.

The guide is **indexed** under countries, counties and places with London Boroughs having a separate index.

We have not included the **Church of Jesus Christ of Latter-day Saints'** (known as "Mormons") Family History Centres. For further information contact The Family History Centre, 64/68 Exhibition Road, South Kensington, London SW7 2PA, Tel 01 589 8561 (from May 1990: 071 589 8561).

For further information about **family history** contact The Administrator of the Federation of Family History Societies, c/o The Benson Room, Birmingham & Midland Institute, Margaret Street, Birmingham B3 3BS

For further information on **local history** contact the British Association for Local History, Phillimore & Co, Shopwyke Hall, Chichester, West Sussex and/or *Local History Magazine*, 3 Devonshire Promenade, Lenton, Nottingham NG7 2DS.

Further Reading

Gibson Guides published by J S W Gibson FSA, FRHistS, FSG, Harts Cottage, Church Hanborough, Oxford OX7 2AB, eg *Record Offices: How to Find Them* plus many other guides of great interest.

You and Your Record Office a free leaflet published by the Association of County Archivists in conjunction with the Federation of Family History Societies.

British Archives: A Guide to Archive Resources in the United Kingdom by Janet Foster and Julia Sheppard (Macmillan 1989).

Genealogical Resources in English Repositories by Joy Wade Moulton (Hampton House, Columbus, Ohio, USA, 1988) obtainable from the Society of Genealogists, 14 Charterhouse Buildings, Goswell Road, London EC1M 7BA.

District Register Offices in England and Wales (East Yorkshire Family History Society).

All the above can be obtained from the *Family Tree Magazine* postal book service, 141 Great Whyte, Ramsey, Huntingdon, Cambs PE17 1HP England, as can details of subscription to the publication.

Terms and Abbreviations

BMD: Births, marriages, deaths
BTs: Bishops' Transcripts
CARN: County Archive Research Network - reader's ticket
CRO: County Record Office
Disabled friendly: Wheelchair access, toilet and assistance
DIY: Do it yourself
IRC: International reply coupons

Minutes: Approximate number of minutes' walk from repository
MIs: Monumental inscriptions
Mss: Manuscripts
NB: *Nota bene* (note well)
O/S: Ordnance Survey maps
PRO: Public Record Office
PRs: Parish registers
Pub: Public House selling food and drink
RO: Record Office
SAE: Stamped addressed envelope
SASE: Self addressed stamped envelope
Ts: Transcripts

ENGLAND

Avon
Bedfordshire
Berkshire
Buckinghamshire
Cambridgeshire
Cheshire
Cleveland
Cornwall
Cumbria
Derbyshire
Devon
Dorset
Durham
Essex
Gloucestershire
Greater Manchester
Hampshire
Hereford and Worcester
Hertfordshire
Humberside
Isle of Wight
Kent
Lancashire
Leicestershire
Lincolnshire
London (central and outer)

Merseyside
Middlesex
Norfolk
Northamptonshire
Northumberland
Nottinghamshire
Oxfordshire
Shropshire
Somerset
Staffordshire
Suffolk
Surrey
Sussex
Tyne and Wear
Warwickshire
West Midlands
Wiltshire
Worcestershire
Yorkshire (North)
Yorkshire (South)
Yorkshire (West)

Isle of Man

IRELAND

Northern (Belfast)
Republic (Dublin)

SCOTLAND

Borders
Central Region
Dumfries and Galloway
Fife
Grampian
Highland
Lothian
Orkney Islands
Shetland Islands
Strathclyde
Tayside

WALES

Clwyd
Dyfed
Glamorgan
Gwent
Gwynedd
Powys

CHANNEL ISLANDS

Guernsey
Jersey

AVON

BATH City Record Office
Guildhall
High Street
Bath BA1 5AW
Telephone: (0225) 461111 Ext 2421

Opening Hours: Mondays to Thursdays 9 am to 1 pm and 2 pm to 5 pm, Fridays 9 am to 1 pm and 2 pm to 4.30 pm. Annual closures: public holidays.
Car Parking: None
Children: No specific ruling.
Disabled: Wheelchair access, lift.
Appointments System: Prior booking for seats unnecessary. Signing in by register. Ten seats.
Document Ordering: Prior orders accepted by letter or telephone. Catalogue numbers unnecessary. Unlimited number at a time. Delivery a few minutes. Photocopying by staff on same day. No facilities for typing or taping. Cameras permitted.
Records: Ts of PRs on open shelves, Bath City records.
Postal Research: Limited, no charge.
Facilities: Toilets, telephone, no refreshments. Cafe/pub two minutes. Shops two minutes (including bookshop with local history publications).
Publications: City maps
Other Repositories: Bath Reference Library, Queen Square, Bath (local history collection); Fashion Research Centre, 4 The Circus (by appointment).
Places of Interest: The Huntingdon Centre (the Countess of Huntingdon's Connexion), Bath Industrial Heritage Centre, Roman Museum, Baths, Pumproom, Abbey, Burrows Toy Museum, Carriage Museum, American Museum in England, Claverton, the Museum of Costume (closed for two years from January 1989).
Tourist Office: Abbey Churchyard, Bath, Avon BA1 1LY. Tel 0225 462831.
Remarks: Historical city map on display.

BRISTOL Record Office
Council House
College Green
Bristol BS1 5TR
Telephone: (0272) 222000 Ext 442 or (0272) 222377

Opening Hours: Mondays to Thursdays 9.30 am to 4.45 pm, Fridays 9.30 am to 4.15 pm, first two Saturdays in each month 9 am to 12 noon. Annual closure: public holiday and last two weeks in January.
Car Parking: Nearby.
Children: Accompanied: no specific ruling. Unaccompanied: fourteen years plus.
Disabled: Use staff entrance and lift at back of building.
Appointments System: Prior booking for seats essential, at least one week. Signing in by register. Ten seats. Two film viewers.
Document Ordering: Prior ordering accepted by letter or telephone for three items only, otherwise unlimited number at a time. Catalogue numbers unnecessary. Delivery approximately 15 minutes. Ordering times: not between 12 noon and 1.30 pm; last orders before 3.30 pm. Photocopying by staff on same day, if large quantity or busy then sent by post; BTs allowed. No facilities for typing/taping. Cameras permitted.
Records: Some Ts of PRs on open shelves. Original PRs on fiche/film. Mainly original PRs. Diocesan archive repository for Bristol. Roman Catholic registers (in process of being filmed).
Postal Research: Charge made.
Facilities: Toilets and public telephone on premises, but no refreshments. Cafe/pub two to five minutes. Shops ten minutes (including bookshop with local history publications).
Publications: Bristol Record Society publications, Bristol Historical Association publications, handlists, information leaflets, maps, postcards, and free leaflets on the Bristol RO.
Other Repositories: Central Library, Deanery Road, Bristol BS1 5TL; University of Bristol, Queens Road, Bristol 1.
Places of Interest: Historic seaport, 12th century cathedral, Corn Exchange, St Mary Redcliffe, Clifton Suspension Bridge, Christmas Steps, Wesley's Chapel, Cabot House, Maritime Heritage Centre, Bristol Industrial Museum.
Tourist Office: Colston House, Colston Street, Bristol BS1. Tel 0272 293891. 14 Narrow Quay, Bristol, Avon BS1. Tel 0272 260767.
Remarks: Solicitors, Land Tax and hospital records require two to three days' prior notice. Bags not allowed. Storage facilities available. Donations box. Historical county map on display. On entry to Council House an identification slip is given by security staff, this must be produced to them on leaving. Researchers are escorted whilst in the building. Some Bristol Diocesan archives are at the Wilts RO.

BEDFORDSHIRE

BEDFORDSHIRE Record Office
County Hall
Cauldwell Street
Bedford MK42 9AP
Telephone: (0234) 228833 or 63222 Ext 2833

Opening Hours: Mondays to Fridays 9 am to 1 pm and 2 pm to 5 pm. Annual closure: public holidays.
Car Parking: Limited.
Children: No specific ruling for accompanied but preferably in older age group. Unaccompanied twelve years plus.
Disabled: Disabled friendly.
Appointments System: Prior booking for seats and viewers unnecessary. Signing in by register plus identification. More than 20 seats, five viewers and seven fiche.
Document Ordering: Prior ordering unnecessary. Four at a time. Delivery approximately five minutes. Photocopying by staff on same day. Typing/taping and cameras permitted.
Records: Ts of PRs/BTs on open shelves. Post 1813 PRs on fiche/film. Original PRs. Diocesan archive repository for Lincoln and Ely.
Postal Research: Up to two hours maximum, charge made.
Facilities: Toilets. No public telephone. Refreshments and drink vending machine plus room for own food. Cafe/pub five minutes. Shops ten minutes plus bookshop with local history publications.
Publications: County maps, publications list, various family history books, photographs, slides, Bedford PR series.
Other Repositories: Bedford Borough Records, Bedford Muniment Room, Town Hall, Bedford MK40 1SJ. Tel 0234 67422.
Places of Interest: Woburn Abbey fourteen miles. Bedford has many associations with Bunyan: the Bunyan Meeting Library and Museum, Georgian houses, museum, Elstow Moot Hall (at Elstow).
Tourist Office: 10 St Paul's Square, Bedford MK40 1SL. Tel 0234 215226.
Remarks: Bags not allowed. Storage facilities available. Donations box. Historical county map on display.

BERKSHIRE

BERKSHIRE Record Office
Shire Hall
Shinfield Park
Reading RG2 9XD
Telephone: (0734) 875444 Ext 3182

Opening Hours: Tuesday and Wednesday 9 am to 5 pm, Thursday 9 am to 9 pm, Friday 9 am to 4.30 pm (closed Mondays). Special arrangements over public holiday period. Annual closure: public holidays and two weeks late October/early November.
Car Parking: Yes
Children: Accompanied: six years plus. Unaccompanied: twelve years plus.
Disabled: Wheelchair access, some steps.
Appointments System: Prior booking for seats by letter only - two to three days minimum, one week if possible. Signing in by register plus CARN. Sixteen seats and fourteen fiche/film viewers.
Document Ordering: Prior ordering accepted by letter. Catalogue numbers necessary. Six at a time issued individually. Delivery ten to fifteen minutes. Ordering times 9.30 am, 10.15 am, 11 am, 11.45 am, 12.30 pm, 2 pm, 2.45 pm, 3.30 pm, 4.15 pm. Thursday only: 5 pm and on demand thereafter. Photocopying by staff and sent by post, PRs off fiche. No facilities for typing or taping. Cameras by special arrangement, fee required.
Records: Ts of PRs/BTs on open shelves. Original PRs on fiche/film. Diocesan archive repository for Archdeaconry of Berkshire.
Postal Research: Limited, charge made.
Facilities: Toilets and public telephone on premises. Refreshments plus room for own food; drink vending machine. Shop on premises.
Publications: County map, handlist of PRs, *Finding your Family.* Free: *Notes for Family Historians, Notes for Intending Visitors.*
Other Repositories: Reading Central Library, Blagrave Street, Reading (local studies collection).
Places of Interest: Museum of Rural Life; Reading Museum; National Dairy Museum, Wellington County Park, Riseley; Blake's Lock Museum; REME Museum, Arborfield.
Tourist Office: Civic Offices, Civic Centre, Reading RG1 7TD. Telephone (0734) 592388/575911.
Remarks: Bags not allowed, storage facilities available. Historical county map on display. For area Roman Catholic registers contact Diocesan Archivist, Diocesan Information Office, St Edmund House, Edinburgh Road, Portsmouth PO1 3QA. The Diocese of Salisbury covers many parishes of Berkshire and the records are in Wilts RO.

BUCKINGHAMSHIRE

BUCKINGHAMSHIRE Record Office
County offices
Walton Street
Aylesbury
Bucks HP20 1UA
Telephone: (0296) 382587

Opening Hours: Tuesday to Thursday 9 am to 5.15 pm, Friday 9 am to 4.45 pm. Late opening first Thursday in each month by appointment. Closed Mondays. Annual closure: public holidays, plus Tuesday following late Spring and Summer public holidays; second full week in February.
Car Parking: None.
Children: Fourteen years plus.
Disabled: No special facilities, and prior notification required.
Appointments System: Prior booking for seats advisable. Viewers unnecessary. Signing in by register plus CARN. Approximately eleven seats, three viewers film and one fiche.
Document Ordering: Prior ordering not allowed. Four at a time, delivered in five to ten minutes. No production between 11.45 am and 1 pm; last orders 45 minutes before closure. Photocopying restricted, carried out by staff and sent by post. No facilities for typing or taping. Cameras by special arrangement.
Records: Some Ts of PRs on open shelves. Some original PRs on fiche/film. Some original PRs. Diocesan archive repository for Lincoln, Oxford and Archdeaconry of Bucks.
Postal Research: Limited specific enquiry, donations invited.
Facilities: Toilets, but no public telephone. No refreshment facilities but cafe/pub five minutes. Shops five minutes including bookshop with local history publications.
Publications: Historical county map. Free: publications list, notes for the guidance of genealogists, list of PRs, *How to Trace the History of Your House*, Aylesbury map with car parks.
Other Repositories: Bucks County Reference Library, Walton Street, Aylesbury.
Places of Interest: King's Head Inn (National Trust), County Museum, St Mary's Church, Grand Union Canal.
Tourist Office: County Hall, Walton Street, Aylesbury HP20 1UA. Telephone (0296) 3950000.
Remarks: Bags not allowed, storage facilities available. Historical county map on display.

CAMBRIDGESHIRE

CAMBRIDGE County Record Office
Shire Hall
Cambridge CB3 0AP
Telephone: (0223) 317281

Opening Hours: Monday to Thursday 9 am to 12.45 pm and 1.45 pm to 5.15 pm, Friday 9 am to 12.45 pm and 1.45 pm to 4.15 pm. Tuesday evenings 5.15 pm to 9 pm by appointment only. Annual closure: public holidays, plus Tuesday following Spring and late Summer public holidays; one additional day adjacent to Christmas.
Car Parking: 40 places.
Children: No specific ruling but dependent on behaviour.
Disabled: Wheelchair access via ramp at rear of building.
Appointments System: Prior booking for seats unnecessary, but advisable for viewers. Signing in by register plus CARN. Eighteen seats, four film viewers and one fiche.
Document Ordering: Prior ordering accepted by letter or telephone. Catalogue numbers unnecessary. Reasonable number at a time permitted. Delivery five to fifteen minutes. Photocopying by staff on same day; PRs allowed. No facilities for typing or taping. Cameras not allowed.
Records: Ts of PRs on open shelves, a few Ts of BTs, some original PRs on fiche/film, original PRs; probate records for Consistory Court of Ely, Archdeaconry of Ely and Peculiar of Thorney.
Postal Research: Very limited, no charge made.
Facilities: Toilets, public telephone and refreshments on premises. Cafe/pub two minutes. Shops twelve minutes including bookshop with local history publications.
Publications: Historical county map, list of PRs, list of PRs and BTs on film, Nonconformist registers, list of Ts of MIs, *Genealogists' Sources in Cambridgeshire*.
Other Repositories: Manuscripts Room, Cambridge University Library, West Road, Cambridge CB3 9DR (holds some local probate records); Wisbech and Fenland Museum, Museum Square, Wisbech, Cambs PE13 1ES (holds parish records for a number of parishes in Cambs and Norfolk near to Wisbech, also bygones and natural history - appointment only) Telephone (0945) 583817.
Places of Interest: Cambridge University, King's College Chapel, Folk Museum, Fitzwilliam Museum, Cambridgeshire Collection at Central Library.

Tourist Office: Wheeler Street, Cambridge CB2 3QB. Telephone (0223) 322640.
Remarks: Bags not allowed, some storage facilities available. Donations box. Historical county map on display. No original BTs held here.

HUNTINGDON County Record Office
Grammar School Walk
Huntingdon
Cambs PE18 6LF
Telephone: (0480) 425842

Opening Hours: Monday to Thursday 9 am to 12.45 pm and 1.45 pm to 5.15 pm, Friday 9 am to 12.45 pm and 1.45 pm to 4.15 pm; second Saturday in each month 9 am to 12 noon by appointment only. Annual closure: public holidays plus Tuesday following late Spring and late Summer public holidays; one additional day adjacent to Christmas.
Car Parking: Nearby
Children: No specific ruling but dependent on behaviour.
Disabled: No facilities so prior arrangement essential. Records may be seen at Cambridge office.
Appointments System: Prior booking for seats unnecessary and for viewers advisable. Signing in by register plus CARN. Twenty seats including viewers. Three film viewers and two fiche.
Document Ordering: Prior ordering accepted by letter or telephone. Catalogue numbers helpful. Number at a time at archivist's discretion. Delivery one to fifteen minutes. Photocopying by staff on same day; if large quantity or busy, sent by post; PRs/BTs allowed. No facilities for typing or taping. Cameras by special arrangement.
Records: Ts of PRs/BTs on open shelves, some original PRs on fiche/film, Diocesan archive repository for Lincoln, Ely and Archdeaconry of Huntingdon.
Postal Research: Limited specific enquiry, no charge made.
Facilities: Toilets, but no public telephone. No refreshment facilities but cafe/pub two minutes. Shops two minutes including bookshop with local history publications.
Publications: Historical county map, lists of PRs, *Notes for Genealogists.*
Other Repositories: Norris Museum and Library, The Broadway, St Ives, Huntingdon, Cambs PE17 4BX.
Places of Interest: Cromwell Museum (illustrates Oliver Cromwell's role from 1640-1660), All Saints Church, Cambridgeshire Regimental Collection is at Ely Museum.

Tourist Office: The Library, Princes Street, Huntingdon PE18 6PH. Telephone (0480) 425831/425801.
Remarks: Bags not allowed, storage facilities available. Donations box. Historical county map on display. Local library has newspapers on microfilm.

CHESHIRE

CHESHIRE Record Office
Duke Street
Chester CH1 1RL
Telephone: (0244) 602574

Opening Hours: Monday to Friday 9.15 am to 4.45 pm. Annual closure: public holidays.
Car Parking: None
Children: Accompanied: eight years plus. Unaccompanied: Fourteen years plus.
Disabled: Access and toilet.
Appointments System: Prior booking for seats necessary (three to five days). Prior booking for viewers necessary. Signing in by Cheshire ROs reader's ticket. 16 seats, 12 film viewers, and two fiche.
Document Ordering: Prior ordering accepted by letter or telephone. Catalogue numbers unnecessary. Three at a time; delivery ten minutes. Photocopying by staff on same day; if large or busy, sent by post. PRs by printout only; BTs allowed. No facilities for typing or taping. Cameras by prior arrangement.
Records: Some Ts of PRs/BTs on open shelves, some original PRs on fiche/film, some original PRs, Chester diocesan records.
Postal Research: Maximum of one hour, charge made.
Facilities: Toilets but no public telephone. No refreshment facilities but cafe/pub five minutes. Shops five minutes including bookshop with local history publications.
Publications: Historical county map, summary guide, census indexes booklet. Free: source sheets on researching ancestors, houses etc.
Places of Interest: Roman and medieval walled city, Chester Heritage Centre, cathedral, Castle Street - Georgian house, Providence House, The Rows, Grosvenor Museum, The Cheshire Military Museum (5th Royal Inniskilling Dragoon Guards, Carabineers, Cheshire Yeomanry, 22nd [Cheshire] Regiment).
Tourist Office: Town Hall, Northgate Street, Chester CH1 2NF. Telephone (0244) 324324. Chester Visitor Centre, Vicar's Lane, Chester CH1 1QX Telephone (0244) 351609.

Remarks: A few public and local authority items and some private deposits stored elsewhere require one week's prior notice. Bags not allowed, storage facilities available. Historical county map on display.

CHESTER City Record Office
Town Hall
Chester CH1 2HJ
Telephone: (0244) 324324 Ext 2108

Opening Hours: Monday to Friday 9 am to 1 pm and 2 pm to 5 pm. Late night Monday 5 pm to 9 pm by appointment only. Annual closure: public holidays.
Car Parking: None.
Children: No specific ruling.
Disabled: Disabled friendly.
Appointments System: Prior booking for seats and viewers unnecessary. Signing in by register. Thirteen seats and one film viewer.
Document Ordering: Prior ordering accepted by letter or telephone. Catalogue numbers necessary. Four at a time, delivery within a few minutes. Last orders 12.45 pm and 4.45 pm. Photocopying by staff on same day. No facilities for typing but taping permitted. Cameras not allowed.
Records: No PRs available. Borough, Quarter Sessions, Nonconformists, Poor Law Union, educational etc.
Postal Research: Limited, no charge made.
Facilities: No toilets or public telephone. No refreshment facilities, cafe/pub a few minutes. Shops nearby.
Publications: *Archives and Records of the City of Chester, Chester Schools, Notes for Family Historians.*
Places of Interest: Has complete circuit of Roman and medieval walls, two watch towers have small museums; black and white timbered buildings; The Rows (covered galleries of shops); cathedral.
Tourist Office: See other Cheshire entry.
Remarks: Donations box.

STALYBRIDGE see GREATER MANCHESTER

CLEVELAND

CLEVELAND County Archives Department
Exchange House
6 Marton Road
Middlesbrough
Cleveland TS1 1DB

Telephone: (0642) 248321
Opening Hours: Monday to Thursday 9 am to 1 pm and 2 pm to 4.30 pm, Friday 9 am to 1 pm and 2 pm to 4 pm. Annual closure: public holidays.
Car Parking: None.
Children: No specific ruling.
Disabled: by prior arrangement.
Appointments System: Prior booking for seats advisable. Viewers necessary. Signing in by register plus CARN. 35 seats, eight film viewers/fiche.
Document Ordering: Prior ordering not allowed. Three at a time; delivery approximately five minutes. Photocopying by staff on same day; PRs and BTs by printout. No facilities for typing or taping. Prior permission for cameras required.
Records: Ts of PRs on open shelves, some original PRs/BTs on fiche/film, some Ts of BTs.
Postal Research: Limited, no charge made.
Facilities: Toilets but no public telephone. No refreshment facilities but cafe/pub two minutes. Shops five minutes including bookshop with local history publications.
Publications: Free brief guide to RO. Genealogical sources, list of Ts.
Other Repositories: British Steel Corporation, Northern Region Records Centre, Unit F2, Commerce Way, Skippers Lane, Middlesbrough, Cleveland TS6 6UT; Cleveland Central Library, Victoria Square, Middlesbrough TS1 2AY.
Places of Interest: St Mary's Roman Catholic Cathedral; Transporter Bridge; Ormesby Hall (3 miles); Captain Cook Birthplace Museum, Stewart Park; Dorman Museum, Linthorpe Road (local and social history); Newham Grange Leisure Farm, Coulby, Newham.
Tourist Office: 51 Corporation Road, Middlesbrough TS1 1LT. Telephone (0642) 243425/245432 Ext 3580.
Remarks: Some records relating to Hartlepool are stored elsewhere and require one week's prior notice. Historical county map on display.

CORNWALL

CORNWALL Record Office
County Hall
Truro
Cornwall TR1 3AY
Telephone: (0872) 73698 or 74282 Ext 3127

Opening Hours: Tuesday to Thursday

9.30 am to 1 pm and 2 pm to 5 pm, Friday 9.30 am to 1 pm and 2 pm to 4.30 pm, Saturday 9 am to 12 noon. Closed Mondays. Annual closure: public holidays plus following day and previous Saturday; first two weeks in December.
Car Parking: Yes
Children: No specific ruling but dependent on behaviour.
Disabled: Disabled friendly.
Appointments System: Prior booking for seats (one week). Prior booking for viewers necessary. Signing in by register plus CARN. Approximately 26 seats and two film viewers.
Document Ordering: Prior ordering accepted by letter or telephone. Two at a time (or five wills). Catalogue numbers helpful. Delivery approximately two minutes. Photocopying by staff on same day or by post; BTs allowed. No facilities for typing or taping. Cameras permitted.
Records: Ts of PRs on open shelves, original PRs, diocesan records.
Postal Research: Limited, charge made.
Facilities: Toilets but no public telephone. No refreshment facilities but cafe/pub five minutes. Shops ten minutes including bookshop with local history publications.
Publications: Historical county map, *Sources for Cornish Family History*, a brief guide to sources, various handlists. Free: *Using the Search Room*, list of publications, *History of a House, Probate, Family History* etc.
Other Repositories: County Local Studies Library, Clinton Road, Redruth, Cornwall TR15 2QE (leaflets on collections, printed Ts and film of PRs and BTs); Royal Institution of Cornwall, County Museum, River Street, Truro, Cornwall.
Places of Interest: County Museum and Art Gallery; 18th century assembly rooms; Truro Pottery and Old Kiln Museum; cathedral; Come to Good (old Quaker Meeting House c1710); Flambards Triple Theme Park, Culdrose Manor, Helston; Duke of Cornwall's Light Infantry (32nd Regt of Foot), The Keep, Bodmin.
Tourist Office: Municipal Buildings, Boscawen Street, Truro TR1 2NE. Telephone (0872) 74555.
Remarks: Bags not allowed. Donations box. Historical county map on display.

CUMBRIA

Cumbria Record Office (BARROW)
140 Duke Street
Barrow in Furness
Cumbria LA14 1XW

Telephone: (0229) 831269

Opening Hours: Monday to Friday 9 am to 5 pm. Annual closure: public holidays, plus Tuesday following Easter and Spring bank holiday.
Car Parking: None
Children: No specific ruling if accompanied. Separate registration system in Cumbria which needs to be stamped by school if unaccompanied.
Disabled: Access, assistance by request.
Appointments System: Prior booking for seats and viewers unnecessary. Signing in by register plus CARN. 13 seats, one film viewer and one fiche.
Document Ordering: Prior ordering accepted by letter or telephone. Catalogue numbers helpful. Two at a time. Delivery within a few minutes. Photocopying by staff on same day; BTs allowed. No facilities for typing or taping. Prior permission required for cameras.
Records: Ts of PRs/BTs on open shelves, some original PRs and BTs.
Postal Research: Limited specific enquiry, no charge made.
Facilities: Toilets, but no public telephone. No refreshment facilities but cafe/pub five minutes. Shops five minutes including bookshop with local history publications.
Publications: Historical county map, *Cumbrian Ancestors*. Free: lists of PRs, local directories and maps, *Ships and Shipbuilding in Furness, Development of Modern Barrow, Local Industries, Introduction to House History*.
Other Repositories: Central Library (next door - closed Thursday pm) has large local history collection and census returns.
Places of Interest: 12th century Furness Abbey, museum, the Port, Castle.
Tourist Office: Civic Hall, 28 Duke Street, Barrow in Furness LA14 2LD. Telephone (0229) 25795.
Remarks: Bags and briefcases in search room (under review). Donations welcome. Historical county map on display.

Cumbria Record Office (CARLISLE)
The Castle
Carlisle CA3 8UR
Telephone: (0228) 23456 Ext 2416

Opening Hours: Monday to Friday 9 am to 5 pm. Annual closure: public holidays, plus Tuesday following Easter and Spring bank holiday.
Car Parking: Yes - restricted to RO searchers
Children: No specific ruling if accompanied. Separate registration system in

Cumbria which needs to be stamped by school if unaccompanied.

Disabled: Always welcome.

Appointments System: Prior booking for seats and viewers unnecessary. Signing in by register plus CARN. 24 seats, one film viewer and one fiche.

Document Ordering: Prior ordering accepted by letter or telephone. Catalogue numbers required. Two at a time; delivery approximately a few minutes. Photocopying by staff on same day; BTs allowed. No facilities for typing or taping. Prior permission required for cameras.

Records: Ts of PRs/BTs on open shelves, some original PRs and BTs.

Postal Research: Limited specific enquiry; charge made for trial period.

Facilities: Toilets, but no public telephone. No refreshment facilities but cafe/pub five minutes. Shops ten minutes including bookshop with local history publications.

Publications: Historical county map, *Cumbrian Ancestors, Railway Records, World War Records. Free: Cumberland Tithe Maps and Awards.*

Other Repositories: Carlisle Museum, Tullie House, Castle Street, Carlisle; Carlisle Library, Globe Lane, Carlisle.

Places of Interest: Hadrian's Wall; Carlisle City Museum - Tullie House Museum; cathedral; Border Regiment History Museum; Guildhall Museum.

Tourist Office: Old Town Hall, Green Market, Carlisle CA3 8JH. Telephone (0228) 25517.

Remarks: Some records are stored elsewhere which require prior notice: Archives of Dean and Chapter of Carlisle Cathedral (one week); Lord Egremont's Estate Archives (two weeks); some local authority, shipping and business records (one day). Historical county map on display. Donations welcome. Bags and briefcases in search room (under review).

Cumbria Record Office (KENDAL)
County Offices
Kendal
Cumbria LA9 4RQ
Telephone: (0539) 21000 Ext 4329

Opening Hours: Monday to Friday 9 am to 5 pm. Annual closure: public holidays, plus Tuesday following Easter and Spring bank holiday.

Car Parking: Limited

Children: No specific ruling if accompanied. Separate registration system in Cumbria which needs to be stamped by school if unaccompanied.

Disabled: Access via rear entrance. Access to toilets is difficult. Assistance by request.

Appointments System: Prior booking for seats and viewers unnecessary. Signing in by register plus CARN. Twelve seats, one film viewer, and two fiche.

Document Ordering: Prior ordering accepted by letter or telephone. Catalogue numbers helpful. Two at a time; delivery within a few minutes. Photocopying by staff on same day if possible; BTs allowed. No facilities for typing or taping. Prior permission required for cameras.

Records: Ts of PRs on open shelves, some original PRs. Some local authority, solicitors, business records are stored in a strongroom and may take longer to produce.

Postal Research: Limited specific enquiry; charge made for trial period.

Facilities: Toilets and public telephone on premises. No refreshment facilities but cafe/pub two minutes. Shops two minutes including bookshop with local history publications.

Publications: Historical county map, various plans of Kendal from 1787, *An Anthology of Kendal Wool 1420-1720, Cumbrian Ancestors.*

Other Repositories: Armitt Library, Ambleside, Cumbria; Dove Cottage, Grasmere, Cumbria; Kendal Library, Strick Landgate, Kendal.

Places of Interest: Art Gallery and Abbot Hall Museum of Lakeland Life and Industry; Holy Trinity Church in Kirkland.

Tourist Office: Town Hall, Highgate, Kendal LA9 4DL. Telephone (0539) 25758 or 33333 Ext 380 (weekdays).

Remarks: Records of Levens Hall manors and estates are stored elsewhere and require four weeks' prior notice. Bags and briefcases in search room (under review). Donations welcome. Historical county map on display.

DERBYSHIRE

DERBYSHIRE Record Office
Ernest Bailey Building
New Street
Matlock
Derbyshire
Telephone: (0629) 580000 Ext 7347

POSTAL ADDRESS:
County Education Department
County Offices
Matlock
Derbyshire DE4 3AG

Opening Hours: Monday to Friday 9.30 am to 1 pm and 2 pm to 4.45 pm. Annual

closure: public holidays.
Car Parking: Limited.
Children: Accompanied: No specific ruling but dependent on behaviour.   Unaccompanied: Twelve years plus.
Disabled: Disabled friendly.
Appointments System: Prior booking for seats advisable (one week) and necessary for viewers. Signing in by register. 12 seats plus two at map tables. Five film viewers plus one reader/printer, and one fiche.
Document Ordering: Prior ordering accepted by letter or telephone. Catalogue numbers helpful. Three at a time may be ordered. Ordering times 9.45 am, 10.30 am, 11.15 am, 12 noon, 12.30 pm, 2.15 pm, 3 pm, 3.45 pm. Photocopying restricted and done by staff, on same day if possible. No facilities for typing or taping. Prior permission required for cameras.
Records: Some Ts of PRs on open shelves. Some Ts of PRs require ordering. Some original PRs on fiche/film and directories on fiche. Some original PRs and pre 1948 National Coal Board records.
Postal Research: Limited to one query; charge made.
Facilities: Toilets but no public telephone. Canteen in County Offices five minutes; cafe/pub two minutes. Shops two minutes including bookshop with local history publications.
Publications: Historical county map and various maps, introduction to main holdings, *Anglican & Nonconformist Registers in RO* (under revision). Free: various notes on sources.
Other Repositories: Derby Local Studies Library, 25b Irongate, Derby; County Local Studies Department, County Library, Matlock DE4 3AG; local history collections at Buxton, Chesterfield, Glossop and Ilkeston Libraries.
Places of Interest: Matlock Bath (19th century Spa with model village and mining museum); Riber Castle and nature reserve; Derbyshire Yeomanry Cavalry; 9th/12th Royal Lancers Museum, Derby.
Tourist Office: The Pavilion, Matlock Bath, DE4 3NR. Telephone (0629) 55082.
Remarks: Local Authority District Council (pre-1974) records are stored elsewhere and require at least one week's prior notice. Bags not allowed, storage facilities available. Historical county map on display.

DEVON

DEVON Record Office
Castle Street

Exeter EX4 3PU
Telephone: (0392) 273509
Opening Hours: Monday to Thursday 9.30 am to 5 pm, Friday 9.30 am to 4.30 pm; first and third Saturday in each month (except bank holidays) 9.30 am to 12 noon. Annual closure: public holidays plus Christmas week.
Car Parking: None
Children: At archivist's discretion.
Disabled: Ramp. Lift may be called by buzzer.
Appointments System: Prior booking for seats and viewers unnecessary. Signing in by card index plus identification. Daily or annual charge (reduced for OAPs); no charge for bona fide students with identification from study centre. 24 seats, four film viewers and 11 fiche.
Document Ordering: Prior ordering accepted by letter or telephone. Catalogue numbers necessary. Three at a time; delivery variable according to where stored. Photocopying by staff on same day; if large quantity or busy, sent by post. PRs and BTs allowed. No facilities for typing or taping. Cameras at archivist's discretion.
Records: A few original PRs but mostly original PRs on fiche/film. Diocesan records for Exeter, county and city records,; pre 1974 Authorities, Inland Revenue wills 1812-1858.
Postal Research: Professional genealogist; charge made.
Facilities: No toilets, public telephone or refreshment facilities, but toilets and refreshment facilities hoped for shortly. Cafe/pub five minutes. Shops five minutes including bookshop with local history publications.
Publications: Guides to sources, historical county map, *Maritime Sources,* postcards, *Poor Law.* Free: publications list, leaflets on history of house, maritime, transport, mining, tithe, crimes and punishments, family history etc.
Other Repositories: West Country Studies Library, Castle Street, Exeter (adjoining RO and on the same floor), extensive Ts of PRs and BTs in Devon and Cornwall Record Society collection - daily charge; Exeter Dean and Chapter archives, Cloister Library, Palace Gate, Exeter EX1 1HX. Tel (0392) 72894/273063 Monday to Friday 2 pm to 5 pm by appointment.
Places of Interest: Cathedral, Exeter Maritime Museum, Devonshire Regiment Museum, 14th century underground passages, Royal Albert Memorial Museum and Art Gallery, Guildhall, Law Courts, Museum of Costume and Lace, St Nicholas Priory.
Tourist Office: Civic Centre, Paris

Street, Exeter EX1 1JJ. Telephone (0392) 265297.

Remarks: Some records stored elsewhere require 48 hours prior notice. Poor Law unions, school boards, hospitals, parishes and private deposits etc are divided among branch offices. Bags not allowed: to be given to search room staff. Historical county map on display.

NORTH DEVON Record Office
Library and Record Office
Tuly Street
Barnstaple
Devon EX32 7EJ
Telephone: (0271) 47068 (search room) or 47119 (Archivist)

Opening Hours: Monday, Tuesday, Friday 9.30 am to 5 pm, Wednesday and Saturday 9.30 am to 4 pm, Thursday 9.30 am to 7 pm. Annual closure: public holidays plus Christmas week.
Car Parking: Nearby
Children: Accompanied: no specific ruling but dependent on behaviour.
Disabled: Lift, toilet.
Appointments System: Prior booking for seats unnecessary. For viewers necessary. Signing in by card index; reader's ticket. Daily or annual charge (reduced for OAPs); no charge for bona fide students with identification from study centre. Approximately 40 seats, five film viewers and four fiche.
Document Ordering: Prior ordering accepted by letter or telephone. Catalogue numbers unnecessary. Number at a time at archivist's discretion. Delivery five minutes. Photocopying by staff on same day; if large quantity or busy, sent by post. PRs by printout only. Prior permission required for typing/taping. Cameras permitted.
Records: Ts of PRs require ordering. Some original PRs/BTs on fiche/film.
Postal Research: Limited; charge made.
Facilities: Toilets, but no public telephone. No refreshment facilities but cafe/pub two minutes. Shops two minutes including bookshop with local history publications.
Publications: Historical county map, *Parish Poor Law in Devon,* location check list, *Parish and Non-parochial Registers in RO.* Free: *Family History* and various leaflets on the RO.
Places of Interest: The Guildhall, Queen Anne's Walk, St Anne's Chapel and Old Grammar School, St Peter's Church, Museum of North Devon.
Tourist Office: North Devon Library, Tuly Street, Barnstaple EX32 7EJ. Telephone (0271) 47177.

Remarks: Historical county map on display. This is also the Local Studies Centre, combined with the North Devon Athenaeum: twenty seats for consultation of printed sources.

WEST DEVON Record Office
Unit 3
Clare Place
Coxside
Plymouth PL4 0JW
Telephone: (0752) 264685

Opening Hours: Monday to Thursday 9.30 am to 4.50 pm, Friday 9.30 am to 4.20 pm; first Wednesday in each month 5 pm to 6.50 pm. Annual closure: public holidays plus Christmas week.
Car Parking: 15 places.
Children: Accompanied: At archivist's discretion. Unaccompanied: twelve years plus.
Disabled: Rear access.
Appointments System: Prior booking for seats unnecessary but for viewers necessary. Signing in by register; card index. Daily or annual charge (reduced for OAPs). No charge for bona fide students with identification from study centre. 20 seats, one film viewer and six fiche.
Document Ordering: Prior ordering not allowed. Three at a time, delivered within a few minutes. Photocopying at archivist's discretion; by staff and sent by post; PRs and BTs allowed. No facilities for typing or taping. Cameras at archivist's discretion.
Records: Ts of PRs/BTs require ordering. Original PRs on fiche/film.
Postal Research: Limited; charge made.
Facilities: Toilets, but no public telephone. No refreshment facilities but cafe/pub two minutes. Shops ten minutes including bookshop with local history publications.
Publications: *Guide to Archives* (Plymouth City Libraries), *Parish and Non Parochial Registers, Devon Poor Law.* Free: sources for family history, location maps.
Other Repositories: Plymouth Central Library, Lending Library, Local Studies Reference Library, Drake Circus, Plymouth PL4 8AL.
Places of Interest: Plymouth Hoe, Elizabethan House, St Andrew's Church, Sutton Harbour, Merchant's House.
Tourist Office: 12 The Barbican, Plymouth PL1 2LS. Telephone (0752) 223806. Civic Centre, Royal Parade, Plymouth PL1 2EW. Telephone (0752) 264849/264851.
Remarks: Historical county map on display.

DORSET

DORSET Record Office
County Hall
Dorchester
Dorset DT1 1XJ
Telephone: (0305) 204411

Opening Hours: Monday to Friday 9 am to 1 pm and 2 pm to 5 pm; Saturday 9.30 am to 12.30 pm (for experimental period). Annual closure: public holidays.
Car Parking: Yes
Children: No specific ruling but dependent on behaviour.
Disabled: Access
Appointments System: Prior booking for seats necessary (one week). Booking for viewers unnecessary. Signing in by card index. 14 seats, seven dual viewers.
Document Ordering: Prior ordering accepted by letter or telephone. Catalogue numbers necessary. Four at a time, delivered in five to twenty minutes. Last orders Monday to Thursday 4.30 pm, Friday 3.40 pm. Photocopying by staff on same day; if large quantity or busy, sent by post. Cameras permitted, but under review.
Records: Ts of PRs/BTs on open shelves, original PRs, diocesan records for Archdeaconries of Sherborne and Dorset.
Postal Research: Yes, charge made.
Facilities: Toilets nearby in County Hall as is public telephone. No refreshment facilities but cafe/pub five minutes. Shops five minutes including bookshop with local history publications.
Publications: *Guide to PRs*, parish map, *List of Diaries and Memoirs, List of Documents Relating to French Invasion 1797-1814*, Shire publications, *Tracing Dorset Ancestors, Dorset County Guide*, postcards.
Places of Interest: Maiden Castle, Maumbury Rings, Roman House, Dorset County Museum, Dorset Military Museum, Dinosaur Museum.
Tourist Office: 7 Acland Rd, Dorchester DT1 1EF. Telephone (0305) 67992.
Remarks: Donations box. Historical county map on display. A new RO is contemplated in the near future. Many Dorset parishes come under the Diocese of Salisbury and these diocesan records are held at Wiltshire RO.

DURHAM

Durham County Record Office
DARLINGTON Branch
Darlington Library

Crown Street
Darlington
Durham DL1 1ND
Telephone: (0325) 462034/469858

Opening Hours: Monday, Tuesday, Thursday, Friday 9 am to 1 pm and 2.15 pm to 7 pm; Wednesday and Saturday 9 am to 1 pm and 2.15 pm to 5 pm. Annual closure: public holidays.
Car Parking: Nearby
Children: Accompanied: No specific ruling. Unaccompanied: twelve years plus.
Disabled: No special arrangements, assistance given.
Appointments System: Prior booking for seats advisable for late night and Saturday, and necessary for viewers. Signing in by register. Twelve seats, two film viewers and one fiche.
Document Ordering: Prior ordering accepted by letter or telephone. Catalogue numbers unnecessary. Three at a time, delivery approximately 15 minutes. Photocopying by staff on same day; PRs by printout only. No facilities for typing or taping. Cameras not allowed.
Records: Ts of PRs on open shelves in Local History Collection, original PRs on fiche/film.
Postal Research: None
Facilities: Toilets, but no public telephone. No refreshment facilities but cafe/pub two minutes. Shops five minutes including bookshop with local history publications.
Publications: *North Eastern Ancestors, Sources for Genealogy in RO*. Free: lists of books on genealogy, leaflet on PRs, *Guide to Darlington Branch*.
Places of Interest: Railway Centre and Museum; Art Gallery; Roman remains, Piercebridge (5 miles); Darlington Museum.
Tourist Office: District Library, Crown Street, Darlington DL1 1ND Telephone (0325) 469858
Remarks: Seats are shared with users of Local History Collection.

DURHAM County Record Office
County Hall
Durham DH1 5UL
Telephone: (091) 386 4411 Ext 2474/2253

Opening Hours: Monday, Tuesday, Thursday 8.45 am to 4.45 pm, Wednesday 8.45 am to 8.30 pm, Friday 8.45 am to 4.15 pm. Annual closure: public holidays.
Car Parking: County Hall car park
Disabled: Prior notice required.
Appointments System: Prior booking for seats essential (two weeks) and for viewers necessary. Signing in by register.

Ten seats, ten film viewers and two fiche. **Document Ordering:** Prior ordering unnecessary except for Wednesday evenings (one day's notice). Approximately three at a time allowed. Delivery two to five minutes. Photocopying by staff on same day; PRs by printout only. Limited typing/taping permitted with prior permission. Cameras permitted.
Records: Ts of PRs on open shelves, original PRs on fiche/film.
Postal Research: None
Facilities: Toilets and public telephone on premises. Refreshments plus room for own food; cafe/pub two minutes. Shops ten minutes including bookshop with local history publications.
Publications: Historical county map, *North Eastern Ancestors.* Free: various leaflets on records held at the RO, publications list.
Other Repositories: Department of Palaeography and Diplomatic, 5 The College, Durham City DH1 3EQ (probate records of Diocese of Durham).
Places of Interest: Durham Castle, Cathedral and Treasury, Durham Light Infantry Museum and Arts Centre, Old Fulling Mill Museum.
Tourist Office: Durham Market Place, Durham DH1 3NJ. Telephone (091) 384 3720.
Remarks: Donations box, historical county map on display.

ESSEX

ESSEX Record Office
County Hall
Chelmsford
Essex CM1 1LX
Telephone: (0245) 492211 Ext 20067

Opening Hours: Monday 10 am to 8.45 pm, Tuesday to Thursday 9.15 am to 5.15 pm, Friday 9.15 am to 4.15 pm. Annual closure: public holidays and day following Boxing Day.
Car Parking: None
Children: At archivist's discretion.
Disabled: Ramp. Parking may be arranged.
Appointments System: Prior booking for seats and viewers essential (a few days for seats and several days for viewers). Signing in by register plus CARN. 28 seats, nine film viewers, three fiche.
Document Ordering: Prior ordering accepted by letter or telephone. Catalogue numbers preferred. Maximum of five single items or one bundle may be ordered at a time. Delivery approximately ten to fifteen minutes. Tuesday to Friday: no production between 12.30 pm and

2 pm (documents can be ordered in advance to cover these times). Photocopying by staff on same day; if large quantity or busy, sent by post; PRs if suitable.
Prior permission required for typing/taping. Cameras not allowed.
Records: Ts of PRs on open shelves, some original PRs on fiche/film; some original PRs, diocesan records for Diocese of London, Archdeaconry of Essex, Diocese of Rochester (19th century).
Postal Research: Professional genealogist; charge made.
Facilities: Toilets, and refreshments plus room for own food and drink vending machine. Cafe/pub two minutes. Shops two minutes including bookshop with local history publications.
Publications: Historical county map, maps, posters, various publications. Free: publications list, Essex RO and its services, genealogical searches in the Essex R.Os.
Other Repositories : Chelmsford Library, County Hall, Chelmsford, Essex.
Places of Interest: St Mary's Cathedral, Shire Hall, Chelmsford and Essex Museum and Essex Regimental Museum.
Tourist Office: E Block, County Hall, Chelmsford CM1 1LX. Telephone (0245) 283400.
Remarks: Modern local authority records, magistrates' court records and uncatalogued material are stored elsewhere and require up to one week's prior notice. Bags not allowed, storage facilities available. Donations box. Historical county map on display. Parish records for the Deanery of Walthamstow are held at Vestry House Museum and Archives, Walthamstow E17 9NH (see under London Boroughs, Walthamstow).

Essex Record Office
COLCHESTER AND NORTH EAST ESSEX Branch
Stanwell House
Stanwell Street
Colchester
Essex CO2 7DL
Telephone: (0206) 572099

Opening Hours: Monday to Thursday 9.15 am to 5.15 pm, Friday 9.15 am to 4.15 pm. Annual closure: public holidays.
Car Parking: None
Children: At archivist's discretion.
Disabled: Lift.
Appointments System: Prior booking for seats and viewers necessary (short notice). Signing in by register plus CARN. Fourteen seats, four film

viewers, one fiche.

Document Ordering: Prior ordering accepted by letter or telephone. Catalogue numbers unnecessary. Number at a time at archivist's discretion. Delivery approximately five minutes. Ordering times: not between 1 pm and 2 pm, and sometimes also between 12 noon and 1 pm; last orders for morning fifteen minutes before lunchtime; last orders in afternoon thirty minutes before closure. Photocopying restricted; done by staff on same day; if large quantity or busy, sent by post; PRs allowed until filmed. No facilities for typing or taping. Cameras not allowed.

Records: Some original PRs on fiche/film, some original PRs.

Postal Research: Limited; charge made.

Facilities: Toilets and public telephone on premises. No refreshment facilities but cafe/pub two minutes. Shops five minutes including bookshop with local history publications.

Publications: Historical county map, maps, posters, various publications. Free: Essex RO at Colchester, introductory notes for enquirers, parish records at branch offices, publications list (all obtainable from Chelmsford).

Other Repositories: University of Essex Library, Wivenhoe Park, Colchester CO4 3SQ; Local Studies Department, Colchester Library, Trinity Square, Colchester CO1 1JR.

Places of Interest: The Castle, St Botolph's Priory, the Dutch Quarter, Holly Trees Museum, Social History Museum, Holy Trinity Church, St John's Abbey Gardens, Tymperley's Clock Museum.

Tourist Office: 1 Queen Street, Colchester CO1 2PJ. Telephone (0206) 712233.

Remarks: Bags not allowed, storage facilities available. Donations box. Historical county map on display.

DAGENHAM see LONDON
HAVERING see LONDON
ROMFORD see LONDON

Essex Record Office
SOUTHEND Branch
c/o Central Library
Victoria Avenue
Southend-On-Sea
Essex SS2 6EX
Telephone: (0702) 612621 Ext 215

Opening Hours: Monday, Wednesday, Thursday 9.15 am to 5.15 pm, Tuesday 9.45 am to 5.15 pm, Friday 9.15 am to 4.15 pm. Annual closure: public holidays.

Car Parking: None

Children: Accompanied: at archivist's discretion. Unaccompanied: twelve years plus.

Disabled: No facilities or arrangements.

Appointments System: Prior booking for seats and viewers necessary. Signing in by register. Six seats, three film viewers and one fiche.

Document Ordering: Prior ordering accepted by letter or telephone. Catalogue numbers necessary. Five at a time may be ordered. Photocopying by staff on same day; if large quantity or busy, sent by post. No facilities for typing or taping. Cameras not allowed.

Records: Ts of PRs require ordering; original PRs on fiche/film.

Postal Research: Not here, but at Chelmsford.

Facilities: Toilets and public telephone on premises. Refreshments but no room for own food. Cafe/pub few minutes. Shops a few minutes' walk including bookshop with local history publications.

Publications: Historical county map. Free: parish records at branch offices, publications list, Essex RO at Southend-on-Sea.

Places of Interest: The Pier (longest in the world), Churchill Gardens, Central Museum, Prittlewell Priory Museum, Southchurch Hall, Beecroft Art Gallery.

Tourist Office: Civic Centre, Victoria Avenue, Southend-on-Sea SS2 6ER. Telephone (0702) 355122.

Remarks: Bags not allowed. Historical county map on display. Donations box.

GLOUCESTERSHIRE

GLOUCESTERSHIRE Record Office
Clarence Row
Alvin Street
Gloucester GL1 2TG
Telephone: (0452) 425295

Opening Hours: Monday to Wednesday and Friday 9 am to 1 pm and 2 pm to 5 pm, Thursday 9 am to 1 pm and 2 pm to 8 pm. Annual closure: public holidays, plus Tuesday following Easter, Spring, August and Christmas bank holidays.

Car Parking: Limited.

Children: No specific ruling but dependent on behaviour.

Disabled: Access; a few steps.

Appointments System: Prior booking for seats and viewers advisable. Signing in by register plus reader's ticket. Charge made except for unwaged and reduction for OAPs. Car registration if parked on premises. Forty seats, six film viewers, thirteen fiche.

Document Ordering: Prior ordering accepted by letter or telephone. Catalogue numbers unnecessary. Only one issued at a time. Delivery approximately 15 minutes. Last orders 4.30 pm, Thursday 7 pm. Photocopying DIY; PRs and BTs by printout only. No facilities for typing or taping. Prior permission required for cameras.

Records: Some Ts of PRs/BTs on open shelves, original PRs/BTs on fiche/film, diocesan records.

Postal Research: Professional genealogist; charge made.

Facilities: Toilets but no public telephone. No refreshments but coffee-room soon. Cafe/pub five to ten minutes. Shops five to ten minutes including bookshop with local history publications.

Publications: Historical county map, handlists of contents of RO, *Gloucestershire Family History*, archive teaching books, postcards.

Other Repositories: Gloucester City Reference Library, Brunswick Road, Gloucester GL1 1HT (local history collection).

Places of Interest: Cathedral, Folk Museum, City Museum and Art Gallery, the Docks, Opie's "Pack Age" collection, Waterways Museum, Transport Museum, Gloucestershire Regimental Museum.

Tourist Office: St Michael's Tower, The Cross, Gloucester GL1. 1PD Telephone (0452) 421188

Remarks: Records stored at Shire Hall and uncatalogued material require prior ordering. Historical county map on display.

**GREATER MANCHESTER
see MANCHESTER**

HAMPSHIRE

**HAMPSHIRE Record Office
20 Southgate Street
Winchester SO23 9EF**
Telephone: (0962) 846154

Opening Hours: Monday to Thursday 9 am to 4.45 pm, Friday 9 am to 4.15 pm. Every Saturday from October to March: 9 am to 12 noon. April to September: second and fourth Saturday in each month, 9 am to 12 noon. Saturdays by appointment only. Annual closure: public holidays plus previous Saturdays, and last full week before Christmas.

Car Parking: Two or three places.

Children: At archivist's discretion.

Disabled: Lifts and wheelchair access.

Appointments System: Prior booking for seats unnecessary but advisable for viewers. Signing in by register plus CARN. 28 seats, one film viewer, ten fiche, and eight fiche/viewers.

Document Ordering: Prior ordering accepted by letter or telephone. Catalogue numbers preferred. Number at a time six; ten on Saturdays. Delivery approximately ten minutes. No ordering between 10 am and 10.20 am, 12.50 pm and 2.10 pm, 3.10 pm and 3.20 pm; last orders 30 minutes before closure. Photocopying by staff on same day; if large quantity or busy, sent by post; PRs by printout only; BTs allowed. No special facilities for typing/taping but arrangements can be made. Cameras not allowed.

Records: Some Ts of PRs on open shelves; some Ts of PRs require ordering. Majority of original PRs on fiche/film; original PRs only if not on fiche/film. Diocesan records; fiche of all Hampshire PRs including those in Guildford Muniment Room, Surrey.

Postal Research: Limited specific enquiry, no charge made.

Facilities: Toilets but no public telephone. No refreshments but room for own food. Cafe/pub two minutes. Shops five minutes including bookshop with local history publications.

Publications: Historical county map, leaflets on maps, wills, transport, estate records of the Bishops of Winchester, *Sources for Genealogy in the RO.* Free: general leaflet on location etc, how to use the RO.

Other Repositories: Local Studies Library, Jewry Street, Winchester; Reference Library, North Walls, Winchester; Winchester Cathedral Library.

Places of Interest: Cathedral; Pilgrim's Hall; The Great Hall, Westgate (King Arthur's Round Table); City Museum; Hampshire Regimental Museum (Green Jackets); Royal Army Pay Corps Museum, Worthy Down; Light Infantry Museum; The Royal Hussars Museum.

Tourist Office: The Guildhall, The Broadway, Winchester SO23 9LJ. Telephone (0962) 67871

Remarks: Some District Council and County Council records stored elsewhere require a minimum of one day's prior notice. Bags not allowed, storage facilities available. Donations box. Historical county map on display.

**PORTSMOUTH City Record Office
3 Museum Road
Portsmouth PO1 2LE**
Telephone: (0705) 829765

Opening Hours: Monday to Wednesday 9.30 am to 1 pm and 1.30 pm to 5 pm; Thursday 9.30 am to 1 pm and 1.30 pm to 5 pm, evening 5 pm to 7 pm by appointment only; Friday 9.30 am to 1 pm and 1.30 pm to 4 pm. Annual closure: public holidays plus Tuesday following Spring and Summer bank holidays.
Car Parking: Limited
Children: At archivist's discretion but dependent on behaviour.
Disabled: Ramps, toilet.
Appointments System: Prior booking for seats and viewers unnecessary. Signing in by register. Twenty seats, three film viewers and six fiche.
Document Ordering: Prior ordering not allowed. Three at a time; immediate delivery. Photocopying by staff on same day; if large quantity or busy, sent by post; PRs by printout only. Typing/taping permitted. Cameras permitted.
Records: Original PRs on fiche/film. Original PRs, city and borough records.
Postal Research: Limited specific enquiry. Donations welcome.
Facilities: Toilets but no public telephone. Room for own food. Cafe/pub five minutes. Shops ten minutes including bookshop with local history publications.
Publications: *Guide to Collections, Sources for Local Studies, Registers of Hampshire and Isle of Wight, Portsmouth Archives Review.* Free: general facilities of the RO, tracing your ancestors, how to use the search room, history of PRs, tracing the history of your house, how to do research, Portsmouth City publications.
Other Repositories: Central Library, Guildhall Square, Portsmouth PO1 2DX.
Places of Interest: Cathedral of Thomas a Becket; Tudor fortifications; Mary Rose Ship Hall and exhibition; D Day Museum; Royal Marines Museum, Southsea; Royal Naval Museum; Charles Dickens' Birthplace Museum; HMS *Victory;* HMS *Warrior.*
Tourist Office: The Hard, Portsmouth PO1 3QJ . Telephone (0705) 826722
Remarks: Bags not allowed, storage facilities available. Donations box.

SOUTHAMPTON City Record Office
Civic Centre
Southampton SO9 4XR
Telephone: (0703) 832251

Opening Hours: Monday to Friday 9 am to 1 pm and 1.30 pm to five pm. Two late evenings a month; contact RO for details. Annual closure: public holidays.
Car Parking: Limited

Children: Accompanied: six years plus. Unaccompanied: ten years plus.
Disabled: Access
Appointments System: Prior booking for seats and viewers unnecessary. Signing in by register. Eight seats and one dual viewer.
Document Ordering: Prior ordering not allowed. Three at a time, delivery approximately five minutes. Photocopying restricted; done by staff, usually on same day. Typing/taping permitted by special arrangement. For the use of cameras a fee or prior permission may be required - depends on use of material.
Records: Some Ts of PRs/BTs on open shelves, some original PRs on fiche/film, some original PRs, city and borough records.
Postal Research: Very limited; no charge made at present.
Facilities: Toilets and public telephone on premises. No refreshment facilities but cafe/pub two minutes. Shops two to ten minutes including bookshop with local history publications.
Publications: *Guide to Official Records, Guide to PRs,* genealogical leaflet. Free: handout on the RO, publications list.
Other Repositories: Southampton Reference Library, Civic Centre, Southampton (Local History Collection); Southampton University Library, Highfield, Southampton (Cope Collection); Southampton Museum, Tudor House, Southampton.
Places of Interest: Southampton City Art Gallery in the Civic Centre, Maritime Museum, Bargate Guildhall Museum, Tudor House Museum, old Southampton, God's House Tower, museum.
Tourist Office: Above Bar Precinct, Southampton. Telephone (0703) 221106.
Remarks: Historical county map available. Some genealogical information for Southampton such as wills and marriage bonds etc are at Hampshire RO, Winchester.

HEREFORD & WORCESTER

HEREFORD and Worcester County Record Office
The Old Barracks
Harold Street
Hereford HR1 2QX
Telephone: (0432) 265441

Opening Hours: Monday 10 am to 1 pm and 2 pm to 4.45 pm, Tuesday to Thursday 9.15 am to 1 pm and 2 pm to 4.45 pm, Friday 9.15 am to 1 pm and 2 pm to 4 pm.

Annual closure: public holidays plus following Tuesday; one week in November.
Car Parking: Limited.
Children: At archivist's discretion.
Disabled: No facilities.
Appointments System: Prior booking for seats unnecessary, but for viewers necessary. Signing in by register plus CARN. Twelve seats, seven film viewers, two fiche.
Document Ordering: Prior ordering not allowed. Two at a time, delivery five minutes. Photocopying DIY; PRs/BTs allowed. No facilities for typing or taping. Cameras permitted but charge made.
Records: Original PRs/BTs. Original PRs/BTs on fiche/film. Hereford diocesan records (diocese includes parts of Shropshire and Powys); Herefordshire county and city records; Quarter Sessions; Leominster Borough, District and Parish Councils originating in Herefordshire; probate; Nonconformists; manorial; Poor Law Unions.
Postal Research: Limited; charge made.
Facilities: Toilets but no public telephone. No refreshment facilities but cafe/pub two minutes. Shops ten minutes including bookshop with local history publications.
Publications: Historical county map, *Guide to PRs.*
Other Repositories: Hereford Cathedral Library, Broad Street, Hereford; Hereford City Library, Broad Street, Hereford.
Places of Interest: Cathedral; Museum of Cider; The Old House (Jacobean); 14th century All Saints Church; Churchill Gardens Museum; Hereford City Museum and Art Gallery; Herefordshire Regiment/Herefordshire Light Infantry Regimental Museum.
Tourist Office: Town Hall Annexe, St Owen's Street, Hereford HR1 2PJ. Telephone (0432) 268430.
Remarks: Bags not allowed, storage facilities available. Historical county map on display. Donations box.

Hereford and WORCESTER
Record Office
County Hall
Spetchley Road
Worcester WR5 2NP
Telephone: (0905) 763763 Ext 3612

Opening Hours: Monday 10 am to 4.45 pm, Tuesday to Thursday 9.15 am to 4.45 pm, Friday 9.15 am to 4 pm. Annual closure: public holidays; two weeks usually in November.
Car Parking: Approximately 200 places.

Children: No specific ruling.
Disabled: Access.
Appointments System: Prior booking for seats unnecessary, but for viewers necessary. Signing in by register plus CARN. 35 seats, thirteen film viewers plus reader/printer, and four fiche.
Document Ordering: Prior ordering not allowed. Three at a time; delivery approximately five minutes except when busy. Photocopying DIY; PRs/BTs by printout only. No facilities for typing or taping. Cameras permitted.
Records: Some Ts of PRs on open shelves; some Ts of PRs require ordering. Some original PRs on fiche/film. Courts of Petty Sessions, Coroners, some hospital and Poor Law Unions, Quarter Sessions, wills, Marriage Bonds and Allegations.
Postal Research: None
Facilities: Toilets and public telephone on premises. Refreshments plus room for own food. Cafe/pub ten minutes. Shops ten minutes.
Publications: Historical county map, maps, postcards, Free: Brief guides to location of records and what you need to know about the RO, *General Resources in Worcestershire ROs,* PRs, *Tracing Your House in the Archives.*
Remarks: Bags not allowed, storage facilities available. Donations box. Historical county map on display. County Hall is approximately three miles from Worcester. Extensive Worcester Photographic Survey available.

Hereford and Worcester
(ST HELENS Branch) Record Office
Fish Street
Worcester WR1 2HN
Telephone: (0905) 763763 Ext 3616

Opening Hours: Monday 10 am to 4.45 pm, Tuesday to Thursday 9.15 am to 4.45 pm, Friday 9.15 am to 4 pm. Occasional lunchtime closure from 1 pm to 2 pm. Annual closure: public holidays; two weeks at the end of November.
Car Parking: Four places.
Children: No specific ruling.
Disabled: One step into search room. Help available.
Appointments System: Prior booking for seats unnecessary, but for viewers necessary. Signing in by register plus CARN. 24 seats, one film viewer and one fiche.
Document Ordering: Prior ordering accepted by letter or telephone. Catalogue numbers necessary. Three at a time, but only one issued. Ordering times, for experimental period, every half hour com-

19

mencing at 9.30 am; no issue 12.30 pm to 1.30 pm. Photocopying DIY. No facilities for typing or taping. Cameras permitted.

Records: No original PRs/BTs or on film. Other parish records eg settlement papers, overseers etc; main repository for non-official Worcestershire records; diocesan records; family collections; Nonconformist; manorial; City of Worcester archives; City Court of Quarter Sessions; local history collection.

Postal Research: None

Facilities: Toilets but no public telephone. No refreshment facilities but cafe/pub two minutes. Shops two minutes including bookshop with local history publications.

Publications: Historical county map, maps, postcards, handlist of whereabouts of PRs. Free: brief guides to location of records and what you need to know about the ROs, how to use St Helen's RO, *Researching the History of a House.*

Other Repositories: Worcester Cathedral Library (Dean and Chapter archives); Worcester City Library (local history collection).

Places of Interest: Cathedral, Museum of Worcester Porcelain, 18th century Guildhall, 15th century Commandery, The Elgar Birthplace, Tudor House Museum, City Museum and Art Gallery, Worcestershire Yeomanry Cavalry Regimental Museum, The Worcestershire Regimental Museum.

Tourist Office: Guildhall, High Street, Worcester WR1 2EY. Telephone (0905) 723471 Exts 201/2/3/4.

Remarks: Bags not allowed, storage facilities available. Donations box. Historical county map on display.

HERTFORDSHIRE

HERTFORDSHIRE Record Office
County Hall
Pegs Lane
Hertford SG13 8DE
Telephone: (0992) 555105

Opening Hours: Monday to Thursday 9.15 am to 5.15 pm, Friday 9.15 am to 4.30 pm. Annual closure: public holidays plus Tuesday following Spring and Autumn bank holidays; one extra day at Christmas.

Car Parking: 200 to 300 places.

Children: No specific ruling but dependent on behaviour.

Disabled: Arrangements can be made to consult records in Local Studies Library on ground floor.

Appointments System: Prior booking for seats essential (at least 48 hours).

Prior booking for viewers necessary. Signing in by register plus CARN.

23 seats, six film viewers and two fiche.

Document Ordering: Prior ordering accepted by letter or telephone. Catalogue numbers helpful. Any number at a time but only one issued. Delivery five to ten minutes. Photocopying by staff on same day; if large quantity or busy, sent by post; BTs allowed. No facilities for typing or taping. Cameras by prior arrangement.

Records: Some Ts of PRs/BTs on open shelves; some Ts of PRs require ordering. Original PRs mainly on fiche/film. Diocesan records.

Postal Research: Yes; charge made.

Facilities: Toilets and public telephone on premises. Refreshments plus room for own food. Cafe/pub five to ten minutes. Shops ten minutes including bookshop with local history publications.

Publications: Historical county map, *Genealogical Sources.* Free: leaflet on facilities of RO.

Other Repositories: Local Studies Library, County Hall, Hertford SG13 8EJ.

Places of Interest: Parliament Square, Bluecoat School, Lombard House, Hertford Museum.

Tourist Office: The Castle, Hertford SG14 1HR, Telephone (0279) 55261.

Remarks: Records of County Council and other local authorities stored elsewhere require one day's prior notice. Historical county map on display.

HUMBERSIDE

HULL City Record Office
79 Lowgate
Kingston-Upon-Hull HU1 2AA
Telephone: (0482) 222015/6

Opening Hours: Monday to Thursday 8.45 am to 12.30 pm and 1.30 pm to 4.45 pm, Friday 8.45 am to 12.30 pm and 1.30 pm to 4.15 pm. Late night alternate Wednesdays until 8 pm, by appointment only. Annual closure: public holidays.

Car Parking: None

Children: At archivist's discretion.

Disabled: By prior arrangement.

Appointments System: Prior booking for seats necessary (one day). Signing in by register. Fifteen seats, and one film viewer.

Document Ordering: Prior ordering accepted by letter or telephone. Catalogue numbers necessary. Three at a time, delivery five minutes. Photocopying by staff on same day. No facilities for typing or taping. Cameras not allowed.

Records: No PRs/BTs. City Council, administration of justice, business, private organisations, charities, Poor Law Unions, schools etc.
Postal Research: None
Facilities: Toilets, but no public telephone. No refreshment facilities but cafe/pub two minutes. Shops five minutes including bookshop with local history publications.
Publications: *Index to the Poll Tax Assessments, The Sieges of Kingston upon Hull 1642 and 1643, History of Kingston upon Hull* (two volumes). Free: sources for genealogy, guide to finding aids, publications list.
Other Repositories: Local Studies Library, Central Library, Albion Street, Hull; The Brynmor Jones Library, The University, Cottingham Road, Hull; The Department of Social and Economic History, The University of Hull, Cottingham Road, Hull; The Yorkshire Archaeological Society, Clarendon Road, Leeds (library and archives relating to whole of the ancient county).
Places of Interest: Town Docks Museum, Queen Victoria Square; High Street Museums; Ferens Art Gallery; Holy Trinity; St Mark's; house of William Wilberforce; Georgian houses; the old Grammar School.
Tourist Office: Central Library, Albion Street, Hull HU1 3TF. Telephone (0482) 223344. 75/76 Carr Lane, Hull HU1 3RD, Telephone (0482) 223559.
Remarks: Deeds of council property and papers relating to their construction stored elsewhere require prior notice, bags not allowed, historical county map on display.

HUMBERSIDE County Record Office
County Hall
Beverley HU17 9BA
Telephone: (0482) 867131 Ext 3394

Opening Hours: Monday to Thursday 9.15 am to 4.45 pm, Friday 9.15 am to 4 pm. Late night opening on Tuesdays until 8 pm. Occasional lunchtime closures from 1 pm to 2 pm, due to staff shortages. Annual closure: public holidays plus Tuesday following Spring and late Summer public holidays; last complete week in January.
Car Parking: Nearby
Children: Accompanied: not allowed. Unaccompanied: ten years plus on authorised project but prior notice required.
Disabled: Wheelchair access, but prior notice helpful.

Appointments System: Prior booking for seats (ten days at least) and also necessary for viewers. Signing in by register (may be joining CARN in near future). Fifteen seats, two film viewers, and one fiche.
Document Ordering: Prior ordering accepted by letter or telephone. Catalogue numbers helpful but not necessary. Six at a time may be ordered on arrival and then hourly; documents for Tuesday evening must be ordered before 4.30 pm on that day. Photocopying by staff and sent by post. Typing not permitted but taping allowed by prior arrangement. Cameras by prior arrangement.
Records: Some Ts of PRs on open shelves, some original PRs, diocesan repository for Archdeaconry of East Riding.
Postal Research: Yes; charge made for searches over fifteen minutes.
Facilities: Toilets, but no public telephone. No refreshment facilities but cafe/pub five minutes. Shops five minutes including bookshop with local history publications.
Publications: *Handlist of PRs, Non Anglican Churches, East Riding Register of Deeds: Guide for Users,* historical map. Free: lists of education records, Quarter Sessions records.
Other Repositories: Beverley Public Library, Local Studies Section, Champney Road, Beverley.
Places of Interest: The Minster, Friary, St Mary's Church, Guildhall, Market Cross, Museum of Army Transport, Skidby Windmill and Museum, Beverley Art Gallery and Museum.
Tourist Office: The Guildhall, Register Square, Beverley HU17 9AU. Telephone (0482) 867430. Museum of Army Transport, Flemingate, Beverley HU17 0NG. Telephone (0482) 867813.
Remarks: Local authority records (eg District Council rate books) stored elsewhere require one week's prior notice. Bags not allowed, storage facilities available. Historical county map on display. Filming of PRs has just commenced so the number of viewers may be increased and original PRs may not be produced.

SOUTH HUMBERSIDE Area Record Office
Town Hall Square
Grimsby
South Humberside DN31 1HX
Telephone: (0472) 353481

Opening Hours: Monday to Thursday 9.30 am to 12 noon and 1 pm to 5 pm,

Friday 9.30 am to 12 noon and 1 pm to 4.15 pm. Late night Tuesday until 9 pm requires appointment made by previous Friday. Annual closure: public holidays plus some following Tuesdays.
Car Parking: Six places.
Children: Accompanied: no specific ruling but dependent on behaviour and ability to do some research. Unaccompanied: at archivist's discretion.
Disabled: Wheelchair access. All public facilities on ground floor.
Appointments System: Prior booking for seats advisable. Signing in by register (may be joining CARN in near future). Six seats.
Document Ordering: Prior ordering accepted by letter or telephone. Catalogue numbers necessary. Number at a time at archivist's discretion. Delivery two minutes. Photocopying by staff and sent by post. Typing/taping permitted if no other searcher objects (manual typewriter only).
Records: Old Clee original PRs only; registers of ships, fishing vessels; crew lists; dock records; merchant marine and fishing apprentice registers; education records. PRs are at Lincoln RO.
Postal Research: Limited, no charge made.
Facilities: Toilets but no public telephone. No refreshment facilities but cafe/pub two minutes. Shops two minutes including bookshop with local history publications.
Publications: *Summary Guide.* Free: leaflets on genealogical sources, shipping records, education records, office brochure.
Other Repositories: Local Collection, Reference Library, Central Library, Town Hall Square, Grimsby DN31 1HG; Welholme Galleries, Welholme Road, Grimsby DN32 9LP.
Places of Interest: "Old World" fishing port, Doughty Museum, Dock Tower.
Tourist Office: Central Library, Town Hall Square, Grimsby DN31 1HG. Telephone (0472) 240410.
Remarks: Winn Papers 1860-1941, Grimsby Borough Engineers' plans and records, Grimsby fishing/merchant vessel crew lists 1864 - 1914 stored elsewhere require one day's prior notice. Some crew lists' indexes (approximately 30,000) available without prior notice, though postal enquiry or preliminary visit is necessary. Bags not allowed, storage facilities available.

ISLE OF MAN

GENERAL REGISTRY
Finch Road
Douglas
Isle of Man
Telephone: (0624) 73358

Opening Hours: Monday to Friday 9 am to 1 pm and 2.15 pm to 4.30 pm. Annual closure: 5 July and Friday of TT Race week.
Car Parking: None
Children: At archivist's discretion.
Disabled: Lift.
Appointments System: No seats (public office counter).
Document Ordering: Prior ordering accepted by letter or telephone. Catalogue numbers unnecessary. Any number at a time. Photocopying by staff on same day. No facilities for typing or taping. Cameras not allowed.
Records: Ts of PRs/BTs require ordering. Church of England baptisms and burials pre 1878, marriage pre 1883, dissenter marriages 1849-83, wills and deeds from 1911 to date.
Postal Research: Limited, charge made.
Facilities: Toilets and public telephone on premises. No refreshment facilities but cafe/pub five minutes. Shops five minutes.
Publications: Free leaflets on holdings etc.
Places of Interest: Snaefell Railway; Laxey Working Water Wheel; Grove Rural Life Museum, Nr Ramsey; Nautical Museum, Castletown; Cregneash Village Folk Museum, Nr Port St Mary, Port Erin.
Tourist Office: 13 Victoria Street, Douglas. Telephone (0624) 74323. Sefton Bureau, Harris Promenade, Douglas. Telephone (0624) 28627.
Remarks: See *The Manx Family Tree (a Beginners Guide to Records in the Isle of Man)* by Janet Narasimham (1986).

MANX MUSEUM LIBRARY
Kingswood Grove
Douglas
Isle of Man
Telephone: (0624) 75522

Opening Hours: Monday to Saturday 10 am to 5 pm. Annual closure: Christmas Day, Boxing Day, New Year's Day, Good Friday, and morning of Tynwald Day.
Car Parking: None
Children: Accompanied: no specific ruling. Unaccompanied: twelve years plus.
Disabled: Lift. Advance notification preferred.

Appointments System: Prior booking for seats and viewers unnecessary. Signing in by register. Approximately thirty seats. Seven film viewers and two fiche.
Document Ordering: Prior ordering not allowed. Delivery two minutes plus. Photocopying restricted; by staff on same day. No facilities for typing or taping. Cameras by special arrangement.
Records: Ts of PRs on film require ordering; some original PRs/BTs on fiche/film.
Postal Research: Limited to indexes, no charge made.
Facilities: Toilets. Public telephone nearby. No refreshment facilities but cafe/pub five minutes. Shops two minutes including bookshop with local history publications.
Places of Interest: See entry for General Registry, Douglas.
Tourist Office: See entry for General Registry, Douglas.

ISLE OF WIGHT

ISLE OF WIGHT County Record Office
26 Hillside
Newport
Isle of Wight PO30 2EB
Telephone: (0983) 823820

Opening Hours: Monday, Tuesday, Thursday, Friday 9.30 am to 5 pm; Wednesday 9.30 am to 8.30 pm. Annual closure: public holidays.
Car Parking: Three places
Children: Accompanied: ten years plus. Unaccompanied: 16 years plus.
Disabled: Entrance via back door but prior notice advisable.
Appointments System: Prior booking for seats unnecessary, but for viewers necessary. Signing in by register. Twelve seats, two film viewers and two fiche.
Document Ordering: Prior ordering accepted by letter only. Catalogue numbers preferred. Six at a time, delivery five minutes. Photocopying by staff on same day or sent by post. No facilities for typing or taping. Cameras permitted.
Records: PRs fully indexed from 1538-1837 (marriages), to 1858 (burials), to 1900 (baptisms), originals withdrawn.
Postal Research: None
Facilities: Toilets but no public telephone. No refreshment facilities but cafe/pub five minutes. Shops five minutes including bookshop with local history publications.
Places of Interest: 12th century Carisbrooke Castle and Museum, Roman Villa, St Thomas the Apostle Church,

Cothey Bottom Heritage Centre.
Tourist Office: Church Litton Car Park, Newport, Isle of Wight. Telephone (0983) 525450.
Remarks: Some local authority records stored elsewhere require two days' prior notice. Bags not allowed, storage facilities available. Historical county map on display. Winchester diocesan records, including BTs, are in Hampshire RO, Winchester.

KENT

BEXLEY see LONDON
BROMLEY see LONDON
GREENWICH see LONDON
LEWISHAM see LONDON

Kent Archives Office
CANTERBURY Archives
The Precincts
Canterbury
Kent CT1 2EH
Telephone: (0227) 463510

This office is due to be merged with Kent Archive Service, so no information available. Contact the office for further information; city and diocesan records

INSTITUTE OF HERALDIC
AND GENEALOGICAL STUDIES
LIBRARY
79-82 Northgate
Canterbury
Kent CT1 1BA
Telephone: (0227) 68664

Opening Hours: Monday, Wednesday, Friday 9.30 am to 1 pm and 2 pm to 4.30 pm. Closed Tuesdays and Thursdays. Annual closure: public holidays and Christmas period.
Car Parking: None
Disabled: No facilities as the building is old with many stairs.
Appointments System: Prior booking for seats and viewers necessary (one week for seats). Signing in by register (entrance fee if not a member). Approximately five seats. Two film viewers, and three fiche.
Document Ordering: Prior ordering accepted by letter or telephone. Catalogue numbers unnecessary. Photocopying by staff on same day. No facilities for typing or taping. Cameras not allowed.
Records: No original source material; Ts of PRs on open shelves; finding aids.
Postal Research: Yes, charge made.
Facilities: Toilets, but no public telephone. Room for own food. Cafe/pub

two minutes. Shops two minutes including bookshop with local history publications.

Publications: Institute series of maps. Other publications at bookshop on premises. Free: leaflets on indexes and a general guide to the library, publications list.

Other Repositories: Dean and Chapter Library, Cathedral Precincts, Canterbury.

Places of Interest: Canterbury Heritage (Time Walk Museum), The Canterbury Centre, Canterbury Pilgrim's Way, The Royal Museum and Art Gallery, Buffs Regimental Museum, Roman Mosaic, the West Gate, Whitstable Museum.

Tourist Office: 34 St Margaret's Street, Canterbury. Telephone (0227) 766567.

Remarks: Catalogues of sources for each parish available. Some specialist indexes, some searched by staff only. Bags not allowed, storage facilities available. Donations box.

HYTHE Town Archives
Town Council Offices
Oaklands
Stade Street
Hythe
Kent CT21 6BG
Telephone: (0303) 66152 or at Folkestone Central Library (0303) 850123

Opening Hours: Wednesday 9.30 am to 1 pm and 2 pm to 4.45 pm, by appointment only.

Car Parking: Ten places

Disabled: By prior arrangement. No lift, offices are on the first floor.

Appointments System: Prior booking for seats essential (as much notice as possible).

Document Ordering: Prior ordering accepted by letter or telephone. Catalogue numbers unnecessary. Number at a time at archivist's discretion. Delivery five minutes. Photocopying restricted; by staff on same day; if large quantity or busy, sent by post. No facilities for typing or taping. Cameras restricted.

Records: No PRs, mainly archives of former borough of Hythe; some parish material.

Postal Research: Very limited, no charge made.

Facilities: Toilets, but no public telephone. No refreshment facilities but cafe/pub five minutes. Shops five minutes including bookshop with local history publications.

Publications: *Town and Cinque Port of Hythe: Catalogue of Documents.*

Places of Interest: Romney, Hythe and Dymchurch Light Railway; Martello Towers; St Leonard's Church. Hythe is one of the Cinque Ports and has old houses and inns. Hythe Local History Room (address above).

Tourist Office: Prospect Road Car Park, Hythe CT21 5NH. Telephone (0303) 67799.

Remarks: Space in this office is extremely limited.

KENT Archives Office
County Hall
Maidstone
Kent ME4 1XQ
Telephone: (0622) 671411 Ext 4363

Opening Hours: Tuesday to Friday 9 am to 4.30 pm (closed Mondays). Annual closure: public holidays; fortnight each Spring and Autumn.

Car Parking: None

Children: Ten years plus.

Disabled: Disabled friendly but no parking.

Appointments System: Prior booking for seats (one week) and viewers necessary. Signing in by CARN. Twelve seats and twelve viewers.

Document Ordering: Prior ordering accepted by letter or telephone. Catalogue numbers necessary. Three at a time; delivery ten minutes. Last orders before 3.30 pm. Photocopying by staff and sent by post or collected later; PRs by printout only. Typing/taping by prior arrangement on Mondays only. Cameras by prior arrangement.

Records: Some Ts of PRs on open shelves. Some original PRs on fiche/film require ordering.

Postal Research: None

Facilities: Toilets, but no public telephone. Refreshments but no room for own food. Cafe/pub five minutes. Shops five minutes.

Publications: (At bookshop on premises) *Guide to RO,* historical county map etc. Free leaflets on house and family history.

Other Repositories: Maidstone Reference Library, St Faith Street, Maidstone, Kent ME14 1LH.

Places of Interest: Museum of Kent Rural Life, Lock Lane, Sandling; The Queen's Own Royal West Kent Regimental Museum; Tyrwhitt Drake Museum of Carriages; 14th century Archbishop's Palace; All Saints Church; Museum and Art Gallery (local history).

Tourist Office: The Gatehouse, Old Palace Gardens, Mill Street, Maidstone, Kent ME15 6YE. Telephone (0625) 602169/67358.

Remarks: Some modern business and local authority records stored elsewhere require one day's prior notice. Bags not allowed, storage facilities available. Historical county map on display, donations box. See *West Kent Sources: A Guide to Genealogical Research in the Diocese of Rochester* (North West Kent FHS, 1989).

Kent Archives Office (MEDWAY area)
Civic Centre
Strood
Kent
Telephone: (92) 732 714

This office should be opening in April 1990.

Remarks: For further information contact Kent Archives Office at Maidstone. See *West Kent Sources: A Guide to Genealogical Research in the Diocese of Rochester* (North West Kent FHS, 1989).

Kent Archives Office
(NORTH EAST KENT area)
Ramsgate Library
Guildford Lawn
Ramsgate
Kent CT11 9A1
Telephone: (0843) 593532

Opening Hours: Thursday 9.30 am to 5 pm, by appointment only (likely to change in the near future).
Car Parking: None
Children: School age.
Disabled: Ramp and access for wheelchairs.
Appointments System: Prior booking for seats essential (as much notice as possible) and for viewers necessary. Eight seats (shared with library). One film viewer, and two fiche (shared with library).
Document Ordering: Prior ordering accepted by letter or telephone. Catalogue numbers unnecessary. Number at a time at archivist's discretion. Delivery five minutes. Photocopying restricted; by staff, sent by post. If large quantity or busy, sent by post. No facilities for typing or taping. Cameras restricted.
Records: Ts and fiche of PRs available for a few parishes in Thanet and adjoining area. A few Ts of Nonconformist registers for Thanet, and some originals.
Postal Research: Very limited, no charge made.
Facilities: No toilets no public telephone. No refreshment facilities but cafe/pub two minutes. Shops two minutes

Publications: Free leaflets on sources for family history, produced by Kent Archive Office.
Places of Interest: Viking Ship, Pegwell Bay; Queen's Court; Maritime Museum Complex; Ramsgate Motor Museum; Ramsgate Museum (local history); Spitfire Memorial Pavilion.
Tourist Office: Argyle Centre, Queen Street, Ramsgate CT11 9EE. Telephone (0843) 591086.
Remarks: Plans and local authority records stored elsewhere require seven days' prior notice. All services are soon to be shared with the local history section of the library, including seating.

Kent Archives Office
(SOUTH EAST KENT area)
Central Library
Grace Hill
Folkestone
Kent CT20 1HD
Telephone: (0303) 850123

Opening Hours: Friday 9 am to 5 pm by appointment; other times by arrangement (liable to alteration in the near future).
Car Parking: None
Disabled: Prior arrangement necessary.
Appointments System: Prior booking for seats essential (as much as possible) and for viewers necessary. Twelve seats (shared with library). One film viewer. One fiche (shared with library).
Document Ordering: Prior ordering accepted by letter or telephone. Catalogue numbers unnecessary. Number at a time at archivist's discretion. Delivery five minutes. Photocopying restricted; by staff on same day; if large quantity or busy, sent by post. No facilities for typing or taping. Cameras restricted.
Records: No PRs kept. Ts and film of PRs in Reference Library. A few Nonconformists baptismal registers; parish and borough.
Postal Research: Limited to under fifteen minutes; no charge made.
Facilities: No toilets or public telephone. No refreshment facilities but cafe/pub two minutes. Shops five minutes including bookshop with local history publications.
Publications: None: see Maidstone RO.
Places of Interest: Folkestone Museum, St Mary and St Eanswythe Church, The Leas, Metropole Arts Centre, Folkestone Museum and Art Gallery.
Tourist Office: Harbour Street, Folkestone CT20 1QN. Telephone (0303) 58594.

Remarks: All maps and plans, uncatalogued and rarely used collections stored elsewhere require seven days' prior notice.

Kent Archives Office
(WEST KENT Area Branch Office)
Sevenoaks Library
Buckhurst Lane
Sevenoaks
Kent TN13 1LQ
Telephone: (0732) 453118/452384

Opening Hours: Monday to Wednesday, and Friday, 9.30 am to 5.30 pm; Thursday 9.30 am to 7 pm; Saturday 9 am to 5 pm. Annual closure: public holidays.
Car Parking: None
Children: No specific ruling.
Disabled: Disabled friendly.
Appointments System: Prior booking for seats helpful, but not essential, and for viewers unnecessary. Approximately four seats. Two film viewers, and one fiche.
Document Ordering: Prior ordering accepted by letter or telephone. Catalogue numbers unnecessary. Approximately three at a time. Delivery within a few minutes. Photocopying DIY. No facilities for typing or taping. Cameras permitted.
Records: Ts of PRs require ordering; some original PRs on fiche/film.
Postal Research: Limited; no charge made.
Facilities: No toilets or public telephone. No refreshment facilities but cafe/pub five minutes. Shops two minutes including bookshop with local history publications.
Places of Interest: Knole House, St Nicholas' Church, Sevenoaks Museum (local history).
Tourist Office: Buckhurst Lane, Sevenoaks TN13 1LQ. Telephone (0732) 450305.
Remarks: The Archivist is normally available Mondays, Wednesdays and Fridays, but documents may be produced at other times by library staff. See *West Kent Sources: A Guide to Genealogical Research in the Diocese of Rochester* (North West Kent FHS, 1989).

LANCASHIRE

BURY see MANCHESTER

LANCASHIRE Record Office
Bow Lane
Preston PR1 2RE
Telephone: (0772) 54868

Opening Hours: Tuesday 10 am to 8.30 pm, Wednesday to Friday 10 am to 5 pm (closed Mondays). Annual closure: public holidays plus Tuesday following Easter and Spring bank holidays.
Car Parking: Ten places.
Children: No specific ruling but dependent on behaviour.
Disabled: Two car parking places, lift.
Appointments System: Prior booking for seats and viewers unnecessary. Signing in by register plus CARN. 42 seats, eight film viewers, and two fiche (due to be increased).
Document Ordering: Prior ordering not allowed. Three at a time; delivery depends on how busy and type of record. Photocopying by staff next day or sent by post; BTs allowed. No facilities for typing or taping. Cameras restricted.
Records: Ts of PRs mostly on open shelves, original PRs only if unavailable in other forms; BTs on film.
Postal Research: Specific enquiry, no charge made.
Facilities: Toilets but no public telephone on premises. No refreshment facilities but cafe/pub two to five minutes. Shops five minutes including bookshop with local history publications.
Publications: Handlist of genealogical sources, *Guide to the RO,* historical maps.
Other Repositories: The Harris Library, Market Square, Preston.
Places of Interest: Elizabethan Astley Hall (8 miles), Harris Museum and Art Gallery, Lancashire County and Regimental Museum, The Loyal Regimental Museum.
Tourist Office: The Guildhall, Lancaster Road, Preston PR1 1HT. Telephone (0772) 53731.
Remarks: Bags not allowed, storage facilities available. Historical county map on display.

WIGAN see MANCHESTER

LEICESTERSHIRE

LEICESTERSHIRE Record Office
57 New Walk
Leicester LE1 7JB
Telephone: (0533) 544566

Opening Hours: Monday to Thursday 9.15 am to 5 pm, Friday 9.15 am to 4.45 pm, Saturday 9.15 am to 12.15 pm. Annual closure: public holidays plus following Tuesdays and preceding Saturdays; first week in October.
Car Parking: Very limited.
Children: Accompanied: no specific ruling but dependent on behaviour. Unaccompanied: 14 years plus.

Disabled: Prior arrangement required.
Appointments System: Prior booking for seats and viewers unnecessary. Signing in by register, ROs own reader's ticket. 35 seats, six film viewers, twelve fiche.
Document Ordering: No prior ordering except for documents stored elsewhere. Three at a time; delivery five to ten minutes. Photocopying by staff on same day; if large quantity or busy, sent by post; PRs/BTs by printout only. No facilities for typing or taping. Cameras permitted.
Records: Some Ts of PRs on open shelves; some original PRs/BTs on fiche/film.
Postal Research: Limited (twenty minutes only), no charge made.
Facilities: Toilets, no public telephone. No refreshment facilities but cafe/pub two minutes.
Shops ten minutes including bookshop with local history publications.
Publications: Map of Leicester, OS maps, posters, *Quarter Sessions in RO, Village History in the Records, Family and Estate records in RO, A Guide to Tracing Your Family Tree in the RO.* Free leaflets on the RO, publications list and record agents.
Other Repositories: Leicestershire Local History Collection, Public Reference Library, Bishop Street, Leicester LE16 6AA; Leicester University Library Archives Section.
Places of Interest: Museum of the Royal Leicester Regiment, Jewry Wall Museum, Roman Baths and Museum, Wygston's House Museum of Costume, Museum and Art Gallery, cathedral, Belgrave Hall, Newarke Houses Museum, Guildhall, Gas Museum.
Tourist Office: 2-6 St Martins Walk, Leicester LE1 5DG. Telephone (0533) 511333.
Remarks: Larger business and family collections, archdeaconry and some local authority records stored elsewhere require one week's prior notice (plus catalogue numbers). Bags not allowed, storage facilities available. Donations box. Historical county map on display.

LINCOLNSHIRE

LINCOLNSHIRE Archives Office
The Castle
Lincoln LN1 3AB
Telephone: (0522) 25158

Opening Hours: Monday to Friday 9.15 am to 4.45 pm. Annual closure: public holidays plus last week in January and first week in February.

Car Parking: None
Children: At archivist's discretion.
Disabled: No facilities.
Appointments System: Prior booking for seats necessary (one week) but for viewers unnecessary. Signing in by register plus reader's ticket. Thirty seats, three film viewers, and eight fiche.
Document Ordering: Prior ordering accepted by letter or telephone. Catalogue numbers unnecessary. Number at a time at archivist's discretion. Delivery twenty minutes, longer at lunchtimes. Photocopying DIY; BTs allowed. No facilities for typing or taping. Cameras not allowed.
Records: Some Ts of PRs on open shelves; some Ts of PRs require ordering. Original PRs if not on film/fiche, diocesan records for Lincoln and Archdeaconry of Lincoln.
Postal Research: None
Facilities: Toilets but no public telephone. No refreshment facilities but cafe/pub two minutes. Shops two minutes including bookshop with local history publications.
Publications: *Your Family History in Lincolnshire Archives, Lists of PRs, Nonconformists, Lincoln Diocesan Archives.*
Other Repositories: Lincoln City Library, (Local Studies). Free School Lane, Lincoln; Lincoln Cathedral Library, The Cathedral, Lincoln.
Places of Interest: Aaron the Jew's House, Cardinal's Hat, castle, cathedral, Usher Gallery, East Gate Roman Tower, Museum of Lincolnshire Life (includes Royal Lincolnshire Regiment Museum), City and County Museum.
Tourist Office: 21 The Cornhill, Lincoln. Telephone (0522) 512971. 9 Castle Hill, Lincoln LN1 3AA. Telephone (0522) 29828.
Remarks: Urban and Rural District Council, Ruston and Hornsby engineering records, some other business records stored elsewhere require one week's prior notice. Bags not allowed, storage facilities available. Donations box. Historical county map on display.

LONDON
CENTRAL & OUTER

PLACES OF INTEREST

General Museums: Bethnal Green Museum of Childhood; British Museum; Cabinet War Rooms; Church Farm House Museum, Hendon; Cuming Museum, Southwark; Geffrye Museum, Shoreditch; Jewish Museum, Tavistock

Square; The London Museum of Jewish Life, The Sternberg Centre, 80 East End Road; London Transport Museum, Covent Garden; Museum of Garden History, Lambeth Palace Road; The Museum of London; The Museum of Methodism, 49 City Road; National Postal Museum; The Royal Hospital Museum, Chelsea; Theatre Museum, Covent Garden; Wimbledon Windmill Museum.

Services' Museums: The Guards Museum, Wellington Barracks; The Honourable Artillery Company, City Road; Inns of Court and City Yeomanry Museum, Lincolns Inn; Museum of Artillery, Repository Road, Woolwich; The Royal Fusiliers Museum, Tower of London; Royal Regiment of Fusiliers, City of London Company 5th Battalion (appointment only), Balham High Road.

Note: The majority of parochial and other records relating to London and the county of Middlesex are deposited in the Greater London Record Office. Similar records for the City of London will be found in the Department of Manuscripts, Guildhall Library, Aldermanbury, London.

MAIN TOURIST OFFICE

British Travel Centre, 12 Regent Street, Piccadilly Circus, London SW1Y 4PQ, Telephone 01 730 3400 (from May 1990: 071 730 3400)
Written enquiries to:
London Tourist Board, 26 Grosvenor Gardens, SW1W 0DU
Telephone information service:
Telephone 01 730 3488 (from May 1990: 071 730 3488)

LONDON BOROUGHS

BOROUGH OF BARKING AND DAGENHAM
BARKING AND DAGENHAM
Local History Studies
Valence Library
Valence House
Becontree Avenue
Dagenham
Essex RM8 3HT
Telephone: 01 592 4500 Ext 4293, but from May 1990: (081) 592 4500 Ext 4293

Opening Hours: House: Monday to Friday 9.30 am to 1 pm and 2 pm to 4.30 pm. Library: Monday, Tuesday, Thursday, Friday 9.30 am to 7 pm; Wednesday and Saturday 9.30 am to 1 pm.
Annual closure: public holidays.

Car Parking: Approximately 20 places
Appointments System: Prior booking for seats and viewers necessary (one week). Signing in by register plus identification. Twenty seats, and two film viewers.
Document Ordering: Prior ordering necessary (by letter or telephone at least one day before visit). Catalogue numbers unnecessary. Up to ten items at a time; delivery on arrival. Photocopying by staff on same day or by post. No facilities for typing or taping. Cameras permitted.
Records: Ts of PRs require ordering; PRs on film.
Publications: Free: list of eight papers to holdings, *Guide to Local History Resources.*
Places of Interest: Valence House Museum.
Remarks: Borough of Barking and Dagenham records and Fanshawe Family records require one week's prior notice.

BOROUGH OF BARNET
London Borough of BARNET Archives and Local Studies
Ravensfield House
The Burroughs
London NW4 4BE
Telephone: 01 202 5625 Ext 55, but from May 1990: (081) 202 5625 Ext 55

Opening Hours: Monday to Wednesday, and Friday, 9.30 am to 5 pm; Thursday 9.30 am to 7 pm; Saturday 9.30 am to 4 pm. Annual closure: public holidays.
Car Parking: Approximately 20 places
Children: Accompanied: no specific ruling. Unaccompanied: seven years plus.
Disabled: No facilities
Appointments System: Prior booking for seats necessary (24 hours) but unnecessary for viewers. Signing in by register. Four seats, one film viewer, and one fiche.
Document Ordering: Prior ordering accepted by letter or telephone. Catalogue numbers preferred. Three at a time; delivery within a few minutes. Photocopying by staff on same day; if large quantity or busy, sent by post; DIY sometimes. No facilities for typing or taping. Cameras not allowed.
Records: Ts of PRs require ordering; original PRs on fiche/film.
Postal Research: Limited, no charge made.
Facilities: Toilets, but no public telephone. No refreshment facilities but cafe/pub 2 to five minutes. Shops five to ten minutes including bookshop with local history publications.
Publications: Books, pamphlets, old

local OS maps, local postcards, town trails, *Finchley Vestry Minutes* (part 2). Publication list available.

Other Repositories: Royal Air Force Museum, Hendon, London NW9 5LL; Barnet Museum, Wood Street, Barnet, Herts.

Places of Interest: Church Farmhouse Museum, Greyhound Hill, Hendon.

Remarks: 19th/20th century rate books for Finchley, East Barnet, Chipping Barnet, Hendon, South Mimms, Friern Barnet, Totteridge require two days notice. Bags not allowed.

BOROUGH OF BEXLEY
BEXLEY Local Studies Centre
Hall Place
Bourne Road
Bexley
Kent DA5 1PQ
Telephone: (0322) 526574

Opening Hours: Monday to Saturday 9 am to 5 pm (4.15 pm in winter). Annual closure: public holidays.

Car Parking: Approximately 200 places

Children: Any age

Disabled: Only one step. Assistance available for wheelchairs. Toilet nearby.

Appointments System: Prior booking for seats and viewers unnecessary.

Signing in by register. Eighteen seats, one fiche, and three fiche/film.

Document Ordering: Prior ordering accepted by letter or telephone. Catalogue numbers usually unnecessary. Delivery approximately five minutes. Photo- copying at staff discretion; by staff usually on same day; PRs by printout only. No facilities for typing or taping. Cameras permitted.

Records: Ts of PRs some on open shelves, some require ordering. Original PRs on fiche/film, original PRs.

Postal Research: Specific enquiry, no charge made.

Facilities: Toilets nearby but no public telephone. No refreshment facilities but cafe/pub two to five minutes. Shops fifteen minutes including bookshop with local history publications.

Publications: *Guide to Local History Resources, Tracing Your Family Tree*, pamphlets on local history.

Places of Interest: Bexley Museum, and gardens: as above address.

Remarks: Modern local records are stored elsewhere and require one week's prior notice. Historical map available on request. See *West Kent Sources: A Guide to Genealogical Research in the Diocese of Rochester* (North West Kent FHS, 1989).

BOROUGH OF BRENT
GRANGE MUSEUM
OF COMMUNITY HISTORY
Neasden Lane
London NW10 1QB
Telephone: 01 908 7432, but from May 1990: (081) 908 7432

Opening Hours: Tuesday and Thursday 12 noon to 5 pm, Wednesday 12 noon to 8 pm, Saturday 10 am to 12 noon and 1 pm to 5 pm (under review). Closed Mondays and Fridays. Annual closure: public holidays.

Car Parking: 20 places

Children: 8 years plus.

Disabled: Library on first floor and no wheelchair access but with prior notice arrangements can be made to view the records on ground floor.

Appointments System: Prior booking for seats and viewers unnecessary.

Signing in by register. Six seats, two film viewers, and two fiche.

Document Ordering: Prior ordering not allowed. Four at a time, delivery approximately fifteen minutes. Photocopying by staff on same day. No facilities for typing or taping. Cameras permitted.

Records: Ts of PRs require ordering. Poor Law, electoral registers, rate books.

Postal Research: Very limited, no charge made.

Facilities: Toilets, but no public telephone. No refreshment facilities but cafe/pub two minutes. Shops five minutes.

Publications: Under preparation.

Places of Interest: Grange Museum.

Remarks: Donations box. It is proposed to open a room where researchers may eat their own food, and to supply a drink vending machine.

BOROUGH OF BROMLEY
Local Studies and Archives Section
Central Library
High Street
BROMLEY
Kent BR1 1EX
Telephone: 01 460 9955 Ext 261, but from May 1990: (081) 460 9955 Ext 261

Opening Hours: Monday, Wednesday, Friday 9.30 am to 6 pm, Tuesday, Thursday 9.30 am to 8 pm, Saturday 9.30 am to 5 pm. Annual closure: public holidays.

Car Parking: None

Children: No specific ruling.

Disabled: Lifts, parking by prior arrangement, toilets nearby.

Appointments System: Prior booking for seats and viewers unnecessary.

Signing in by register. More than twenty seats. Two or three film viewers and fiche.

Document Ordering: Prior ordering accepted by letter or telephone. Catalogue numbers not always necessary. Number at a time at staff discretion. Delivery usually under ten minutes but may be delayed during lunch time. Photocopying by staff usually on same day. No facilities for typing or taping. Cameras not allowed.

Records: Ts of PRs on open shelves, original PRs on fiche/film.

Postal Research: Very limited, no charge made.

Facilities: Toilets nearby. Public telephone on premises. No refreshment facilities but cafe/pub two minutes. Shops two minutes including bookshop with local history publications.

Publications: Local history publications. Free leaflet on PRs, others in preparation.

Remarks: Historical map on display and for sale. See *West Kent Sources: A Guide to Genealogical Research in the Diocese of Rochester* (North West Kent FHS, 1989).

BOROUGH OF CAMDEN
Local Studies Library
HOLBORN Library
32-38 Theobalds Road
London WC1X 8PA
Telephone: 01 405 2705 Ext 337.
Reference Library Extensions 330/331.
From May 1990: 071 405 2705 Ext 337

Opening Hours: Contact Holborn Library for opening hours and appointment; open three days per week including evenings and restricted Saturday opening. Annual closure: public holidays.

Car Parking: None

Children: No specific ruling.

Disabled: Access but not to outstore.

Appointments System: Prior booking for seats essential (24 hours notice). Prior booking for viewers necessary. Four seats, two film viewers, one fiche/film viewer.

Document Ordering: Prior ordering accepted by letter or telephone. Catalogue numbers unnecessary. Reasonable number at a time permitted. Delivery ten to fifteen minutes. Photocopying restricted; DIY. No facilities for typing or taping. Cameras permitted.

Records: Ts of PRs require ordering. Rate books, former Holborn Borough Council archives, Highgate Cemetery registers.

Postal Research: None

Facilities: Toilets and public telephone on premises. No refreshment facilities but cafe/pub two minutes. Shops five minutes. Underground: Holborn/Chancery Lane.

Publications: *Guide to London Local Library Resources: London Borough of Camden.* Free *Guide to Collections.*

Remarks: Council and Vestry Committee minutes 1856 to c1978, rate books 1900-1966 and various modern council records require prior notice.

BOROUGH OF CAMDEN
Local Studies Library
SWISS COTTAGE Library
88 Avenue Road
London NW3 3HA
Telephone: 01 586 5989 Ext 234, but from May 1990: 071 586 5989 Ext 234

Opening Hours: Monday and Thursday 9.30 am to 8 pm, Tuesday 9.30 am to 5 pm, first and third Saturday in month 9.30 am to 5 pm. May be closed for lunch from 1 pm to 2 pm. Closed Wednesdays and Fridays: it may be possible for the library to be open additional hours by prior arrangement. Annual closure: public holidays.

Car Parking: Nearby

Children: No specific ruling.

Disabled: Access

Appointments System: Prior booking for seats unnecessary but for viewers necessary. Eight seats, two film viewers, one fiche. **Document Ordering:** Prior ordering accepted by letter or telephone. Catalogue numbers unnecessary. Reasonable number at a time. Delivery approximately ten minutes. Photocopying restricted; DIY. Typing permitted but not taping. Cameras permitted.

Records: Ts of PRs require ordering. Some PRs on fiche/film. Borough vestry minutes, rate books, manorial, private records, deeds, photographs, paintings, prints, Kentish Town Rolls (19th century drawings), periodicals, newspapers, directories, special collections, maps and plans, records relating to the former boroughs of St Pancras and Hampstead, MIs, one original PR.

Postal Research: None

Facilities: Toilets but no public telephone. No refreshment facilities but cafe/pub two minutes. Shops five minutes.

Publications: *Guide to London Local Library Resources: London Borough of Camden.* Free *Guide to Collections.*

Remarks: Local material in several local history organisations in Camden; also see Holborn Library.

ST CATHERINE'S
see GENERAL REGISTER OFFICE

COLINDALE see BRITISH LIBRARY,
NEWSPAPER LIBRARY

CHELSEA see KENSINGTON
CHISWICK see HOUNSLOW

BOROUGH OF CHISWICK
CHISWICK District Library (Reference Library)
Duke's Avenue
Chiswick
London W4 2AB
Telephone: 01 994 5295/1008, but from May 1990: (081) 994 5295/1008

Opening Hours: Monday to Wednesday 9 am to 8 pm, Thursday 9 am to 1 pm, Friday 9.30 am to 5 pm, Saturday 9 am to 5 pm. Annual closure: public holidays.
Car Parking: Ten places
Children: Accompanied: no age limit. Unaccompanied: ten years plus.
Disabled: Access to lending library on ground floor; material from reference library can be made available there.
Appointments System: Prior booking for seats and viewers unnecessary. Approximately thirty seats, one film viewer, and one fiche.
Document Ordering: Prior ordering essential (by letter or telephone). Catalogue numbers unnecessary. Unlimited number at a time. Delivery five to ten minutes. Photocopying by staff on same day or by post depending on availability of staff; DIY. No facilities for typing or taping. Cameras permitted.
Records: PRs on fiche, books, maps, prints, paintings, photographs, local newspapers, rate books, local directories, census, local authority minutes: all for areas of Brentford, Strand on the Green and Chiswick.
Postal Research: Yes, charge for photocopying plus postage.
Facilities: Toilets but no public telephone. No refreshment facilities but cafe/pub five minutes. Shops two minutes.
Publications: *Guide to London Local History Resources: London Borough of Hounslow*, local history books.
Other Repositories: Gunnersbury Park Museum, Gunnersby Park, London W3 8LQ.
Places of Interest: Chiswick House, Burlington Lane, Chiswick; Hogarth's House, Hogarth Lane, Great West Road, Chiswick

Borough of CROYDON
CROYDON Local Studies Library
Katharine Street
Croydon
Surrey CR0 6ND
Telephone: 01 760 5570, but from May 1990: (081) 760 5570

Opening Hours: Monday 9.30 am to 7 pm, Tuesday to Friday 9.30 am to 6 pm, Saturday 9 am to 5 pm. Annual closure: public holidays.
Car Parking: None
Children: Accompanied: ten years plus. Unaccompanied: twelve years plus.
Disabled: Entrance via Lending Library in Mint Walk.
Appointments System: Prior booking for seats and viewers unnecessary. Two film viewers and three fiche.
Document Ordering: Prior ordering accepted by letter or telephone. Catalogue numbers unnecessary. Photocopying by staff on same day or by post; DIY. No facilities for typing or taping. Cameras permitted.
Records: Original PRs/BTs on fiche/film. Original PRs.
Postal Research: None
Facilities: No toilets. Public telephone on premises. No refreshment facilities but cafe/pub two minutes. Shops five minutes including bookshop with local history publications.
Publications: Free leaflets
Tourist Office: Katharine Street, Croydon, Surrey CR9 1ET, Telephone 01 760 5400 Exts 2984/5 or 01 760 5630 (from May 1990 Telephone [081] 760 5400 or [081] 760 5630).
Remarks: Many records stored elsewhere require seven days' prior notice. Donations box. No archives are held here for the London Borough of Croydon.

DAGENHAM see BARKING

BOROUGH OF EALING
Local History Library
EALING Central Library
103 Ealing Broadway Centre
Ealing
London W5 5JY
Telephone: 01 567 3656 Ext 37, but from May 1990: (081) 567 3656 Ext 37

Opening Hours: Tuesday, Thursday,

Friday 9 am to 7.45 pm; Wednesday and Saturday 9 am to 5 pm (closed Mondays). Annual closure: public holidays.

Car Parking: Nearby

Disabled: Generally no facilities but possibility of some arrangements.

Appointments System: Prior booking for seats and viewers advisable. Approximately six to ten seats. One dual viewer (in Reference Library).

Document Ordering: Prior ordering accepted by letter or telephone. Catalogue numbers unnecessary. Generally one at a time permitted; delivery within a few minutes. No facilities for typing or taping. Cameras not allowed.

Records: Small collection of archives: rate books pre 1936, education records (mainly minutes), local societies' material, electoral registers, maps, Poor Law, vestry records.

Postal Research: Very limited, no charge made.

Facilities: No toilets or public telephone. No refreshment facilities but cafe/pub two minutes. Shops two minutes including bookshop with local history publications.

Publications: Local history publications eg *Ealing As It Was, Acton As It Was, Environs of Ealing, Ealing in the Thirties and Forties, History of Southall, Historical Notes on the Borough, Short History of Northolt* etc.

Other Repositories: Council records at London Borough of Ealing, Chief Executive's Department, Civic Centre, 14 Uxbridge Road, Ealing W5.

Places of Interest: Pitshanger Museum.

Remarks: One week's notice required for local periodicals. Reference library on ground floor. Most parish records at Greater London RO including rate books post 1835.

BOROUGH OF ENFIELD
Archives and Local History Unit
London Borough of ENFIELD Libraries
Southgate Town Hall
Green Lanes
London N13 4XD
Telephone: 01 982 7453, but from May 1990: (081) 982 7453

Opening Hours: Monday to Saturday 9 am to 5 pm. Annual closure: public holidays.

Car Parking: 30 places

Children: No specific ruling, but no access to original documents.

Disabled: Special parking bay, ramp (not Saturdays).

Appointments System: Prior booking unnecessary for seats but necessary for

viewers. Signing in by register. Six seats, one film viewer.

Document Ordering: Prior ordering accepted by letter or telephone. Catalogue numbers unnecessary. Number at a time at staff's discretion; delivery ten minutes. Photocopying by staff on same day. No facilities for typing or taping. Cameras permitted.

Records: Ts of PRs on open shelves, original documents.

Postal Research: Limited, no charge made.

Facilities: Toilets but no public telephone. No refreshment facilities but cafe/pub ten minutes. Shops five minutes.

BOROUGH OF FINSBURY
FINSBURY Local History Collection
Finsbury Library
245 St John Street
London EC1V 4NB
Telephone: 01 609 3051 Ext 266, but from 1990: 071 609 3051 Ext 266

Opening Hours: Monday, Tuesday, Thursday 9 am to 8 pm; Wednesday and Friday 9 am to 1 pm; Saturday 9 am to 5 pm (no appointment before 10 am). Annual closure: public holidays.

Car Parking: None

Children: At staff discretion.

Disabled: Not accessible for wheelchairs but special arrangements can be made according to situation and requirements.

Appointments System: Prior booking for seats and viewers essential (24 hours for seats). Signing in by register. Six seats, two film viewers, one fiche.

Document Ordering: Prior ordering unnecessary. Catalogue numbers unnecessary. Number at a time at staff's discretion; delivery five minutes. Last orders thirty minutes before closure. Photocopying of some printed material only; by staff on same day or by post; DIY depending on items required. Typing/taping not generally permitted. Cameras not allowed.

Records: Ts of PRs and printed PRs on open shelves: those of the former Metropolitan Borough of Finsbury and parishes which preceded it, including some Poor Law and workhouse records; some baptismal registers for Claremont Chapel (Nonconformist), some unofficial records.

Postal Research: Limited, no charge made.

Facilities: Toilets and public telephone on premises. No refreshment facilities but cafe/pub two minutes. Shops two minutes.

Publications: List available from Special Services, Islington Central Library, 2

Fieldway Crescent, London N5 1PF.
Remarks: Bags not allowed, storage facilities available. Parish map on display. Also see Islington.

FULHAM see HAMMERSMITH

BOROUGH OF GREENWICH
GREENWICH Local History Library
Woodlands
90 Mycenae Road
Blackheath
London SE3 7SE
Telephone: 01 858 4631, but from May 1990: (081) 858 4631

Opening Hours: Monday, Tuesday, Thursday 9 am to 8 pm; Saturday 9 am to 5 pm. Closed Wednesdays and Fridays. Annual closure: public holidays.
Car Parking: Twelve places
Children: No specific ruling.
Disabled: Limited facilities. Access to viewers very difficult, but documents can be brought to ground floor. Prior notification required.
Appointments System: Prior booking for seats unnecessary but for viewers necessary. Fourteen seats, two film viewers, two fiche. **Document Ordering:** Prior ordering accepted by letter or telephone. Catalogue numbers unnecessary. Reasonable number at a time. Photo- copying by staff on same day; DIY. No facilities for typing or taping. Cameras permitted.
Records: Ts of PRs on open shelves. Original PRs; administrative records of the borough from the 1630s; church records; local business and organisations' records; local pictures, postcards, maps, pamphlets, books and other publications.
Postal Research: Yes; charge for photocopying.
Facilities: Toilets, but no public telephone. No refreshment facilities but cafe/pub five minutes. Shops two minutes including bookshop with local history publications.
Publications: *Guide to the Collection.*
Places of Interest: Plumstead Local History Museum, Plumstead Library, Plumstead High Street.
Tourist Office: 46 Greenwich Church Street, London SE10. Telephone 01 858 6376 (from May 1990 Telephone (081)858 6376).
Remarks: Specific advice offered for family historians with ancestry in the borough. Blackheath JPs minutes and various other material, including some rate books, require one week's notice. Woodlands is a Georgian villa and also has an art gallery. See *West Kent Sources: A Guide to Genealogical Research in the*

Diocese of Rochester (North West Kent FHS, 1989).

GREENWICH
NATIONAL MARITIME MUSEUM
(Reading Room)
Romney Road
Greenwich
London SE10 9NF
Telephone: 01 858 4422, but from May 1990: (081) 858 4422

Opening Hours: Monday to Friday 10 am to 4.45 pm; Saturdays by appointment only. Annual closure: public holidays; last two weeks in February.
Car Parking: By the observatory
Children: Accompanied: generally not allowed. Unaccompanied: 16 to 18 years (for exam study).
Disabled: Facilities for Reading Room only.
Appointments System: Prior booking for seats and viewers unnecessary. Signing in by register plus reader's ticket. Eight to ten seats, two film viewers, two fiche.
Document Ordering: Prior ordering accepted by letter or telephone. Catalogue numbers required sometimes. Six at a time, delivery 20 to 30 minutes. No ordering of documents during lunch hour; last orders 3.45 pm. Photocopying by staff and sent by post (printed books only, not manuscripts except for masters' certificates and crew lists); DIY sometimes. No facilities for typing or taping. Cameras generally not allowed.
Postal Research: Limited to one hour maximum (donations appreciated).
Facilities: Toilets and public telephone on premises. Refreshments plus seats in the Colonnades for own food. Cafe/pub two to five minutes. Shops ten minutes including bookshop with local history publications.
Publications: *Guide to the Manuscripts* (two vols).
Tourist Office: *Cutty Sark* Gardens, Greenwich, London SE10. Telephone 01 858 6376 (from May 1990 Telephone (081)858 6376).
Remarks: Masters' certificates, crew lists, Lloyds Surveys, business records (except P & O), most ship plans, most older charts all require two to three weeks notice. Bags not allowed, storage facilities available.
Donations box in museum.

BOROUGH OF HACKNEY
HACKNEY Archives Department
Rose Lipman Library
De Beauvoir Road

London N1 5SQ
Telephone: 01 241 2886, but from May 1990: 071 241 2886
Opening Hours: Monday, Tuesday and first and third Saturday in month 9.30 am to 1 pm and 2 pm to 5 pm.
Annual closure: public holidays and last two weeks in February.
Car Parking: Yes
Children: Accompanied: no specific ruling; creche facilities. Unaccompanied: at archivist's discretion (about nine years plus).
Disabled: Disabled friendly
Appointments System: Prior booking for seats and viewers essential (at least 24 hours). Signing in by register. Ten seats, three film viewers, one fiche, one dual.
Document Ordering: Prior ordering accepted by letter or telephone (due to staff shortages a month's notice is sometimes required). Catalogue numbers unnecessary. Number at a time normally five but depends on size and nature. Delivery five to twenty minutes. Ordering times under review. Photocopying by staff on same day; if large quantity or busy, sent by post; DIY for printed material. No facilities for typing. Taping at staff's discretion. Cameras not allowed (department has own photographic service).
Records: Ts of PRs on open shelves, some PRs on fiche/film. Some post 1837 Nonconformist registers, burial ground registers, MIs.
Postal Research: Under review to see if a paid service can be introduced.
Facilities: Toilets and public telephone on premises. No refreshment facilities but cafe fifteen minutes, pub five minutes. Shops fifteen minutes.
Publications: Books, pamphlets, postcards, maps, posters. Free list of PRs, chapels, places of deposit of certain local cemeteries, copying service, publications, genealogical sources and information for teachers. (MUST be accompanied by SAE)
Remarks: On occasions there will be additional closures due to staff leave or sickness. Hours may be reviewed and extended. Donations box maintained by The Friends of Hackney Archives User Group who publish newsletters, organise talks and lectures, provide a forum for members to exchange information and arrange visits to places of interest.

BOROUGHS OF HAMMERSMITH AND FULHAM
HAMMERSMITH AND FULHAM Archives
Shepherds Bush Library
7 Uxbridge Road
London W12 8LJ

Telephone: 01 743 0910 or 01 748 3020 Ext 3850, but from May 1990: (081) 743 0910 or (081) 748 3020 Ext 3850
Opening Hours: Monday to Friday 10 am to 5 pm by appointment only. Late evening on Tuesdays to 8 pm by special arrangement. Annual closure: public holidays.
Car Parking: None
Children: At archivist's discretion.
Disabled: Ramp into library on ground floor but no lift to archives. Special arrangements can be made.
Appointments System: Prior booking for seats essential (24 hours or more) and for viewers necessary. Signing in by register. Four seats and one film viewer.
Document Ordering: Prior ordering not allowed. Number at a time at archivist's discretion. Delivery five to fifteen minutes. Photocopying by staff on same day (not bound volumes). No facilities for typing or taping. Cameras permitted.
Records: Original PRs, vestry records, Fulham Board of Works, borough records, church records.
Postal Research: Limited, no charge made. Donations welcome.
Facilities: Toilets but no public telephone. No refreshment facilities but cafe/pub two minutes. Shops five minutes.
Publications: Local interest publications. Free information leaflet.
Other Repositories: The archives and local history collections are divided between this office, Hammersmith Local History Collection, Hammersmith Central Library, Shepherds Bush Road, London W6 7AT, Telephone 01 748 3020 Ext 3812 (from May 1990 Telephone (081) 748 3020 Ext 3812) for printed material about Hammersmith, and Fulham Local History Collection, Fulham Library, 598 Fulham Road, London SW6 5NX, Telephone 01 748 3020 Ext 3875 (from May 1990 Telephone (081)748 3020 Ext 3875) for printed material about Fulham.
Remarks: Wise to telephone for general enquiry about the collections. All three repositories contain photographs, prints, maps, newspapers, directories, voter's lists and ephemera.

BOROUGH OF HARINGEY
HARINGEY Archives Department
Bruce Castle
Lordship Lane
London N17 8NU
Telephone: 01 808 8772, but from May 1990: (081) 808 8772

Opening Hours: Usually afternoons - please telephone for details. Annual clo-

sure: public holidays.
Car Parking: Yes

Children: Accompanied: no specific ruling but dependent on behaviour. Unaccompanied: ten years plus.
Disabled: No facilities but material can be taken into museum.
Appointments System: Prior booking for seats and viewers essential (one week at least). Signing in by register. Six seats and two film viewers.
Document Ordering: Prior ordering accepted by letter or telephone. Catalogue numbers unnecessary. Number at a time at librarian's discretion. Delivery within a few minutes. Photocopying by staff on same day. No facilities for typing or taping. Cameras not allowed.
Records: Ts of PRs on open shelves, original PRs on fiche/film.
Postal Research: Very limited, no charge made.
Facilities: No toilets or public telephone. No refreshment facilities but drink vending machine. Cafe/pub five minutes. Shops ten minutes.
Publications: Free nine page handlist outlining the holdings of the department.
Places of Interest: Bruce Castle Museum.

BOROUGH OF HARROW
Local History Library
Civic Centre Library
PO Box 4
Civic Centre
HARROW
Middlesex HA1 2UU
Telephone: 01 863 5611, but from May 1990: (081) 863 5611

Places of Interest: Middlesex Regiment (Duke of Cambridge's Hussars), Yeomanry Museum, Harrow; Harrow Museum and Heritage Centre, Headstone Manor.
Tourist Office: Civic Centre, Station Road, Harrow HA1 2UH. Telephone 01 863 5611 Ext 2100/2/3 (Tel No from May 1990 [081] 863 5611 Ext 2100/2/3).
Remarks: Declined to answer questionnaire but known to hold a considerable number of local records.

BOROUGH OF HAVERING
London Borough of HAVERING
Reference and Information Library
St Edwards Way
Romford
Essex RM1 3AR
Telephone: (0708)46040 Exts.3169/3174

Opening Hours: Monday to Friday 9.30 am to 8 pm, Saturday 9.30 am to 5 pm. Annual closure: public holidays.
Car Parking: None
Children: No specific ruling.
Disabled: Lift and access to staff toilets available on request to staff.
Appointments System: Prior booking for seats unnecessary but advisable for viewers. Eighty seats, two film viewers, and one fiche.
Document Ordering: Prior ordering accepted by letter or telephone. Catalogue numbers unnecessary. Approximately three at a time; delivery ten to fifteen minutes. Last orders 30 minutes before closure. Photocopying by staff on same day or by post; DIY; charge for printouts. No facilities for typing or taping. Cameras permitted.
Records: Ts of PRs require ordering. PRs on film, Local Board of Health c1850 plus, Municipal Records c1895 plus, limited amount of material from other sources (very few maps).
Postal Research: Yes, charge for photocopying plus postage.
Facilities: Toilets and public telephone nearby. No refreshment facilities but cafe/pub two minutes. Shops two minutes including bookshop with local history publications.
Publications: Summary list of holdings mainly for staff reference.
Other Repositories: Passmore Edwards Museum, 29 Romford Road, London E15.
Remarks: The library is not a recognised place of deposit for local archives.

BOROUGH OF HILLINGDON
Local Studies Collection
HILLINGDON Borough Libraries
Central Library
High Street
Uxbridge
Middlesex UB8 1HD
Telephone: (0895) 50600

Opening Hours: Monday to Friday 9.30 am to 8 pm, Saturday 9.30 am to 5 pm. Annual closure: public holidays.
Car Parking: None
Children: No specific ruling.
Disabled: Lifts. Toilet facilities on request.
Appointments System: Prior booking for seats advisable but unnecessary for viewers. Signing in by register. Five seats, two film viewers, and two fiche.
Document Ordering: Prior ordering accepted by letter or telephone. Catalogue numbers unnecessary. Number at a time unlimited. Photocopying by staff on same

day or by post; DIY. No facilities for typing or taping. Cameras permitted.

Records: Ts of PRs require ordering. Rate books and 19th and early 20th century voters' lists, records of St John's Church, Hillingdon.

Postal Research: Limited, no charge made.

Facilities: No toilets but public telephone on premises. No refreshment facilities but cafe/pub two minutes. Shops two minutes including bookshop with local history publications.

Tourist Office: Central Library, High Street, Uxbridge, Middx UB8 1JY. Telephone (0895) 50706.

Remarks: Council minutes for Hillingdon and previous authorities stored elsewhere require three days' prior notice. Historical area map available on request.

HOLBORN see CAMDEN
HOUNSLOW see CHISWICK

BOROUGH OF HOUNSLOW
HOUNSLOW Library Centre
24 Treaty Centre
High Street
Hounslow
London TW3 1ES
Telephone: 01 570 0622 Ext 296, but from May 1990: (081) 570 0622 Ext 296

Opening Hours: Monday, Wednesday, Friday, Saturday 9.30 am to 5.30 pm; Tuesday and Thursday 9.30 am to 8 pm. Annual closure: public holidays.

Car Parking: Nearby

Children: Accompanied: no specific ruling. Unaccompanied: ten years plus.

Disabled: Lifts

Appointments System: Prior booking for seats and viewers unnecessary. 47 seats, one film viewer, one fiche.

Document Ordering: Prior ordering accepted by letter or telephone. Catalogue numbers unnecessary. Unlimited number at a time, delivery five minutes. Photocopying by staff on same day or by post subject to staffing; DIY. Typing/taping permitted. Cameras permitted.

Records: Ts of PRs require ordering. PRs on fiche, original PRs, books, maps, prints, paintings, photographs, local newspapers, rate books, local directories, census, local authority minutes.

Postal Research: Yes, charge for photocopying plus postage.

Facilities: Toilets and public telephone on premises. Refreshments but no facilities for own food; cafe/pub two minutes. Shops two minutes.

Publications: *Guide to London Local History Resources: London Borough of Hounslow*, local history publications.

Other Repositories: See entry for Chiswick.

Remarks: Historical map on display; covers areas of Hounslow, Heston, Isleworth, Cranford, Hanworth, Feltham and Bedfont.

HOUSE OF LORDS see Westminster

BOROUGH OF ISLINGTON
ISLINGTON Archives
Islington Central Library
2 Fieldway Crescent
London N5 1PF
Telephone: 01 609 3051 Exts 216/217, but from May 1990: 071 609 3051 Exts 216/217

Opening Hours: Monday to Thursday 9 am to 8 pm, Friday and Saturday 9 am to 5 pm (for library). Appointment hours 10 am to 12 noon, 2 pm to 4 pm, 5 pm to 7 pm, depending on staff availability. Annual closure: public holidays.

Car Parking: None

Children: At staff's discretion.

Disabled: Lifts accessible by wheelchair. Assistance available and special arrangements can be made.

Appointments System: Prior booking by letter or telephone for seats (at least one day) and viewers necessary. Signing in by register plus identification. Six seats, but no more than three appointments at the same time. One film viewer, one fiche.

Document Ordering: Prior ordering and catalogue numbers unnecessary. Number at a time at staff's discretion; delivery five to ten minutes. Photocopying by staff on same day or by post; DIY unless large order; restricted copying of printed material. Typing/taping not generally permitted. Cameras permitted.

Records: Original PRs on fiche/film, Metropolitan Borough of Islington, civil parish of St Mary's, other miscellaneous records.

Postal Research: Limited, no charge made. Donations welcome.

Facilities: No toilets. Public telephone on premises. No refreshments but drink vending machine. Cafe/pub two minutes. Shops two minutes including bookshop with local history publications.

Publications: For details apply to Special Services, Islington Central Library.

Remarks: Historical parish map on display. Donations box. Original PRs at Greater London RO. Check on opening hours prior to visit. Also see Finsbury.

ROYAL BOROUGH OF KENSING-TON AND CHELSEA
CHELSEA Public Library
Local Studies Department
Old Town Hall
King's Road
London SW3 5EZ
Telephone: 01 352 6056/2004, but from May 1990:071 352 6056/2004

Opening Hours: Monday, Tuesday, Thursday 10 am to 8 pm; Wednesday 10 am to 1 pm; Friday and Saturday 10 am to 5 pm. Annual closure: public holidays plus Saturdays before Easter and August bank holiday.
Car Parking: None
Children: Accompanied: no specific ruling. Unaccompanied: 13 years plus.
Disabled: Bell at street level for assistance to lift.
Appointments System: Prior booking for seats unnecessary, but necessary for viewers. Signing in by register. Four seats, one film viewer, one fiche.
Document Ordering: Prior ordering accepted by letter or telephone. Catalogue numbers unnecessary. Number at a time at librarian's discretion. No ordering between 12 noon and 2 pm on Saturdays. Photocopying by staff and sent by post; DIY. No facilities for typing or taping. Cameras not allowed.
Records: Ts of PRs require ordering. Original PRs on fiche/film. Parish records, rate books, voters lists, deeds, census. Histories and other records relating to former Metropolitan Borough of Chelsea, mainly after 1700.
Postal Research: Limited, charge made.
Facilities: Toilets and public telephone on premises. No refreshment facilities but cafe/pub two minutes. Shops two minutes.
Publications: Free leaflets: *Finding Out About Censuses, Finding Out About your Family, Images of the Past, Past and Present in Kensington and Chelsea, Your House and its History.*
Places of Interest: Carlyle's House, Cheyne Row.
Remarks: Available for use in department: lists of holdings, Chelsea records. Lists of Chelsea records not at Chelsea.

BOROUGH OF KENSINGTON
KENSINGTON Local Studies Collection
Royal Borough of Kensington and Chelsea Libraries and Arts Service
Central Library
Phillimore Walk
London W8 7RX
Telephone: 01 937 2542 Ext 3038, but from May 1990: 071 937 2542 Ext 3038

Opening Hours: Monday, Tuesday, Thursday, Friday 10 am to 8 pm; Wednesday 10 am to 1 pm; Saturday 10 am to 12 noon and 2 pm to 5 pm. Annual closure: public holidays.
Car Parking: None
Children: Accompanied: no specific ruling. Unaccompanied: school age.
Disabled: Advance notice required. Ramps and lift for wheelchairs.
Appointments System: Prior booking for seats and viewers unnecessary. Signing in by register. Four seats, two film viewers, one fiche.
Document Ordering: Prior ordering accepted by letter or telephone. Catalogue numbers necessary. Approximately three at a time. Delivery ten to twenty minutes, last orders thirty minutes before closure. Photocopying by staff on same day or post; DIY sometimes. No facilities for typing or taping. Cameras permitted subject to copyright.
Records: Ts of PRs on open shelves.
Postal Research: Limited, no charge made.
Facilities: Toilets nearby. No public telephone. No refreshment facilities but cafe/pub two minutes. Shops two minutes including bookshop with local history publications.
Publications: OS maps, historic maps, old postcards, prints, colour slides, historical walks, *St Mary Abbot's Church, PR Marriages 1676-1775*, publications list.
Places of Interest: Kensington Palace - Court Dress Collection; Commonwealth Institute, Kensington High Street.
Remarks: Historical map on display.

KEW see Public Record Office

ROYAL BOROUGH OF KINGSTON-UPON-THAMES
KINGSTON Museum and Heritage Centre
Wheatfield Way
Kingston-Upon-Thames
Surrey KT1 2PS
Telephone: 01 546 5386, but from May 1990: (081) 546 5386

Opening Hours: Monday to Saturday 10 am to 5 pm. Annual closure: public holidays.
Car Parking: Nearby

Appointments System: Prior booking for seats essential (two or three days). Photocopying service available.
Records: Newspapers, books, pictures, photographs, maps, oral history archive.
Publications: Local history publications, photographs, prints, postcards etc, *Guide to Borough Archives* (1971).
Tourist Office: Heritage Centre: as above. Telephone 01 546 5386. (Tel No from May 1990 [081] 546 5386).
Remarks: Most of the borough's archives are in Surrey RO.

BOROUGH OF LAMBETH
LAMBETH Archives Department
Minet Library
Knatchbull Road
London SE5 8QY
Telephone: 01 733 3279, but from May 1990: 071 733 3279

Opening Hours: Please telephone for information. Annual closure: public holidays.
Car Parking: Nearby
Children: Accompanied: no specific ruling. Unaccompanied: eleven years plus.
Disabled: Wheelchair access and access to toilet.
Appointments System: Prior booking for seats and viewers necessary (24 hours for seats and a few days for viewers). Signing in by register. Nine seats, three film viewers, one fiche.
Document Ordering: Prior ordering accepted by letter or telephone. Catalogue numbers unnecessary. Number at a time at archivist's discretion. Delivery five minutes. Photocopying by staff on same day. No facilities for typing or taping. Cameras not allowed.
Records: Ts of PRs require ordering. Archives and local history material relating to Borough of Lambeth and its predecessors, considerable material on Surrey, council records, appointed place for certain public records, manorial repository, private deposits.
Postal Research: Limited, no charge made.
Facilities: No toilets or public telephone. No refreshment facilities but cafe/pub five minutes.
Publications: Postcards. Free: list of holdings, list of genealogical searchers, *Brief Guide to Records for the Local and Family Historian.* Other titles in preparation.
Other Repositories: Reference Library, Brixton Central Library, Brixton Oval, London SW2 1JG; Lambeth Palace Library, London SE1 7JU.

BOROUGH OF LEWISHAM
LEWISHAM Library Service
Local History Centre
The Manor House
Old Road
Lee
London SE13 5SY
Telephone: 01 852 5050/7087, but from May 1990: (081) 852 5050/7087

Opening Hours: Monday and Saturday 9.30 am to 5 pm, Tuesday and Thursday 9.30 am to 8 pm, Friday 9.30 am to 1 pm. Closed Wednesdays. Annual closure: public holidays plus Saturday before; first two full weeks in December.
Car Parking: Approximately twelve places
Children: No specific ruling.
Disabled: No facilities at present. Standard access to ground floor proposed but centre is on first floor with no lift.
Appointments System: Prior booking for seats unnecessary but necessary for viewers. Signing in by register for archive collection. Eight to ten seats, three film viewers.
Document Ordering: Prior ordering accepted by letter or telephone. Catalogue numbers unnecessary. Three at a time, delivery five to ten minutes. Last orders 30 minutes before closure. Photocopying by staff on same day; PRs depending on condition. No facilities for typing or taping. Cameras permitted, subject to copyright etc.
Records: Ts of some PRs on open shelves, original PRs held elsewhere on fiche/film. Original PRs, Poor Rate books, Church and Highway Rate books, registers of graves, Nonconformist registers, Poll books, electoral registers, MIs, local newspapers, cemetery burial records, interview tapes and local films, local directories.
Postal Research: Limited, no charge made.
Facilities: Toilets, but no public telephone. No refreshment facilities but cafe/pub two minutes. Shops ten minutes.
Publications: Pamphlets, prints, historical walks, maps, local history information pack plus other local history publications. Free: *Sources for Family History in Lewisham Local History Centre,* general guide leaflet on centre.
Other Repositories: Morden College, 19 St German's Place, London SE3.
Tourist Office: Lewisham Library, Lewisham High Street, London SE13 6LG. Telephone 01 690 8325 (from May 1990 Telephone [081] 690 8325).
Remarks: Industrial and local authority records stored elsewhere require ten days

prior notice. See *West Kent Sources: A Guide to Genealogical Research in the Diocese of Rochester* (North West Kent FHS, 1989).

BOROUGH OF MARYLEBONE
Archives and Local Studies Section
MARYLEBONE Library
Marylebone Road
London NW1 5PS
Telephone: 01 798 1030, but from May 1990: 071 798 1030

Opening Hours: Monday to Friday 9.30 am to 7 pm, Saturday 9.30 am to 1 pm and 2 pm to 5 pm. Annual closure: public holidays.
Car Parking: None
Children: At archivist's discretion.
Disabled: Prior notice required. Steps into library. Lift to search room, but not for wheelchairs.
Appointments System: Prior booking for seats and viewers unnecessary. Signing in by register. Seven seats, four film viewers and one fiche.
Document Ordering: Prior ordering accepted by letter or telephone (essential to see particular documents). Catalogue numbers unnecessary. Approximately four at a time. Ordering times 9.30 am to 11.30 am and 2 pm to 3.15 pm. Photocopying by staff or DIY; microfilm copies have a handling charge. No facilities for typing or taping. Cameras permitted, but prior arrangement essential.
Records: Ts of PRs on open shelves, rate books, poor law records for area, wills (Commissary Court of Dean and Chapter of Westminster 1504-1829 for parish of St Margaret and St John the Evangelist, Westminster), local directories.
Postal Research: Professional genealogist, charge made. Appointment needed: send for form.
Facilities: No toilets or public telephone. No refreshment facilities but cafe/pub five minutes. Shops five minutes.
Publications: *Plan of the Parish of St Marylebone c1832.* Free: leaflet on the collection and the Victoria Library collection, *List of Nonconformist Registers and Ts, Lists of Ts and PRs, Guide to Tracing the History of a House in Westminster.*
Places of Interest: Cricket Memorial Gallery, Lord's Ground, London NW8 8QN.
Remarks: City of Westminster drainage plans stored elsewhere require one week's prior notice. Historical map on display. Donations box. Staffing very limited.

BOROUGH OF MERTON
MERTON Central Reference Library
Wimbledon Hill Road
London SW19 7NB
Telephone: 01 946 1136, but from May 1990: (081) 946 1136

Declined to answer questionnaire but known to contain local material. See Morden Library.

BOROUGH OF MITCHAM
MITCHAM Public Library
London Road
Mitcham
Surrey CR4 2YR
Telephone: 01 648 4070, but from May 1990: (081) 648 4070

Opening Hours: Monday, Tuesday, Thursday, Friday 9.30 am to 7 pm; Wednesday 9.30 am to 1 pm; Saturday 9.30 am to five pm. Annual closure: public holidays.
Car Parking: 20 places
Children: No specific ruling.
Disabled: Access for wheelchairs.
Appointments System: No prior booking for the 32 seats. Self-service photocopying. No facilities for typing or taping. Cameras are not allowed.
Records: Census returns, local directories etc.
Postal Research: Limited, charge made for photocopying.
Facilities: No toilets or public telephone. No refreshment facilities but cafe/pub two minutes. Shops five minutes.
Publications: Books on many aspects of local history, maps, walks, postcards etc.
Remarks: Most records have been transferred to Surrey RO.

BOROUGH OF MORDEN
Local Studies Library
MORDEN Library
Morden Road
London SW19 3DA.
Telephone: 01 542 2842/1701, but from May 1990: (081) 542 2842/1701

Opening Hours: Monday, Tuesday, Thursday, Friday 9.30 am to 7 pm; Wednesday 9.30 am to 1 pm; Saturday 9.30 am to 5 pm. Annual closure: public holidays.
Car Parking: Approximately twelve places
Children: No specific ruling.
Disabled: Access but toilet on first floor.
Appointments System: Prior booking

for seats unnecessary but appreciated. Three fiche viewers.

Document Ordering: Prior ordering essential; by letter or telephone. Catalogue numbers unnecessary. Self-service photocopying. No facilities for typing or taping. Cameras permitted.
Records: Ts of PRs require ordering. Parish rate books mid 19th century onwards, electoral registers from 1891 to date, photographs, census, local histories and directories.
Postal Research: Limited, no charge made.
Facilities: Toilets, but no public telephone. No refreshment facilities but cafe/pub two minutes. Shops a few minutes.
Publications: at bookshop: various books etc on aspects of local history.
Other Repositories: Wimbledon Reference Library, Compton Road, London SW19.
Remarks: Historical map on request. Local collection for Merton.

NATIONAL MARITIME MUSEUM
see GREENWICH

BOROUGH OF NEWHAM
London Borough of NEWHAM Local Studies Library
Stratford Reference Library
Water Lane
London E15 4NJ
Telephone: 01 534 4545 Ext 25662 (office hours) or 01 534 1305 (evenings or Saturdays), but from May 1990: (081) 534 4545 or (081) 534 1305

Opening Hours: Monday, Tuesday, Thursday, Friday 9 am to 7 pm; Wednesday and Saturday 9 am to 5 pm. Annual closure: public holidays, Christmas week and Easter weekend.
Car Parking: None
Children: Accompanied: at librarian's discretion. Unaccompanied: not allowed.
Disabled: Access by prior arrangement.
Appointments System: Prior booking for seats and viewers essential (one day). Signing in by register. Eight seats, three film viewers and two fiche.
Document Ordering: Prior ordering by letter or telephone. Catalogue numbers unnecessary. Reasonable number at a time. No ordering at lunch times (12 noon to 2 pm). Photocopying by staff usually on same day; DIY. No facilities for typing. Taping not usual but possible. Cameras not allowed.
Records: Ts of PRs on open shelves, orig-

inal PRs on fiche/film. Poor Law Union records.

Postal Research: Limited; charge made for photocopies etc.
Facilities: No toilets. Public telephone nearby. No refreshment facilities but cafe/pub five minutes. Shops five minutes. Underground: Stratford.
Publications: Local studies notes: *Interested in Finding Out More About Newham?* how to reach the library, numerous leaflets on family and local history.
Other Repositories: Passmore Edwards Museum, Romford Road, London E15 (PRs for West Ham).
Places of Interest: Passmore Edwards Museum.
Remarks: Local authority Council minutes and rate books stored elsewhere require two days' prior notice (at least). Historical map on display. Bags not allowed, storage facilities available.

PUBLIC RECORD OFFICE
Ruskin Avenue
Kew
Richmond
Surrey TW9 4DK
Telephone: (01) 876 3444, but from May 1990: (081) 876 3444

Opening Hours: Monday to Friday 9.30 am to 5 pm. Annual closure: public holidays plus Friday before Spring bank holiday; first two full weeks in October.
Car Parking: Approximately 100 places
Children: Accompanied: any age. Unaccompanied: 16 years plus.
Disabled: Disabled friendly.
Appointments System: Prior booking for seats and viewers unnecessary. Signing in by register plus reader's ticket. Approximately 300 seats, 21 film viewers, and seven fiche.
Document Ordering: Prior ordering by letter or telephone. Catalogue numbers essential. Three at a time. Delivery approximately 30 minutes. Last orders 3.30 pm (documents ordered after this time will be produced on next working day). Photocopying by staff on same day or sent by post. Typing/taping permitted. Cameras not allowed.
Records: Generally the modern records of government departments (some departments, eg Admiralty and War Office, have been in existence for several centuries).
Postal Research: None
Facilities: Toilets and public telephone on premises. Refreshments plus room for own food, also drink vending machine. Cafe/pub ten minutes. Shops ten

minutes.

Publications: For sale: *The Current Guide to PRO,* handbooks, postcards etc. Free: More than 100 leaflets on a wide range of topics, available on a self-help basis.

Places of Interest: Kew Bridge Steam Museum, Green Dragon Lane, Brentford; Kew Gardens.

Tourist Office: Old Town Hall, Whittaker Avenue, Richmond, Surrey TW 9 1TP. Telephone (01) 940 9125 (from May 1990 Telephone (081) 940 9125).

Remarks: Bags not allowed, storage facilities available; PRO has another repository at Chancery Lane, London (see entry).

RICHMOND see also
PUBLIC RECORD OFFICE

BOROUGH OF RICHMOND
RICHMOND Local Studies Library
Old Town Hall
Whittaker Avenue
Richmond
Surrey TW9 1TP
Telephone: (01) 940 5529 Ext 32, but from May 1990: (081) 940 5529 Ext 32

Opening Hours: Tuesday 10 am to 5 pm; Wednesday 1 pm to 8 pm; Thursday and Friday 10 am to 6 pm; Saturday 10 am to 5 pm (closed Mondays). Closed each lunch-time from 12.30 pm to 1.30 pm. Annual closure: public holidays.

Car Parking: None

Children: No specific ruling.

Disabled: No access to search room but material may be viewed in Reference Library by prior arrangement.

Appointments System: Prior booking essential for seats and necessary for viewers. Signing in by register. Ten seats, one film viewer, one fiche.

Document Ordering: Prior ordering by letter or telephone. Catalogue numbers unnecessary. Photocopying by staff on same day; DIY. No facilities for typing or taping. Cameras permitted, permission required.

Records: Ts of PRs on open shelves. Local collections for Barnes, East Sheen, Ham, Kew, Mortlake, Petersham and Richmond; general books on county of Surrey; microfilm of newspapers; cuttings; local publications; maps; archives; photographs; paintings; prints.

Postal Research: Very limited

Facilities: Toilets and public telephone on premises. Restaurant/canteen. Cafe/pub five minutes. Shops five minutes, including bookshop with local history publications.

Publications: For Sale: postcards of paintings and prints, reproductions of engravings. Free: series of short guides to local history material.

Places of Interest: Museum of Richmond.

Tourist Office: Old Town Hall, Whittaker Avenue, Richmond, Surrey TW9 1TP, Telephone (01) 940 9125 (Tel No from May 1990 (081) 940 9125).

Remarks: Local History Society publications are on sale in Tourist Centre. Many archives relating to the area are held in the Chief Executive and Town Clerk's Department at York House: apply either by writing or in person to the Reference Library staff. Local material may be referred to in the Reference Study Room by prior arrangement if Local Studies Library is closed.

SOMERSET HOUSE
see PRINCIPAL REGISTRY
OF THE FAMILY DIVISION

BOROUGH OF SOUTHWARK
SOUTHWARK Local Studies Library
211 Borough High Street
Southwark
London SE1 1JA
Telephone: (01) 403 3507, but from May 1990: (071) 403 3507

Opening Hours: Monday and Thursday 9.30 am to 12.30 pm and 1.30 pm to 8 pm; Tuesday and Friday 9.30 am to 12.30 pm and 1.30 pm to 5 pm; Saturday 9.30 am to 1 pm (by appointment only). Closed Wednesdays. Annual closure: public holidays plus preceding Saturdays.

Car Parking: None

Children: No specific ruling.

Disabled: Access, toilets.

Appointments System: Prior booking for necessary for viewers but unnecessary for seats. Signing in by register. Sixteen seats, one film viewer, one fiche and one dual viewer.

Document Ordering: Prior ordering unnecessary. Two or three at a time. Delivery five to ten minutes. Photocopying at archivist's discretion. Typing/taping permitted but only one person at a time. Cameras permitted.

Records: Poor Law, Council, Ts of PRs on open shelves (very brief sections of two parishes), rate books on film/fiche, vestry minutes, civil records of the ten ancient parishes of Southwark, electoral registers, directories, maps, newspapers, photographs, books.

Postal Research: None

41

Facilities: Toilets and public telephone on premises. No refreshment facilities but cafe/pub two minutes. Shops ten minutes. Underground: Borough.

Publications: For Sale: leaflets on publications and holdings of library.

Other Repositories: Southwark Cathedral Library and Archives, Chapter House, St Thomas Street, Southwark.

Remarks: Poor Law, Council records and less frequently requested items stored elsewhere require seven to fourteen days' prior notice. Modern borough map with civil parishes on display.

ST CATHERINE'S
see GENERAL REGISTER OFFICE

BOROUGH OF SUTTON
Sutton Central Library
St Nicholas Way
Sutton
Surrey SM1 1EA
Telephone: (01) 770 4782, but from May 1990 (081) 770 4782.

Opening Hours: Tuesday to Friday 9.30 am to 8 pm. Saturdays 9.30 am to 5 pm. Closed Mondays.

Car Parking: Nearby.

Children: At Librarian's discretion.

Disabled: Ramps, lift.

Appointments System: Prior booking advisable. 78 seats. Some film/fiche, some with printout facilities. Photocopying. Cameras permitted.

Records: Ts of PRs, rate books, vestry, churchwardens etc. Manor, Nonconformists, private deposits, local histories, business, maps, education deeds, newspapers.

Facilities: Toilets. Drinks available. Cafe/pub and shops two minutes.

Publications: Local histories, leaflets.

Places of Interest: Heritage Centre (local history), Honeywood, Carshalton, Surrey.

BOROUGH OF TOWER HAMLETS
Local History Library and Archives
Bancroft Library
277 Bancroft Road
London E1 4DQ
Telephone: (01) 980 4366 Ext 47/32, but from May 1990: (081) 980 4366 Ext 47/32

Opening Hours: Monday to Thursday 9 am to 8 pm, Friday and Saturday 9 am to 5 pm. Annual closure: public holidays.

Car Parking: None

Children: No specific ruling.

Disabled: Entrance ramp and lift.

Appointments System: Prior booking for viewers necessary but unnecessary for seats. Signing in by register. Approximately twenty seats, three film viewers, and one fiche.

Document Ordering: Prior ordering by letter or telephone. Catalogue numbers unnecessary. Three at a time. Delivery approximately five minutes. Photocopying by staff and sent by post; DIY. No facilities for typing or taping. Cameras permitted.

Records: Ts of PRs require ordering; original PRs on fiche/film. Original PRs, Nonconformists, parish etc.

Postal Research: Specific enquiry, no charge made.

Facilities: Toilets and public telephone on premises. No refreshment facilities but cafe/pub five minutes. Shops five minutes.

Publications: Free: *Brief Guide to Genealogical Sources in Tower Hamlets Local History Library, Brief Guide to Census Returns in Library, Parish and Nonconformist Registers Available in Library.*

Tourist Office: Mayfield House, Cambridge Heath Road, London E2 9LJ. Telephone (01) 980 4831 Exts 5313/5 (from May 1990 Telephone [081] 980 4831).

Remarks: Bags not allowed. Lengthy general postal research not undertaken.

BOROUGH OF TWICKENHAM
TWICKENHAM Local Studies Library
Garfield Road
Twickenham
Middlesex TW1 3JS
Telephone: (01) 891 7271, but from May 1990: (081) 891 7271

Opening Hours: Monday and Friday 10 am to 12 noon and 2 pm to 6 pm, Tuesday 1 pm to 8 pm, Wednesday and Saturday 10 am to 12 noon and 2 pm to 5 pm. Closed Thursdays. Annual closure: public holidays.

Car Parking: None

Children: No specific ruling.

Disabled: No access to search room but material may be viewed in library by prior arrangement.

Appointments System: Prior booking for seats essential and for viewers necessary. Signing in by register. Nine seats and one viewers fiche.

Document Ordering: Prior ordering by letter or telephone. Catalogue numbers unnecessary. Photocopying by staff on same day; DIY. No facilities for typing or taping. Cameras permitted (sometimes special permission required).

Records: Ts of PRs on open shelves, PRs on fiche; local collections for The Hamp-

tons, Teddington, Twickenham and Whitton; maps from 1635; photographs; paintings; prints.
Postal Research: Very limited, no charge made.
Facilities: No toilets or public telephone. No refreshment facilities but cafe/pub five minutes. Shops five minutes including bookshop with local history publications.
Publications: Series of short guides to local history material relating to specific parishes, reproduction of engravings and prints, Local History Societies' publications.
Places of Interest: Orleans House Gallery.
Tourist Office: District Library, Garfield Road, Twickenham, Middx TW1 3JS. Telephone (01) 892 0032 (Tel No from May 1990 [081] 892 0032.
Remarks: Material may be referred to in the Reference Study Room by prior arrangement when the Local Studies Library is closed. Some local church vestries still retain ecclesiastical records for their areas.

THE UNITED SYNAGOGUE
Office of the Chief Rabbi
Adler House
Tavistock Square
London WC1 9HN
Telephone: (01) 387 1066, but from May 1990: (071) 387 1066

Remarks: There is no public access to the archives for purely genealogical purposes. The major classes of pre-1837 registers have been microfilmed by the Church of Latter-day Saints and are available in their libraries.

BOROUGH OF WALTHAMSTOW
WALTHAM FOREST Archives
Vestry House Museum
Vestry Road, Walthamstow
London E17 9NH
Telephone: (01) 509 1917, but from May 1990: (081) 509 1917

Opening Hours: Tuesday to Friday 10.30 am to 1 pm and 2 pm to 5.30 pm; Saturday 10.30 am to 1 pm and 2 pm to 5 pm (closed Mondays). Annual closure: public holidays.
Car Parking: None
Children: No specific ruling.
Disabled: No facilities but given all possible assistance.
Appointments System: Prior booking for seats and viewers essential (two days). Signing in by register. Fourteen seats,

two film viewers, and one fiche.
Document Ordering: Prior ordering by letter or telephone. Catalogue numbers unnecessary. Up to eight at a time. Delivery ten minutes. Last orders 40 minutes before closure. Photocopying by staff and sent by post; PRs photocopied. No facilities for typing. Taping permitted. Cameras not allowed.
Records: Some Ts of PRs/BTs require ordering; Waltham Ts of PRs on open shelves; original PRs on fiche/film. Quarter Sessions, parish, Poor Law union, education, manorial etc.
Postal Research: Minimal searches free; detailed research by prior payment only.
Facilities: Toilets but no public telephone. No refreshment facilities but cafe/pub two minutes. Shops five minutes including bookshop with local history publications.
Publications: *Brief Guide to Formation of Modern Parishes in Waltham Forest;* maps of area 1894-1914; photographic histories of Waltham Forest; VCH parish histories of Chingford, Leyton and Walthamstow. Free: handlists of PRs, Ts of PRs, brief guide to family history sources.
Other Repositories: Passmore Edwards Museum, Stratford, holds PRs for West Ham.
Places of Interest: Vestry House Museum.
Remarks: Up to three weeks' prior notice required for 20th century rate books, some local newspapers, Essex County collection material. Donations box. Map of modern parishes in Archdiocese available.

BOROUGH OF WANDSWORTH
Local History Library
BATTERSEA Library
265 Lavender Hill
London SW11 1JB
Telephone: (01) 871 7467, but from May 1990: (081) 871 7467

Opening Hours: Tuesday 10 am to 1 pm and 2 pm to 8 pm, Wednesday and Friday 10 am to 1 pm and 2 pm to 5 pm, Saturdays by appointment only, closed Mondays and Thursdays. Annual closure: public holidays; when librarian is on holiday (restricted service from Reference Department).
Car Parking: None
Children: No specific ruling.
Disabled: Access to Reference Library only.
Appointments System: No prior booking for seats, but advisable for viewer. Signing in by register. Twelve seats and

one film viewer.

Document Ordering: Prior ordering by letter or telephone. Catalogue numbers unnecessary. Delivery ten to fifteen minutes. Photocopying by staff on same day; if large quantity or busy, sent by post. No facilities for typing. Taping can be arranged. Cameras permitted.

Records: Ts of PRs on open shelves, one PR on film, parish, education, wills etc.

Postal Research: Very limited, no charge made.

Facilities: No toilets or public telephone. No refreshment facilities but cafe/pub two minutes. Shops two minutes.

Places of Interest: Wandsworth Museum.

Remarks: 48 hours prior notice required for some rate books from 1900 to 1950. Limited sources, telephone for details before visit.

WESTMINSTER
WESTMINSTER ABBEY
Muniment Room and Library
London SW1P 3PA
Telephone: (01) 222 5152 Ext 228, but from May 1990: (071) 222 5152 Ext 228

Opening Hours: Monday to Saturday 10 am to 1 pm and 2 pm to 4.45 pm. Annual closure: public holidays plus some others; liable to closure at short notice.

Car Parking: None

Children: Accompanied: no specific ruling. Unaccompanied not allowed.

Disabled: No facilities - spiral staircase.

Appointments System: Prior booking for seats essential (as much notice as possible). Signing in by register (students require letter of introduction from supervisor). Four seats.

Document Ordering: Prior ordering by letter or telephone. Catalogue numbers necessary. Reasonable number at a time. Delivery five minutes. Photocopying restricted; by staff on same day. No facilities for typing or taping. Cameras permitted.

Records: Original PRs of St Margaret's, Westminster, and the Abbey; administration documents of the Abbey from Anglo-Saxon times to present day; personal papers; various stray material.

Postal Research: Limited; charge made.

Facilities: Toilets but no public telephone. No refreshment facilities but cafe/pub five minutes. Shops five minutes.

Publications: *The Nature and Use of the Westminster Abbey Muniments,* for consultation only.

Remarks: This library and its archives are not comparable to a CRO, it holds the records of the Dean and Chapter of West-

minster so facilities are very limited. Donations box.

BOROUGH OF Westminster
CITY OF Westminster Archives
Victoria Library
160 Buckingham Palace Road
London SW1W 9UD
Telephone: (01) 798 2180, but from May 1990: (071) 798 2180

Opening Hours: Monday to Friday 9.30 am to 7 pm, Saturday 9.30 am to 1 pm and 2 pm to 5 pm. Annual closure: public holidays.

Car Parking: None

Children: Any age admitted but dependent on behaviour. **Disabled:** Ramp access.

Appointments System: Prior booking for seats and viewers unnecessary. Signing in by register. Nine seats, six film viewers, and two fiche.

Document Ordering: Prior ordering not allowed. Ten at a time. Delivery fifteen minutes. Photocopying: printouts only from film; by staff on same day. No facilities for typing or taping. Cameras by appointment only.

Records: Some printed Ts of PRs on open shelves, original PRs on film, original PRs, borough, parish, maps, manorial, private etc.

Postal Research: Professional researcher; charge made; write for details.

Facilities: No toilets or public telephone. No refreshment facilities but cafe/pub two minutes. Shops five minutes.

Publications: Free leaflets: *Westminster City Archives and Local History, Guide to London Local History Resources (City of Westminster), Tracing the History of a House in Westminster, Sources for a Family Historian held by Westminster City Archives, Registers of Nonconformist Churches Deposited in Westminster City Archives, Registers of Anglican Churches Deposited in Westminster City Archives.*

Places of Interest: Buckingham Palace, Pall Mall, St James Park.

Remarks: Westminster Deeds (South), *Bishop's Move* accounting records stored elsewhere require one week's prior notice (can be made available at Marylebone Library). Donations welcome. Historical map on display, children's library available in building.

WESTMINSTER Diocesan Archives
16A Abingdon Road
Kensington
London W8 6AF
Telephone: 01 938 3580, but from May 1990: 071 938 3580

Opening Hours: Monday to Friday 10 am to 5 pm but closed at lunchtime (usually 1 pm to 2 pm). Annual closure: public holidays, and sometimes extended to adjacent days, therefore please enquire if planning to use the facilities around the time of public holidays.
Car Parking: None
Children: Not allowed.
Disabled: No facilities.
Appointments System: Prior booking for the three seats essential.
Document Ordering: Prior ordering accepted by letter or telephone. Catalogue numbers unnecessary. Delivery five to ten minutes. No ordering at lunch time. Photocopying by staff. No facilities for typing or taping. Cameras not allowed.
Records: Some original PRs. Organisation of Catholics in London area and Home Counties, including correspondence with other areas, 16th to 19th century.
Postal Research: Very limited, charge made.
Facilities: Toilets, but no public telephone. No refreshment facilities but cafe/pub two minutes. Shops two minutes.
Publications: For reference only: *The Westminster Archives* by P Hughes, *Dublin Review* (1937); *Archives of St Edmund's College* (Report of the Commission on Historical Manuscripts, 1972).
Other Repositories: Kensington Central Library, Hornton Street, London W8 7RX.

Westminster
HOUSE OF LORDS Record Office
House of Lords
London SW1A 0PW
Telephone: (01) 219 3074, but from May 1990: (071) 219 3074

Opening Hours: Monday to Friday 9.30 am to 5 pm. Annual closure: public holidays and last two weeks in November.
Car Parking: None
Children: Accompanied: eleven years plus. Unaccompanied 16 years plus.
Disabled: Lift.
Appointments System: Prior booking for seats necessary (three days) but unnecessary for viewers. Signing in by register. Eight seats, one film viewer, and one fiche.
Document Ordering: Prior ordering by letter or telephone. Catalogue numbers unnecessary. Six at a time. Delivery 9.30 am, 11 am, 12 noon, 3 pm, 4 pm; other times subject to staff availability. Photo-

copying by staff on same day. No facilities for typing or taping. Cameras by special arrangement
Records: Plans, associated documents and minutes of evidence for canals, railways, roads, docks etc from 1794 on; Estate and Enclosure Acts from 16th century on; Protestation Returns 1641/2; Parliamentary collections etc.
Postal Research: Very limited, no charge made.
Facilities: Toilets but no public telephone. No refreshment facilities but cafe/pub five minutes. Shops five minutes.
Publications: List available.
Places of Interest: Houses of Parliament, St Margaret's Church.

OTHER
LONDON REPOSITORIES

National ARMY MUSEUM (Archives)
Royal Hospital Road
London SW3 4HT
Telephone: 01 730 0717 Ext 222, but from May 1990: 071 730 0717 Ext 222

Opening Hours: Tuesday to Saturday 10 am to 4.30 pm (closed Mondays). Annual closure: public holidays.
Car Parking: Yes
Children: 14 years plus.
Disabled: Lift and toilet.
Appointments System: No prior booking for seats but necessary for viewers. Signing in by register plus identification with address. Twenty seats, one film viewer, two fiche.
Document Ordering: Prior ordering accepted by letter or telephone. Catalogue numbers helpful. Number at a time: no specific ruling. Delivery ten minutes. No ordering between 12 noon and 2 pm; last orders 4.15 pm. Photocopying by staff on same day; if large quantity or busy, sent by post. Typing/taping permitted. Cameras are not allowed.
Records: Private papers: officers and men of the British Army (17th century onwards, but main strength late Victorian period); a few collections of business archives and regimental books, photographs.
Postal Research: Specific enquiry, no charge made.
Facilities: Toilets but no public telephone. Canteen/restaurant and room for own food. Cafe/pub five minutes. Shops five minutes plus bookshop with local history publications.
Remarks: Reader's ticket issued to regular researchers. Bags not allowed, stor-

age facilities available. Donations box.

Refer to *The National Army Museum Archive Collection 1960-1985* in the *Journal* of the Society of Archivists Vol 8, No 1, April 1986.

BRITISH LIBRARY
INDIA OFFICE Library and Records
197 Blackfriars Road
London SE1 8NG
Telephone: 01 928 9531, but from May 1990: 071 928 9531

Opening Hours: Monday to Friday 9.30 am to 5.45 pm, Saturday 9.30 am to 12.45 pm. Annual closure: public holidays and one week in February.
Car Parking: None
Children: Not encouraged, but at archivist's discretion.
Disabled: No facilities
Appointments System: Prior booking for seats and viewers unnecessary.
Signing in by register plus personal identification. 73 seats, seven film viewers, five fiche.
Document Ordering: Prior ordering accepted by letter or telephone. Catalogue numbers necessary. Number at a time: six records or six manuscripts or eight books, plus one box of films or three microfilms. Delivery twenty to thirty minutes. Some restrictions on ordering if short of staff. Photocopying by staff and sent by post. Typing/taping permitted. Cameras are not allowed.
Records: Archives of the East India Company, Board of Control, India Office, Burma Office, map collection, prints and drawings, private papers, newspapers.
Postal Research: None
Facilities: Toilets and public telephone on premises. No refreshments but room for own food, also drink vending machine. Cafe/pub two minutes. Shops two minutes. Underground: Waterloo or Blackfriars.
Publications: *Brief Guide to Biographical Sources.* Free: general introductory booklet on library and records, *Sources for Family History Research, Ecclesiastical Returns, Using the Records and the Library.*
Remarks: Some printed books need 48 hours prior notice. Map of India showing ecclesiastical divisions on display. Bags not allowed, storage facilities available. Reader's ticket needed for long-term use (completed declaration required endorsed by approved sponsor).

Department of MANUSCRIPTS
BRITISH LIBRARY
Great Russell Street
London WC1B 3DG
Telephone: 01 323 7513/4, but from May 1990: 071 323 7513/4

Opening Hours: Monday to Saturday 10 am to 4.45 pm; last admissions and enquiries 4.30 pm. Annual closure: public holidays and normally second week in November.
Car Parking: None
Children: No-one under 21 years admitted.
Disabled: Accessible by wheelchairs
Appointments System: Prior booking for seats and viewers unnecessary.
Signing in by reader's ticket. Sixty seats, three film viewers and one fiche.
Document Ordering: Prior ordering accepted by letter or telephone. Catalogue numbers required. Six at a time, delivery Thirty to sixty minutes. Photocopying by staff and sent by post. No facilities for typing or taping. Cameras are not allowed.
Records: Ts of PRs require ordering.
Postal Research: Limited; no charge.
Facilities: Toilets and public telephone on premises. Refreshments but no room for own food. Cafe/pub two minutes. Shops five minutes including bookshop with local history publications.
Publications: *The British Library: Guide to the Catalogues and Indexes of Department of Manuscripts, Index of Manuscripts in the British Library:* ten volumes, published and unpublished catalogues and indexes to particular collections. Free: leaflets on regulations and guide to the use of students' room.
Remarks: Lord Chamberlain's Plays 1852-1930 require 48 hours prior notice, manuscripts on exhibition require 24 hours prior notice plus special permission. Donations box. Apply in advance for a form for reader's ticket.

BRITISH LIBRARY
NEWSPAPER Library
Colindale Avenue
London NW9 5HE
Telephone: Main switchboard 01 636 1544; Enquiry desk 01 323 7353/5/6. From May 1990: 071 636 1544; 071 323 7353/5/6

Opening Hours: Monday to Saturday 10 am to 4.45 pm. Annual closure: public holidays and week after the last complete week in October.

Car Parking: Very limited number
Children: Under 21 years require prior permission.
Disabled: Lift to Reading Room. Magnifying glasses can be supplied.
Appointments System: Prior booking for seats not allowed and unnecessary for viewers. Signing in by form for reader's ticket (identification required). 65 seats, 31 film viewers and one fiche.
Document Ordering: Prior ordering accepted by letter or telephone. Catalogue numbers required for foreign material only. Four at a time (volumes or films), delivery twenty to sixty minutes: longer if busy. Last orders 4.15 pm. Photocopying by staff and sent by post. Typing/taping permitted. Cameras permitted.
Records: Newspapers (mainly 18th to 20th century): English, Welsh, Scottish, Irish, London after 1801, Commonwealth and foreign.
Postal Research: Limited; charge for photocopying.
Facilities: Toilets and public telephone on premises. Snack machines, room for own food and drink vending machine. Cafe/pub five minutes. Underground: Colindale.
Publications: *Newspapers* and other British Library books. Free: leaflets on newspapers in the British Library, photocopying charge list, catalogue on films for sale, newspaper history, indexes in library, family history advice.
Other Repositories: RAF Museum, Hendon.
Places of Interest: RAF Museum, Hendon.
Remarks: The Burney collection of newspapers 1603-1800 and Thomason collection 1641-1663 are housed in the main library at Bloomsbury. South Asian newspapers in English are at the India Office Library. Cloakroom and storage facilities for bags available if needed.

CORPORATION OF LONDON RECORDS OFFICE
PO Box 270
Guildhall
London EC2P 2EJ
(Entrance via Basinghall Street)
Telephone: 01 260 1251, but from May 1990: 071 260 1251

Opening Hours: Monday to Friday 9.30 am to 4.45 pm. Annual closure: public holidays.
Car Parking: Nearby
Children: No specific ruling.
Disabled: Use Guildhall Yard entrance; lift. Prior notice advisable.
Appointments System: No prior book-

ing for seats. Signing in by register. Ten seats, two film viewers, two fiche.

Document Ordering: Prior ordering accepted by letter or telephone. Catalogue numbers not normally necessary. Six at a time, delivery up to 20 minutes. Photocopying by staff and sent by post; subject to severe restrictions. No facilities for typing or taping. Cameras permitted by prior arrangement.
Records: Freedom records, deeds, court records, drawings of buildings, City of London Sessions (trials at Old Bailey).
Postal Research: Limited, donations welcome.
Facilities: Toilets and public telephone on premises. Drinks trolley service. Cafe/pub two minutes. Shops five minutes. Underground: Bank or St Paul's or Moorgate.
Publications: Free: leaflets on the Record Office, how to get to Guildhall, *Freedom Records* (others in preparation). Various publications for sale in Guildhall Library bookshop.
Places of Interest: Museum of London, Barbican Centre and Art Gallery, St Paul's Cathedral, Guildhall Library.
Remarks: Rate books of the City of London 1908-to-date need 24 hours notice. No PRs at this office.

SOCIETY OF GENEALOGISTS
14 Charterhouse Buildings
Goswell Road
London EC1M 7BA
Telephone: (01) 251 8799, but from May 1990: (071) 251 8799

Opening Hours: Tuesday, Friday, Saturday 10 am to 6 pm; Wednesday and Thursday 10 am to 8 pm (closed Mondays). Annual closure: public holidays plus preceding Friday afternoon; first complete week in February.
Car Parking: None
Children: Twelve years plus.
Disabled: No facilities.
Appointments System: No prior booking for seats but advisable for viewers. Signing in by register plus entrance fee for non-members; reader's ticket for members. 96 seats, five film viewers, eighteen fiche and two readers/printers.
Document Ordering: No prior ordering. Three at a time (only applies to unbound material and some fiche). Delivery two minutes; certain documents stored in basement cannot be fetched during lunch time on Saturdays (12.30 pm to 2.30 pm). Photocopying by staff and sent by post; mainly DIY; no Ts. No facilities for typing or taping. Cameras not allowed.

Records: Mainly English records relating to pre 1837. Printed and Ts of PRs on open shelves, MIs, directories, poll books, genealogical indexes etc.
Postal Research: Yes; charge made.
Facilities: Toilets but no public telephone. Tea and coffee can be made and there is a room for own food. Cafe/pub five minutes. Shops five minutes. Underground: Barbican.
Publications: Catalogues of several sections of holdings and other publications. Free: leaflets, floor guide, publications list.
Places of Interest: Barbican Centre and Art Gallery.
Remarks: Cloakroom and storage facilities available. Historical county maps on display and for sale. Donations box.

GENERAL REGISTER OFFICE
Office of Population Censuses & Surveys
St Catherine's House
10 Kingsway
London WC2B 6JP
Telephone: 01 242 0262, but from May 1990: 071 242 0262

Opening Hours: Public Search Room: Monday to Friday 8.30 am to 4.30 pm. Electoral Roll: 9.30 am to 5 pm. Library 9.30 am to 4 pm. Annual closure: public holidays.
Car Parking: None
Children: Accompanied: no age limit. Unaccompanied: not allowed.
Disabled: Special toilet nearby.
Appointments System: Prior booking not required for search room or for viewers; three to four days notice required for electoral roll and three working days for library. No signing in for search room; form required for electoral roll; bookings required for library. Ten seats for electoral roll, six in library. Three film viewers in search room, two fiche in library. Photocopying library only - by staff for certain documents only. Typing/taping not permitted in search room but permission may be given in certain specific circumstances in other places. Cameras are not allowed.
Records: Public Search Room deals with sale of birth, marriage and death certificates in England and Wales from 1837. Electoral roll copies may be inspected by public free of charge (market researchers charged). Library has various publications, reports and sets of statistics but no genealogical information.
Facilities: Toilets and public telephone on premises. No refreshment facilities

but cafe/pub two to ten minutes. Shops two minutes including bookshop with local history publications.
Publications: Free: information leaflets and descriptions of holdings, guide to electoral roll. Library: bibliographies, journal holdings and sectional lists.
Places of Interest: St Bride's Crypt Museum, Fleet Street; Dr Johnson's House, 17 Gough Square, (off Fleet Street).
Remarks: Messengers and security guards are helpful with regard to disabled and facilities for their use. Other records held include Consular, Army, RAF, Royal Navy etc. Public are only allowed to consult indexes.

GREATER LONDON Record Office
40 Northampton Road
London EC1R 0HB
Telephone: 01 633 6851, but from May 1990: 071 633 6851

Opening Hours: Tuesday 9.30 am to 7.30 pm; Wednesday to Friday 9.30 am to 4.45 pm (closed Mondays). Annual closure: public holidays and third and fourth weeks in October.
Car Parking: Approximately ten places
Children: No specific ruling.
Disabled: Special bell for assistance. Ramp to loading bay access. Lift.
Appointments System: Prior booking for seats and viewers unnecessary. Signing in by register. 55 seats.
Document Ordering: Prior ordering accepted by letter or telephone. Catalogue numbers required. Five at a time, delivery approximately ten to twenty minutes. Ordering times 10 am, 10.30 am, 11 am, 11.45 am, 12.30 pm, 1.15 pm, 2 pm, 2.45 pm, 3.30 pm and 4 pm. Photocopying by staff and sent by post. Typing/taping limited and prior notification required. Cameras are not allowed.
Records: Ts of PRs/BTs on open shelves and require ordering; original PRs on fiche/film. Parish records and other deposited records relating to persons, places, institutions etc within the former counties of London and Middlesex; photograph library; maps; prints; drawings collection.
Postal Research: None
Facilities: Toilets but no public telephone. Room for own food, also drink vending machine. Cafe/pub two minutes. Shops two minutes. Underground: Faringdon or Angel.
Publications: Three guides to PRs in area covered, *Guide to Middlesex Quarter Sessions Records, Guide to Predecessors of London County Council.*
Places of Interest: Clerkenwell (Lon-

don's hidden village) leaflet available.
Tourist Office: Heritage Centre, 35 St John's Square, London EC1M 4DN, Telephone 01 250 1039 (from May 1990 Telephone 071 250 1039).
Remarks: Official archives of London and Middlesex County Councils and predecessors back to 16th century stored elsewhere require one working day's prior notice. Bags not allowed, storage facilities available. Historical map on display.

GUILDHALL LIBRARY
Department of Manuscripts
Aldermanbury
London EC2P 2EJ
Telephone: Direct 01 260 1863, Exchange 01 606 3030 Ext 1863; but from May 1990: Direct 071 260 1863, Exchange 071 606 3030 Ext 1863

Opening Hours: Monday to Saturday 9.30 am to 4.45 pm. Annual closure: public holidays plus Saturdays immediately before and after Christmas, New Year and Easter.
Car Parking: None
Children: No specific ruling.
Disabled: Ramps, toilet, car parking with prior notice. Stair lift for wheelchairs to be fitted.
Appointments System: Prior booking for seats and viewers unnecessary. Signing in by register. 31 seats, eleven film viewers, two fiche, and one dual viewer.
Document Ordering: Prior ordering accepted by letter, or telephone on day of visit. Catalogue numbers necessary. Three at a time. Delivery ten to fifteen minutes. No ordering between 12 noon and 2 pm on Saturdays. Photocopying of unbound material only; by staff and sent by post; PRs by printout. No facilities for typing or taping. Cameras permitted, subject to copyright.
Records: Ts of PRs/BTs generally on open shelves in printed books section of library; original PRs on fiche/film; original PRs; City of London, diocese of London, archdeaconry of London, Christ's Hospital School etc.
Postal Research: None
Facilities: Toilets. Public telephone nearby. No refreshment facilities but cafe/pub five minutes. Shops five minutes.
Publications: Various guides and handlists, eg PRs, *Genealogical Sources in the Library;* maps; other publications in Guildhall Library bookshop. Free: leaflets on probate records, marriage licences, Livery Companies, fire insurance records, sources for genealogy, bookshop

stock list.
Places of Interest: Guildhall, Monument to Great Fire of London.
Remarks: Less frequently requested records (mainly business records) and originals needed for photography require 24 hours prior notice. Historical map on display and for sale. See also Corporation of London RO, Guildhall.

THE HUGUENOT SOCIETY
of Great Britain and Ireland
The Huguenot Library
University College
Gower Street
London WC1E 6BT
Telephone: 01 380 7094, but from May 1990: 071 380 7094

Remarks: Not open to members of the public, only to Fellows of the Society: apply in writing for details. Printed and published records by the society are to be found in most major reference libraries.

IMPERIAL WAR MUSEUM
Department of Documents
Lambeth Road
London SE1 6HZ
Telephone: 01 735 8922 Exts 220/1/2/3, but from May 1990: 071 735 8922 Exts 220/1/2/3

Opening Hours: Monday to Friday 10 am to 5 pm; Saturday 10 am to 5 pm by appointment only. Annual closure: public holidays including Maundy Thursday afternoon and Friday preceding Spring bank holiday; one extra day immediately before or after Christmas; first two weeks in November.
Car Parking: None
Children: Accompanied: no specific ruling. Unaccompanied: fifteen years plus.
Disabled: Prior notice for special arrangements.
Appointments System: Prior booking for seats essential (24 hours) but for viewers unnecessary. Signing in by card index. Approximately 25 seats and four viewers.
Document Ordering: Prior ordering accepted, by letter or telephone. Catalogue numbers unnecessary. Four at a time, Delivery fifteen to thirty minutes. Last orders 4 pm. Photocopying by staff and sent by post. Typing/taping permitted with own equipment. Cameras permitted, negotiable fee.
Records: Collections fall into two main groups: British private papers and captured German material.
Postal Research: None

Facilities: Toilets and public telephone on premises. Refreshments plus room for own food, also vending machine. Cafe/pub five minutes. Shops five to ten minutes including bookshop with local history publications.
Publications: List available. Free: leaflets.
Places of Interest: HMS *Belfast*, Morgans Lane, Tooley Street. Underground: Elephant and Castle or Lambeth North.
Remarks: Some documents stored elsewhere require three days' prior notice. Charge for entry to the Museum·Public Galleries. Bags not allowed, storage facilities available. Donations box.

INDIA OFFICE: See British Library

NATIONAL MARITIME MUSEUM: See London Boroughs - Greenwich

DEPARTMENT OF MANUSCRIPTS: See British Library

NEWSPAPER LIBRARY: See British Library

PRINCIPAL REGISTRY OF THE FAMILY DIVISION
Somerset House
Strand
London WC2R 1LP
Telephone: (01) 936 6000, but from May 1990: (071) 936 6000

Opening Hours: Monday to Friday 10 am to 4.30 pm. Annual closure: public holidays.
Car Parking: None
Children: Accompanied: no specific ruling. Unaccompanied: 16 years plus.
Disabled: No facilities - steps to entrance.
Appointments System: No prior booking. Ten fiche viewers.
Document Ordering: Prior ordering by letter or telephone. Number at a time unlimited, delivery approximately fifteen to twenty minutes. Small charge for viewing. Photocopying by staff and sent by post (approximately ten days). No facilities for typing or taping. Cameras not allowed.
Records: Wills of deceased persons which have been proved or administrations granted (from 1858 to the present); Divorce Registry.
Postal Research: None
Facilities: Toilets and public telephone on premises. No refreshment facilities but cafe/pub five minutes. Shops a few minutes' walk including bookshop with

local history publications. Underground: Temple.

PUBLIC RECORD OFFICE
Chancery Lane
London WC2A 1LR
Telephone: (01) 876 3444, but from May 1990: (081) 876 3444

Opening Hours: Monday to Friday 9.30 am to 5 pm. Annual closure: public holidays and first two weeks in October.
Car Parking: None
Children: 12 years and over (letter from school required if unaccompanied).
Disabled: No facilities.
Appointments System: Signing in by register plus reader's ticket.
Document Ordering: Prior ordering by letter or telephone. Catalogue numbers necessary. Three at a time; last orders 3.30 pm. Photocopying by staff and sent by post. Cameras not allowed.
Records: Original Nonconformist registers on fiche/film; some Ts of Nonconformist registers on open shelves. Generally the older and legal records of government eg Assize, Chancery, Exchequer, Home Office census (1841 to 1851), Inland Revenue (estate duty wills), Prerogative Court of Canterbury etc. Many records are now on microfilm.
Postal Research: None
Facilities: Toilets and public telephone on premises. Room for own food, also drink vending machine. Cafe/pub two minutes.
Publications: (At entrance) various seals, posters, postcards and handbooks. Free series of information leaflets.
Places of Interest: Public Record Office Museum.
Remarks: Consult *Tracing your Ancestors in the Public Record Office* (HMSO 1984). Certain material stored in the Hayes repository requires ten days' prior notice. Bags not allowed, storage facilities available. Census returns on microfilm will be moved from Portugal Street office to Chancery Lane sometime in the near future, when reader's tickets will be needed. 1891 census will be available in 1992.

THE UNITED REFORMED CHURCH HISTORY SOCIETY (URC)
86 Tavistock Place
London WC1H 9RT
Telephone: (01) 837 7661, but from May 1990: (071) 837 7661

Opening Hours: Library open, by prior arrangement only (by letter or telephone), on Tuesdays, Thursdays, Fridays

11.30 am to 3.30 pm.
Publications: *The Journal:* issued free to members (annual subscription).
Remarks: All entries in Nonconformist registers in this library have been filmed by the Church of Latter-day Saints and are on the IGI. The Society's work is to encourage interest in the historical background to the URC. It's scope covers the history of Congregationalism, Presbyterianism and allied historical studies. Postal enquiries are dealt with as soon as possible but must have SAE. The library contains over 6,000 books, 2,500 pamphlets and a considerable amount of archival material. All work is done by volunteer members of this learned society in their spare time.

DR WILLIAMS'S Library
14 Gordon Square
London WC1H 0AG
Telephone: 01 387 3727, but from May 1990: 071 387 3727

Opening Hours: Please telephone for details.
Children: No-one under 18 admitted.
Publications: *Bulletin of Dr Williams's Library* (published annually), *Guide to the Manuscripts in Dr Williams's Library, Nonconformist Congregations in Great Britain, List of Histories and Other Material in Dr Williams's Library.*
Remarks: This library has a large collection of material both in manuscript and in print relating to the history of English Protestant dissent, particularly in its Presbyterian/Unitarian and Congregational forms. Few non-parochial registers. Sometimes able to assist with enquiries about ministers in the above denominations. Since 1982 the Congregational Library, formerly at Memorial Hall, Farringdon Street, has been in part of the building and under the same librarian. Nonconformist registers can be found in PRO and CROs. See *London Local Archives* (2nd edition GLAN 1989).

GREATER MANCHESTER

Local Studies Section
BOLTON Reference Library
Central Library
Le Mans Crescent
Bolton BL1 1SE
Telephone: (0204) 22311 Ext 2173

Opening Hours: Monday, Tuesday, Thursday, Friday 9.30 am to 7.30 pm; Wednesday 9.30 am to 1 pm; Saturday

9.30 am to 5 pm. Annual closure: public holidays.
Car Parking: None
Children: Accompanied: 7 years plus. Unaccompanied: 11 years plus.
Disabled: Ramp, lift, Vistel, Kurzweil reading machine.
Appointments System: Prior booking for seats and viewers unnecessary. Signing in by register. Eighty seats, six film viewers, and three fiche.
Document Ordering: Prior ordering not allowed. Number at a time at librarian's discretion. Delivery approximately five minutes. Photocopying by staff usually on same day. No facilities for typing or taping. Cameras permitted.
Records: Ts of PRs require ordering, some original PRs/BTs on fiche/film. Filmed newspapers, MIs, filmed Nonconformist registers (before 1838), Burgess Rolls and electoral registers for Bolton borough.
Postal Research: None
Facilities: Toilets and public telephone on premises. Refreshments but no room for own food. Cafe/pub two minutes. Shops two minutes including bookshop with local history publications.
Publications: *Tracing Your Ancestors in Bolton.* Free: leaflet about the Local Studies Collection.
Other Repositories: See entry for Manchester City Archives.
Places of Interest: 13th century Ye Old Man and Scythe Inn.
Tourist Office: See Bolton.
Remarks: Historical county map on display.

BOLTON Metropolitan Borough Archive Service
Central Library
Civic Centre
Le Mans Crescent
Bolton BL1 1SE
Telephone: (0204) 22311 Ext 2179

Opening Hours: Monday, Tuesday, Friday 9.30 am to 4.30 pm; Wednesday 9.30 am to 12.30 pm; Thursday 9.30 am to 7 pm. Annual closure: public holidays.
Car Parking: None
Children: Accompanied: seven years plus. Unaccompanied: 11 years plus.
Disabled: Ramp, lift, Vistel, Kurzweil reading machine.
Appointments System: Prior booking for seats essential (three days). Signing in by register. Six seats.
Document Ordering: Prior ordering by letter or telephone. Catalogue numbers unnecessary. Number at a time at archivist's discretion. Delivery two to ten

minutes generally. Photocopying by staff usually on same day. No facilities for typing or taping. Cameras permitted.

Records: Original Nonconformist registers, including Methodists, after 1838; Poor Law and workhouse admission etc; public and local authority; family; estate; business; Quarter Sessions; charities; maps and plans.

Postal Research: None

Facilities: Toilets and public telephone on premises. Refreshments but no room for own food. Cafe/pub two minutes. Shops two minutes including bookshop with local history publications.

Publications: Guide to the Bolton Archive Service, *Tracing your Ancestors in Bolton*. Free: leaflet about the Archive Service.

Other Repositories: Reference Library in same building.

Places of Interest: Museum of Local History, Museum and Art Gallery, Smithills Hall, Hall i' th' Wood Museum, Tonge Moor Textile Museum, 13th century inn, Bolton Steam Museum.

Tourist Office: Town Hall, Bolton BL1 1RU. Telephone (0204) 22311.

Remarks: Business records of several local engineering and cotton manufacturing firms and some local authority records stored elsewhere require two weeks' prior notice. Historical county atlas available on request. Film/fiche copies of records are administered by the Local Studies Section of the Reference Library only.

BURY Archive Service
22A Union Arcade
Bury BL9 0QF

ADDRESS FOR CORRESPONDENCE:
Libraries and Arts Department
Bury Metropolitan Borough Council
Textile Hall
Manchester Road
Bury BL9 0DR
Telephone: (061) 797 6697; out of hours (061) 705 5871

Opening Hours: Tuesday 10 am to 1 pm and 2 pm to 5 pm. By appointment only for other weekdays (opening hours as Tuesday). Annual closure: public holidays plus one day after Christmas; Monday and Tuesday following third week in September.

Car Parking: Nearby

Children: At archivist's discretion.

Disabled: No facilities. Advance notice for possibility of documents being produced at Central Library.

Appointments System: Prior booking for seats essential (a few days). Signing in

by register plus card index and CARN. Four seats.

Document Ordering: Prior ordering accepted by letter or telephone. Catalogue numbers unnecessary. Two at a time; delivery five minutes. Photocopying restricted; by staff on same day.

Typing/taping at archivist's discretion. Cameras at archivist's discretion.

Records: Local authority, Nonconformist, business, trade unions.

Postal Research: Limited to 20 minutes, no charge made.

Facilities: No toilets or public telephone. No refreshment facilities. Cafe/pub two minutes. Shops two minutes including bookshop with local history publications.

Publications: *General Information for Users, Archives in Greater Manchester, Routes: A Guide to Family History in the Bury Area.*

Other Repositories: Central Library (Reference Department), Manchester Road, Bury BL9 0DR.

Places of Interest: Transport Museum, Baldingstone House, Art Gallery.

Remarks: This service is still in the course of development as to premises etc, so check with archivist prior to visit. Donations box.

IRLAM see SALFORD, MANCHESTER

CITY OF MANCHESTER
Archives Department
Manchester Central Library
St Peter's Square
Manchester M2 5PD
Telephone: (061) 236 9422 Ext 269

Opening Hours: Monday 1 pm to 9 pm, Tuesday and Thursday 10 am to 12 noon and 1 pm to 5 pm, Wednesday 1 pm to 5 pm, Friday 10 am to 1 pm. Annual closure: public holidays.

Car Parking: None

Children: Allowed for school purposes only.

Disabled: Ramped access to Local Studies Library where filmed records available.

Appointments System: Prior booking for seats advisable (essential for Monday evenings). Fill in application form on first visit. Ten seats. Viewers in Local History Library (floor above).

Document Ordering: Prior ordering by letter or telephone. Catalogue numbers unnecessary. Eight at a time, delivery five to ninety minutes depending on where located. Produced from 10.40 am to 11.50

am, 1 pm to 3 pm and 3.30 pm to 4.30 pm (4 pm on Mondays). Photocopying by staff on same day, if large quantity or busy, sent by post. No facilities for typing or taping. Cameras not allowed.
Records: Ts of PRs require ordering. Original PRs, original PRs on fiche/film, local authority including Poor Law Unions, Manchester diocesan, Jewish, trade unions, Manchester Ship Canal.
Postal Research: Limited to twenty minutes, no charge made.
Facilities: Toilets. Public telephone next door. Snack bar in basement, but no room for own food. Cafe/pub two minutes. Shops ten minutes including bookshop with local history publications.
Publications: Lists of holdings (for consultation in departments only). Free: *Greater Manchester Archives: A Guide to Local Repositories.*
Other Repositories: Chetham's Library, Long Millgate, Manchester M3 1SB; Documentary Photography Archive, c/o Cavendish Building, Cavendish Street, Manchester M15 6BG; Greater Manchester Museum of Science and Industry, Liverpool Road, Castlefield, Manchester M3 4JP; North West Film Archive, Manchester Polytechnic, Minshull House, 47-49 Chorlton Street, Manchester M1 3EU; Greater Manchester Police Museum, Newton Street, Manchester M1 1ES; Jewish Museum, Spanish and Portuguese Synagogue, 190 Cheetham Hill Road, Manchester; Probate Registry, Astley House, Quay Street, Manchester 3.
Places of Interest: Aircraft Collection, City Art Gallery, Craft Centre, Gallery of English Costume, Chinatown, Pankhurst Centre.
Tourist Office: Town Hall Extension, Lloyd Street, Manchester M60 2LA. Telephone (061) 234 3157/8.
Remarks: Minutes of various Council committees and rate books stored elsewhere require one week's prior notice. Maps are in Local History Library.

GREATER MANCHESTER
County Record Office
56 Marshall Street
New Cross
Manchester M4 5FU
Telephone: (061) 832 5284

Opening Hours: Monday to Friday 9 am to 5 pm, second and fourth Saturday in the month 9 am to 12 noon. Annual closure: public holidays.
Car Parking: Nearby
Children: No specific ruling but dependent on behaviour.
Disabled: Steps to lift. Doorbell for help.

Appointments System: Prior booking for seats (six weeks) and viewers necessary. Signing in by register plus CARN. 20 seats, six film viewers, and two fiche.
Document Ordering: Prior ordering not normally necessary. Three at a time. Delivery five to ten minutes. Photocopying by staff on same day. Typing/taping permitted. Cameras not allowed.
Records: Some Ts of PRs on open shelves, printed probate index 1858-1930, local authority, coroners, hospitals, charity commissioners, business, Rochdale Canal, family, trade unions, solicitors, societies, filmed indexes of civil registration 1837-1912 etc.
Postal Research: Limited, no charge made.
Facilities: Toilets and public telephone on premises. Refreshments and room for own food. Cafe/pub two minutes. Shops ten minutes including bookshop with local history publications.
Publications: *Summary of Collection.* Free: *Probate Records for Greater Manchester County,* RO newsletter, *Greater Manchester Archives: A Guide to Local Repositories, Guide to Civil Registration in Great Britain.*
Other Repositories: See entry for Manchester City Archives.
Places of Interest: Art Gallery, 15th century cathedral, Museum of Science and Industry, Railway Museum, Manchester Police Museum, also see entry for Manchester City Archives.
Tourist Office: See entry for Manchester City Archives.
Remarks: Bags not allowed.

JOHN RYLANDS UNIVERSITY
LIBRARY OF MANCHESTER
Deansgate
Manchester M3 3EH
Telephone: (061) 834 5343/6765

Opening Hours: Monday to Friday 10 am to 5.30 pm, Saturday 10 am to 1 pm. Annual closure: between Christmas and New Year.
Car Parking: None
Children: No-one under 18 admitted.
Disabled: No facilities, but staff prepared to assist.
Appointments System: Prior booking for seats not allowed. Signing in by card index plus Manchester University ticket (need letter of introduction). Approximately 60 seats.
Document Ordering: Prior ordering by letter or telephone. Catalogue numbers preferred. No formal limit on number at a time. Delivery ten to fifteen minutes. Ordering time preferably before 4 pm.

Photocopying by staff on same day, if large quantity or busy, sent by post. No facilities for typing or taping.
Cameras not allowed.
Records: Rare books and manuscripts (Division of the University Library), Nonconformist, business, private etc.
Postal Research: None
Facilities: Toilets but no public telephone. No refreshment facilities. Cafe/pub two minutes. Shops two minutes including bookshop with local history publications.
Publications: Various publications and guides.
Other Repositories: See entry for Manchester City Archives. Manchester Central Library, St Peter's Square, Manchester 2; Methodist Connexional Archives, Church Archivist, c/o John Rylands University Library (address as above), for Methodist records excluding Circuit and Chapel records.
Tourist Office: See entry for Manchester City Archives.
Remarks: Donations box. Bags not allowed, storage facilities available. Newspapers, Manchester Medical Society, English textile companies records stored elsewhere: enquiries to archivist.

SALFORD City Archives Centre
658/662 Liverpool Road
Irlam
Manchester M30 5AD
Telephone: (061) 775 5643

Opening Hours: Monday to Friday 9 am to 4.30 pm. Annual closure: public holidays.
Car Parking: Six places.
Children: No specific ruling.
Disabled: Toilet.
Appointments System: Prior booking for seats essential. Signing in by register plus card. Eight seats.
Document Ordering: Prior ordering by letter or telephone. Catalogue numbers unnecessary. Number at a time at archivist's discretion. Delivery five to ten minutes. Photocopying by staff and sent by post. No facilities for typing or taping. Cameras permitted.
Records: Rate books, printed sources, local authority, public records including Quarter Sessions, religious (including Nonconformist), family, business, trade unions, charities, societies, Poor Law Union.
Postal Research: Limited to one hour, no charge made.
Facilities: Toilets, but no public telephone. Refreshments and room for own food. Cafe/pub ten minutes. Shops ten

minutes.
Publications: Catalogue of records available for consultation. Free: *Genealogical Sources for the City of Salford, The History of Houses.*
Other Repositories: See entry for Manchester City Archives. Salford Local History Library, Peel Park Crescent, Salford M5 4WU; Salford Mining Museum, Buile Hill Park, Eccles Old Road, Salford M6 8GL; The Clifford Whitworth University Library, University of Salford, Salford M5 4WT.
Places of Interest: Museum and Art Gallery, Ordsall Hall Museum, Photographic Heritage Centre, Monks Hall Museum.
Tourist Office: Art Gallery and Museum, The Crescent, Salford. Telephone (061) 736 3353/2649.
Remarks: Some local authority records and one large estate collection stored elsewhere require 24 hours prior notice.

STOCKPORT Archive Service
Central Library
Wellington Road South
Stockport
Cheshire SK1 3RS
Telephone: (061) 474 4534/4530

Opening Hours: Monday to Friday 9 am to 8 pm, Saturday 9 am to 4 pm. Archivist only available Monday to Friday 9 am to 5 pm. Items should be requested in advance for evenings and Saturdays. Annual closure: public holidays.
Car Parking: None
Children: No specific ruling.
Disabled: No facilities.
Appointments System: Prior booking for seats unnecessary, but for viewers necessary. Signing in by register. Four film viewers and four fiche.
Document Ordering: Prior ordering by letter or telephone. Catalogue numbers unnecessary. Delivery five minutes. Photocopying by staff on same day. No facilities for typing or taping. Cameras permitted.
Records: Ts of PRs/BTs require ordering, some original PRs on fiche/film.
Postal Research: Limited specific enquiry, no charge made.
Facilities: No toilets. Public telephone on premises. No refreshment facilities. Cafe/pub two minutes. Shops five minutes including bookshop with local history publications.
Publications: Publications list of booklets, books, maps, postcards and prints (of immense interest to family and local historians).
Places of Interest: The town is a product of the industrial revolution and the rail-

way age, having mills and great chimneys; Vernon Park Museum with local history items; Stockport Museum, Bramhall; Lyme Hall and Park, Disley.
Tourist Office: 9 Princes Street, Stockport, Greater Manchester SK1 1SL. Telephone (061) 480 0315.
Remarks: Some local authority, public records and privately, recently acquired collections stored elsewhere require prior notice. Donations accepted.

TAMESIDE Archive Service
Stalybridge Library
Trinity Street
Stalybridge
Cheshire SK15 2BM
Telephone: (061) 338 2708/3831

Opening Hours: Monday to Wednesday plus Friday 9 am to 7.30 pm, Saturday 9 am to 4 pm (closed Thursdays). Annual closure: public holidays and period between Christmas and New Year.
Car Parking: Nearby
Children: No specific ruling.
Disabled: Prior notification essential. Use side entrance with help from staff because of steps.
Appointments System: Prior booking for seats unnecessary but for viewers necessary. Signing in by register. Twelve seats, two film viewers, and one fiche.
Document Ordering: Prior ordering by letter or telephone. Catalogue numbers preferred. Three at a time, delivery five minutes. Photocopying by staff on same day. No facilities for typing or taping. Depositor's permission required for use of cameras.
Records: Some original PRs on fiche/film, local authority, extensive selection of books and other printed material relating to towns now in Tameside.
Postal Research: Limited, no charge made.
Facilities: No toilets or public telephone. No refreshment facilities. Cafe/pub two minutes. Shops two minutes including bookshop with local history publications.
Publications: *Tameside Bibliography, Guide to Archive Collection,* catalogues and indexes. Free: various leaflets by the Local Studies Library, *Tracing Your Family Tree, Guide to Local Repositories of Greater Manchester,* list of 19th and 20th century copies of photographs.
Other Repositories: See entry for Manchester City Archives.
Places of Interest: Astley Cheetham Art Gallery.
Remarks: Some local authority records stored elsewhere require minimum of 24 hours prior notice. Search room is in local studies library.

WIGAN Record Office
Town Hall
Leigh
Wigan
Lancs WN7 2DY
Telephone: (0942) 672421 Ext 266

Opening Hours: Monday to Friday 10 am to 4 pm. Annual closure: public holidays.
Car Parking: Approximately 100 places.
Children: Any age - dependent on behaviour.
Disabled: Lift to floor below, then stairs.
Appointments System: Prior booking for seats and viewers essential. Signing in by register. Approximately eight seats, three film viewers, and one fiche.
Document Ordering: Prior ordering advisable (by letter or telephone). Catalogue numbers preferred, but not necessary. Three volumes at a time.
Ordering times 11.30 am and 2.15 pm, microfilm on demand. Photocopying by staff and sent by post. No facilities for typing or taping. Cameras not allowed.
Records: Ts of PRs on open shelves, most original PRs on fiche/film. Trade unions, Nonconformist churches, local authority, Poor Law Unions, Quarter Sessions, family, business, education.
Postal Research: Limited, no charge made.
Facilities: Toilets. No public telephone. Refreshments and Drink vending machine. Cafe/pub two minutes. Shops two minutes including bookshop with local history publications.
Publications: *Guide to Genealogical Sources,* leaflets on coal mining, maps and plans, administration of Wigan, local government, *History of your House, Those Dark Satanic Mills* (illustrated history of area). Free: *Wigan RO.*
Other Repositories: Wigan Reference Library, Rodney Street, Wigan (holds electoral registers, directories, census); Leigh Library, Market Square, Leigh (holdings as Wigan Reference Library).
Places of Interest: Industrial town and one of the oldest boroughs in Lancashire, Wigan Pier, Powell Museum, Heigh Hall Country Park (approximately two miles).
Tourist Office: Trencherfield Mill, Wigan Pier, Wigan WN3 4BX. Telephone (0942) 323666.
Remarks: Historical county on display.

GREATER MANCHESTER: OTHER LOCAL REPOSITORIES

OLDHAM LIBRARY SERVICE
Local Studies Library
84 Union Street
Oldham OL1 1DN
Telephone (061) 678 4654

Opening Hours: Monday, Wednesday to Friday 10 am to 7 pm, Tuesday 10 am to 1 pm, Saturday 10 am to 4 pm.
Records: Local authority, family, business, trade unions.

ROCHDALE CENTRAL LIBRARY
(Local Studies)
The Esplanade
Rochdale OL16 1AQ
Telephone (0706) 47474 Ext 4915

Opening Hours: Monday, Tuesday, Thursday 9.30 am to 7.30 pm, Wednesday 9.30 am to 5 pm, Friday 9.30 am to 5.30 pm, Saturday 9.30 am to 4 pm.
Records: Local authority (including Turn Pike Trust), Poor Law Union, Nonconformists, family and manorial, business, trade unions, societies.

TRAFFORD LIBRARY SERVICE
Sale Library
Tatton Road
Sale M33 1YH
Telephone (061) 973 3142 Ext 3458

Opening Hours: Monday, Tuesday, Thursday, Friday 10 am to 7.30 pm, Wednesday 10 am to 1 pm, Saturday 10 am to 4 pm.
Records: Local authority. Also Altrincham Library, Stamford New Road, Altrincham, Telephone (061) 928 0317; Stretford Library, Kingsway, Stretford. Telephone (061) 865 2218; Urmston Library, Crofts Bank Road, Urmston. Telephone (061) 748 0774.

MERSEYSIDE

ST HELEN'S Local History and Archives Library
Central Library
Gamble Institute
Victoria Square
St Helen's
Merseyside WA10 1DY
Telephone: (0744) 24061 Ext 2952

Opening Hours: Monday and Wednesday 9.30 am to 8 pm, Tuesday plus Thursday to Saturday 9.30 am to 5 pm. Annual closure: public holidays.
Car Parking: None
Children: Accompanied: no age restriction. Unaccompanied: primary school age and above.
Disabled: Ramp, lift.
Appointments System: Prior booking for seats unnecessary but for viewers necessary. Signing in by register.
Approximately 30 seats, five film viewers, and two fiche.
Document Ordering: Prior ordering advisable, by letter or telephone. Catalogue numbers necessary. Reasonable number at a time; delivery depends on number of staff. Photocopying by staff on same day. No facilities for typing or taping. Cameras: each case considered separately.
Records: Some Ts of PRs on open shelves, some Ts of PRs require ordering; some original PRs on fiche/film.
Postal Research: None
Facilities: No toilets. Public telephone on premises. No refreshment facilities but cafe/pub two minutes. Shops two minutes including bookshop with local history publications.
Publications: Genealogical holdings list, guide to search room.
Other Repositories: Pilkington Plc, Records Section, Prescot Road, St Helens (access at archivist's discretion).
Places of Interest: Pilkington Glass Museum, Museum and Art Gallery.
Remarks: Some records stored elsewhere require prior notice. Historical county map on request.

LIVERPOOL Record Office
Liverpool City Libraries
and Arts Department
William Brown Street
Liverpool L3 8EW
Telephone: (051) 207 2147

Opening Hours: Monday to Friday 9 am to 9 pm, Saturday 9 am to 5 pm. Annual closure: public holidays plus Tuesday following Spring and Autumn bank holidays.
Car Parking: None
Children: Accompanied: any age. Unaccompanied: 16 plus years at archivist's discretion.
Disabled: Access
Appointments System: Prior booking for seats not allowed. Signing by register plus Liverpool RO ticket. 64 seats. Two cassette film viewers due shortly.
Document Ordering: Prior ordering not allowed. Five volumes or one bundle at a

time. Delivery within a few minutes.

Ordering on the hour and half hour, commencing at 9.30 am, last orders 8.30 pm weekdays, 4.30 pm Saturdays. Photocopying restricted, by staff on same day, if large quantity or busy, sent by post. No facilities for typing or taping. Cameras restricted

Records: Ts of PRs require ordering. Original PRs. Cemetery registers and electoral registers are being filmed (use of originals will be restricted when programme complete). Civil registration indexes on film.

Postal Research: Limited to twenty minutes, no charge made.

Facilities: Toilets and public telephone on premises. Refreshments, but no room for own food; drink vending machine in cafe. Cafe/pub five minutes. Shops ten minutes including bookshop with local history publications.

Publications: Free: guides on title deeds, census, probate records, PRs, Methodist, *Tracing Your Ancestry,* general information, Nonconformists.

Other Repositories: Liverpool University Archives Unit, PO Box 147, Liverpool L69 3BX; Local History Library, Sefton Libraries and Arts Services, 220 Stanley Road, Bootle, Liverpool.

Places of Interest: The King's Regiment Collection (Liverpool Museum), Museum of Labour History, Maritime Museum, Central Museum, Library and Walker Art Gallery, Anglican Cathedral, Roman Catholic Cathedral, Bluecoat Chambers, Speke Hall, Dental Hospital Museum.

Tourist Office: 29 Lime Street, Liverpool L11 1JG. Telephone (051) 709 3631.

Remarks: Viewers are in Microfilm Unit and can be booked in advance. Map of Liverpool Church of England parishes on display.

MERSEYSIDE MARITIME MUSEUM
Maritime Records Centre
Block D
Albert Dock
Liverpool L3 4AA
Telephone (051) 207 0001

Opening Hours: Monday to Friday 10.30 am to 4.30 pm. Annual closure: public holidays.

Car Parking: Ample nearby

Children: School pupils by arrangement only.

Disabled: Ramp

Appointments System: Prior booking for seats and viewers unnecessary.

Signing in register and entrance fee. Twenty seats, two film viewers and one fiche.

Document Ordering: Prior ordering by letter or telephone. Catalogue numbers unnecessary. Three at a time, delivery ten minutes. Photocopying by staff on same day. No facilities for typing or taping. Cameras not allowed.

Records: Documents relevant to the Port of Liverpool.

Postal Research: Limited to thirty minutes, charge for photocopies.

Facilities: Toilets and public telephone on premises. Refreshments, but no room for own food. Cafe/pub five minutes. Shops two minutes plus bookshop with local history publications.

Publications: For sale and free.

Places of Interest: See entry for Liverpool RO.

Tourist Office: See entry for Liverpool RO.

Remarks: Archives stored elsewhere require two weeks' prior notice. Bags not allowed, storage facilities available.

Cheshire RO contains all Merseyside diocesan records.

WIRRAL Archives Service
Information Services
Birkenhead Reference Library
Borough Road
Birkenhead L41 2XB
Telephone: (051) 652 6106/7/8

Opening Hours: Monday to Friday 10 am to 8 pm, Saturday 10 am to 1 pm and 2 pm to 5 pm. Annual closure: public holidays.

Car Parking: Nearby

Children: No specific ruling - dependent on behaviour.

Disabled: Access through right-hand side door. Lift.

Appointments System: Prior booking for seats unnecessary but advisable for viewers. Approximately 50 seats, two film viewers and two fiche.

Document Ordering: Prior ordering advisable, by letter or telephone (three days). Catalogue numbers unnecessary. Usually three at a time, delivery within a few minutes. Photocopying DIY. No facilities for typing or taping. Cameras permitted.

Records: Ts of PRs require ordering, original PRs on fiche/film. School, workhouse, hospital, society, local, rate books, valuation lists, court registers.

Postal Research: Very limited, no charge made.

Facilities: Toilets. No public telephone. No refreshment facilities. Cafe/pub five minutes. Shops five minutes including bookshop with local history publications.

Publications: *A Guide to Sources for*

Family Historians. Free: archive lists.
Other Repositories: Modern Records Centre (Merseyside Residency Body), Mann Island, Liverpool L3 4DY; Port Sunlight Heritage Centre, P.O.Box 139, Greendale Road, Port Sunlight L62 4ZP.
Places of Interest: Williamson Museum and Art Gallery, Hamilton Square, Town Hall, Birkenhead Priory.
Tourist Office: Central Library, Borough Road, Birkenhead L41 2XB. Telephone (051) 652 6106 Ext 36.

MIDLANDS see WEST MIDLANDS

MIDDLESEX see LONDON

NORFOLK

NORFOLK Record Office
Central Library
Bethel Street
Norwich NR2 1NJ
Telephone: (0603) 761349

Opening Hours: Monday to Friday 9 am to 5 pm, Saturday 9 am to 12 noon. Annual closure: public holidays plus preceding Saturday; Tuesday following Easter, Spring and Summer bank holidays; one additional day at Christmas.
Car Parking: None
Children: At archivist's discretion.
Disabled: Two parking places, ramp, lift.
Appointments System: Prior booking for seats advisable (two to four weeks) but for viewers unnecessary. Signing in by registration form plus CARN. Sixteen seats, and eight film viewers.
Document Ordering: Prior ordering by letter or telephone. Catalogue numbers unnecessary. Four at a time; delivery five to thirty minutes. Ordering times 9.10 am, 9.30 am and thereafter at half hourly intervals until 12.30 pm; half hourly from 2 pm to 4.30 pm; no more than a total of twelve documents allowed on Saturdays; Saturday ordering 9.10 am to 11.30 am. Photocopying restricted; by staff and post; PRs restricted. No facilities for typing or taping. Cameras at archivist's discretion.
Records: A few Ts of PRs mostly on open shelves, some require ordering; some original PRs/BTs on fiche/film; borough records.
Postal Research: Yes; charge made.
Facilities: Toilets. No public telephone. No refreshment facilities but cafe/pub two minutes. Shops two minutes including bookshop with local history publications.

Publications: *List of PRs, Guide to Genealogical Sources,* parish map, *Guide to Great Yarmouth Borough Records.* Free: How to use the search room, local record agents.
Other Repositories: Norwich Central Library, Local Studies Department.
Places of Interest: Colman's Mustard Museum, Sainsbury Centre for Visual Arts, Norwich Castle Museum, Bridewell Museum (local craft and industry), Stranger's Hall, ancient cathedral city with medieval streets.
Tourist Office: Guildhall, Gaol Hill, Norwich NR2 1NF. Telephone (0603) 666071.
Remarks: Great Yarmouth charters and assembly books, Kings Lynn borough archives and some modern local authority records stored elsewhere require two to three weeks' prior notice. Donations box. Historical county map on display.

NORTHAMPTONSHIRE

NORTHAMPTONSHIRE
Record Office
Delapre Abbey
London Road
Northampton NN4 9AW
Telephone: (0604) 762129

Opening Hours: Monday to Wednesday 9 am to 4.45 pm, Thursday 9 am to 7.45 pm, Friday 9 am to 4.15 pm, two Saturdays a month 9 am to 12.15 pm.
Annual closure: public holidays.
Car Parking: Approximately 20 places plus others nearby.
Children: At archivist's discretion (approximately 8 years if accompanied or 10 to 12 if unaccompanied).
Disabled: Access
Appointments System: Prior booking for seats essential for Thursday evening and Saturdays. Booking for viewers advisable. Signing in by register. Approximately 30 seats, five film viewers, and five fiche.
Document Ordering: Prior ordering by letter or telephone. Catalogue numbers unnecessary. Reasonable number at a time; four at a time issued. Delivery five to ten minutes if not busy. Ordering times restricted between 12 noon and 2 pm. Photocopying restricted; by staff on same day; if large quantity or busy, sent by post; PRs by printout only. Typing/taping not presently permitted.
Cameras permitted.
Records: Ts of PRs on open shelves, some original PRs/BTs on fiche/film (in process); some original PRs.

Postal Research: Limited; charge made for photocopies.
Facilities: Toilets but no public telephone. Refreshments and room for own food. Cafe/pub five minutes by car. Shops ten minutes by car, including bookshop with local history publications.
Publications: Annual reports and accessions list, *List of PRs, Guide to RO*, various other guides. Free: *Tracing Your Family Tree, History of Your House, Education Records, History of Village, Wills and How to Find Them*, search room rules.
Other Repositories: Northampton Central Library, Abington Street, Northampton NN1 2BA.
Places of Interest: Museum of Leathercraft, Turner's Musical Merry-go-round, Althorp (6 miles), the Abbey building and garden, Northamptonshire Regiment and Northamptonshire Yeomanry Museum, Abington Park.
Tourist Office: 21 St Giles Street, Northampton NN1 1JA. Telephone (0604) 22677/34881 Ext 404.
Remarks: Some 20th century administration records eg Urban and Rural District Council records, stored elsewhere require at least 24 hours prior notice. Bags not allowed. Historical county map on display. Headquarters of Northamptonshire Record Society in historical library: staff may borrow books for use of visitors in search room only.

NORTHUMBERLAND

(Also see TYNE AND WEAR)

BERWICK Branch Record Office
Berwick Borough Council Offices
Wallace Green
Berwick Upon Tweed
Northumberland TD15
Telephone: (091) 2362680;
on Wednesday (0289) 330044

Opening Hours: Wednesday 10 am to 1 pm and 2 pm to 5 pm. Annual closure: public holidays.
Car Parking: None
Children: No specific ruling.
Disabled: No facilities.
Appointments System: Prior booking for seats and viewers unnecessary. Signing in by register. Three seats and one film viewer.
Document Ordering: Prior ordering by letter or telephone. Catalogue numbers unnecessary. Three at a time, delivery five minutes. Photocopying by staff on

same day; if large quantity or busy, sent by post. No facilities for typing or taping. Cameras permitted.
Records: Ts of PRs on open shelves. Original PRs. Original PRs on fiche/film. Manorial, Borough of Berwick upon Tweed (Freemen's records), parish, salmon fisheries' records.
Postal Research: Yes; charge made.
Facilities: Toilets and public telephone on premises. No refreshment facilities but cafe/pub two minutes. Shops two minutes including bookshop with local history publications.
Publications: *Berwick Borough Archives* (describes classes of records at branch office).
Places of Interest: Museum and Art Gallery, Museum of King's Own Scottish Borderers.
Tourist Office: Castlegate Car Park, Berwick upon Tweed TD15 1ED. Telephone (0289) 330733.
Remarks: Donations box.
Proposed move to new office shortly with special entrance for disabled.

NORTHUMBERLAND Record Office
Melton Park
North Gosforth
Newcastle Upon Tyne NE3 5QX
Telephone: (091) 2362680

Opening Hours: Monday 9 am to 9 pm, Tuesday to Thursday 9 am to 5 pm, Friday 9 am to 4.30 pm. Annual closure: public holidays.
Car Parking: Eighteen places
Children: No specific ruling.
Disabled: Assistance given when required.
Appointments System: Prior booking for viewers necessary but not for seats. Signing in by register. Twelve seats, nine film viewers and four fiche.
Document Ordering: Prior ordering by letter or telephone. Catalogue numbers unnecessary. Three at a time; delivery five minutes. Ordering: restricted service between 1 pm and 2 pm. Photocopying by staff and sent by post; PRs by printout only. Typing/taping permitted by special arrangement. Cameras permitted.
Records: Ts of PRs on open shelves, original PRs, original PRs on fiche/film.
Postal Research: Yes; charge made.
Facilities: Toilets. Telephone: use ROs (for cost). Refreshments and room for own food; no facilities nearby.
Publications: Leaflets on various sources, eg coal mining, genealogy, education; RO exhibition catalogues; *North Eastern Ancestors (Sources for Genealogists)*; annual reports.

Places of Interest: Trinity Maritime Centre, John George Joicey Museum (includes the 15th/19th King's Royal Hussars and Northumberland Hussars Museum), Castle Keep Museum, Military Vehicle Museum, Mining Engineering Museum, Plummer Tower Museum, Black Friars Priory ruins, Greek Museum.

Tourist Office: Monk Street, Newcastle upon Tyne NE1 4XW, Telephone (091) 2615367.

Remarks: Donations box. Bags not allowed, storage facilities available. Historical county map on display. Essential to check repositories in Tyne and Wear.

NOTTINGHAMSHIRE

NOTTINGHAMSHIRE Archives Office
County House
High Pavement
Nottingham NG1 1HR
Telephone: (0602) 504524

Opening Hours: Monday and Wednesday to Friday 9 am to 4.45 pm, Tuesday 9 am to 7.15 pm, Saturday 9 am to 12.15 pm. Annual closure: public holidays.
Car Parking: None
Children: No specific ruling but dependent on behaviour.
Disabled: Some items can be made available on ground floor by special arrangement.
Appointments System: Prior booking for seats and viewers unnecessary. Signing by register plus CARN. 36 seats, three film viewers and twelve fiche plus reader/printer.
Document Ordering: No prior ordering, except for records stored elsewhere. Three per hour; delivery ten to fifteen minutes. Ordering times (for original records only) hourly from 9.15 am; last orders 3.15 pm, Tuesday 6.15 pm, Saturday 11.15 am. Photocopying by staff and sent by post; PRs by printout only. No facilities for typing or taping. Cameras permitted.
Records: Some Ts of PRs on open shelves, all pre 1900 PRs on fiche, BTs on film.
Postal Research: Limited specific enquiry, no charge made.
Facilities: Toilets. No public telephone. No refreshment facilities but cafe/pub two minutes. Shops two minutes including bookshop with local history publications.
Publications: List of PRs, archive resource packs on Victorian schools and Great War. Free: information sheets.

Other Repositories: County Library, Angel Row, Nottingham.
Places of Interest: Lace Centre, Castle Museum, Castlegate Costume and Textile Museum, Sherwood Foresters Museum (45th/95th Foot), Industrial Museum, Wollaton Park, Wollaton Hall Natural History Museum, Canal Museum, Brewhouse Yard Museum.
Tourist Office: 14-16 Wheeler Gate, Nottingham NG1 2NB. Telephone (0602) 470661.
Remarks: County council, city, district councils, courts, diocesan and some private deposits require one day's notice; modern city and some private reports require one week's notice. Bags not allowed. Historical county map on display. RO contains Belper library and general reference library.

Department of Manuscripts
and Special Collections
NOTTINGHAM UNIVERSITY
LIBRARY
University Park
Nottingham NG7 2RD
Telephone: (0602) 484848 Ext 3440

Opening Hours: Monday to Friday 9 am to 4.45 pm.
Car Parking: Nearby
Children: Accompanied: 12 years plus. Unaccompanied: 16 years plus.
Disabled: Access
Appointments System: Prior booking for seats and viewers unnecessary. Signing in by register. One film viewer, and one fiche (for catalogues only).
Document Ordering: Prior ordering by letter or telephone. Catalogue numbers necessary. Ten at a time; delivery ten to thirty minutes. Photocopying by staff and sent by post. No facilities for typing or taping. Cameras not allowed.
Records: Family collections eg deeds, manorial and estate; business; Archdeaconry of Nottingham; Nonconformists; hospital; trade unions.
Postal Research: None
Facilities: Toilets and public telephone on premises. Room for own food, also drink vending machine. Cafe (student facilities) five minutes.
Publications: Free leaflet: *A Guide to the Department, Its Holdings and Services.*
Places of Interest: See entry for Nottingham RO.

OXFORDSHIRE

OXFORDSHIRE ARCHIVES
County Record Office
County Hall
New Road
Oxford OX1 1ND
Telephone: (0865) 815203

Opening Hours: Monday to Thursday 9 am to 5 pm, Friday 9 am to 4 pm. Annual closure: public holidays and two weeks during the year.
Car Parking: None
Children: Accompanied: 5 years plus. Unaccompanied: 13 years plus.
Disabled: Lift
Appointments System: Prior booking for seats necessary (two to three days) and also for viewers. Signing by register plus CARN (requires photograph). Nine to twelve seats, one film viewer and one fiche.
Document Ordering: Prior ordering not allowed. Three volumes, three items or one bundle/box at a time. Delivery approximately ten minutes. Ordering times restricted between 12 noon and 2 pm; last orders Monday to Thursday before 4.45 pm, Friday before 3.45 pm. Photocopying by staff on same day; if large quantity or busy, sent by post; PRs only with written permission from incumbent. No facilities for typing or taping. Cameras permitted.
Records: Ts of PRs on open shelves. Original PRs only if not in Ts or if searcher thinks a mistake or an omission made, or signature needs to be checked.
Postal Research: Yes; charge made.
Facilities: Toilets and public telephone on premises. Drink vending machine. Cafe/pub five minutes. Shops five minutes including bookshop with local history publications.
Publications: *Handlist of Enclosure Acts, Plans for Proposed Railways, Oxfordshire Election 1754.* Free: leaflet on main holdings and indexes, for reference only in RO *Oxford CRO and its Records, Oxfordshire - A Handbook for Students of Local History.*
Other Repositories: Oxford Central Library, Local History Collection, Westgate, Oxford OX1 1DJ; Bodleian Library, Broad Street, Oxford OX1 3BG. Many of the Colleges also contain material of use to local historians.
Places of Interest: Oxford Colleges; Museum of History and Science; Museum of Oxford; River Thames; Pitts Rivers Museum; Botanical Gardens; Ashmolean Museum; rivers Isis and Charwell; "The Oxford Story," Broad Street.
Tourist Office: St Aldates, Oxford OX1 1DY. Telephone (0865) 726873/4.

Remarks: Quarter Sessions after 1830, rural and urban district councils, some modern county council, some privately deposited records and newspapers require at least one week's prior notice. Historical county map on display.

SHROPSHIRE

Local Studies Library
Castle Gates
SHREWSBURY SY1 2AS
Telephone: (0743) 61058

Opening Hours: Monday and Wednesday 9.30 am to 12.30 pm and 1.30 pm to 5.30 pm, Tuesday and Friday 9.30 am to 12.30 pm and 1.30 pm to 7.30 pm, Saturday 9.30 am to 12.30 pm and 1.30 pm to 5 pm (closed Thursdays). Annual closure: public holidays.
Car Parking: Nearby
Children: No specific ruling.
Disabled: Access to other parts of building, so staff will attend there.
Appointments System: Prior booking necessary for viewers but unnecessary for seats. Signing in by card index if original documents required. 27 seats, four film viewers and four fiche.
Document Ordering: Prior ordering by letter or telephone. Catalogue numbers unnecessary. Unlimited number at a time. Delivery five minutes. Photo- copying by staff on same day. No facilities for typing.
Taping and cameras permitted.
Records: Ts of PRs on open shelves, original PRs on fiche/film. Maps, photographs, printed books, newspapers, IGI, census, local directories.
Postal Research: Limited, no charge made.
Facilities: Toilets but no public telephone. No refreshment facilities but cafe/pub two minutes. Shops two minutes including bookshop with local history publications.
Publications: Free: *Local Studies in Shropshire.*
Remarks: Historical county map on display. Probability that this library and Shropshire RO will be amalgamated in one building at some time in the future.

SHROPSHIRE Record Office
Shire Hall
Abbey Foregate
Shrewsbury SY2 6ND
Telephone: (0743) 252851

Opening Hours: Monday, Tuesday, Thursday 9.30 am to 12.40 pm and 1.20 pm to 5 pm; Friday 9.30 am to 12.40 pm and 1.20 pm to 4 pm (closed Wednesdays). Annual closure: public holidays; two weeks usually in November
Car Parking: Yes
Children: At archivist's discretion, but preferably able to use records properly.
Disabled: Access; prior notice required
Appointments System: Prior booking for seats and viewers necessary (at least one week for seats). Signing by register plus card index (on first visit). Twelve seats, three film viewers and two fiche.
Document Ordering: Prior ordering by letter or telephone. Catalogue numbers necessary. Three at a time, delivery five to 30 minutes. Photocopying restricted (copyright declaration signed by researcher); by staff on same day. No facilities for typing or taping.
Cameras permitted.
Records: Ts of PRs require ordering. Original PRs (if no Ts). PRs on fiche/film.
Postal Research: Limited; charge made.
Facilities: Toilets and public telephone on premises. Refreshments and drink vending machine. Cafe/pub five minutes.
Publications: List of original PRs; printed, filmed and Ts of PRs and Non-conformist registers; Enclosure; *Gazetteer of Shropshire Place Names; Guide to Shropshire Records;* parish and field name maps. Free leaflet on Shropshire wills.
Other Repositories: Wenlock Town Council, Town Clerk, Corn Exchange, Much Wenlock, Shropshire; Oswestry Town Council, Town Clerk, Powis Hall, Oswestry; Ironbridge Gorge Museum Trust Ltd, The Wharfage, Ironbridge, Telford, Shropshire.
Places of Interest: Clive House, Shropshire Regimental Museum, medieval timber framed buildings, St Mary's Church, castle, Rowley's House Museum, Ironbridge Gorge (ten miles), Haughmond Abbey, Bear Steps Hall.
Tourist Office: The Square, Shrewsbury SY1 1LH. Telephone (0743) 50761/2.
Remarks: Donations box. Historical county map on display.

SOMERSET

SOMERSET Record Office
Obridge Road
Taunton TA2 7PU
Telephone: (0823) 337600 (appointments only), 278805 (enquiries)

Opening Hours: Monday 10.30 am to 5 pm, Tuesday to Thursday 9 am to 5 pm, Friday 9 am to 4.30 pm, Saturday 9.15 am to 12.15 pm.
Annual closure: public holidays.
Car Parking: Eleven places.
Appointments System: Prior booking for seats necessary (three days) but unnecessary for viewers. Signing in by register. 28 seats, five film viewers and eight fiche.
Document Ordering: Prior ordering by letter or telephone. Catalogue numbers unnecessary. Four at a time; delivery ten to thirty minutes. No ordering between 1 pm and 2 pm; last orders 4 pm (3.30 pm Fridays). Photocopying by staff usually on same day. Use of own word processors permitted. Taping not allowed.
Cameras permitted.
Records: Ts of PRs require ordering; original PRs on fiche/film; original PRs only if not on film.
Postal Research: Yes; charge made.
Facilities: Toilets. No public telephone. Drink vending machine. Cafe/pub five minutes. Shops five minutes.
Publications: *Primary Genealogical Holdings* (list of PRs), *Your Somerset House* (sources in RO).
Other Repositories: Local History Library, Taunton Central Library, The Castle, Castle Green, Taunton.
Places of Interest: British Telecom Museum, Somerset County and Military Museum, The Castle, St Mary Magdalen Church.
Tourist Office: The Library, Corporation Street, Taunton TA1 4AN. Telephone (0823) 274785/270479.
Remarks: Donations box. Historical county map on display. Many aspects of the service are under review and may be altered during next 15 months including reader's tickets, bag storage and production times.

STAFFORDSHIRE

LICHFIELD Joint Record Office
Lichfield Library
Bird Street
Lichfield
Staffs WS13 6PN
Telephone: (0543) 256787

Opening Hours: Monday, Tuesday, Thursday, Friday 10 am to 5.15 pm, Wednesday 10 am to 4.30 pm. Annual closure: public holidays plus Tuesday following

Late Spring and Summer bank holidays; Christmas Day to New Year's Day inclusive.

Car Parking: None

Children: 12 years plus.

Disabled: Lift to first floor and three steps down to RO. Parking by arrangement.

Appointments System: Prior booking for seats necessary (as long as possible) and for viewers essential. Signing in register plus card index and reader's ticket. Ten seats, two film viewers and one fiche.

Document Ordering: Prior ordering by letter or telephone. Catalogue numbers necessary in some cases. Number at a time: maximum ten in morning and ten in afternoon (total twenty). Delivery five to ten minutes, longer if busy. Ordering times 10 am, 12.30 pm, 2.30 pm, 4 pm (3.45 pm Wednesday). Photocopying at archivist's discretion; by staff and sent by post; no volumes; BTs allowed. No facilities for typing or taping. Cameras permitted.

Records: Some Ts of PRs/BTs on open shelves, original Lichfield PRs, original BTs, some PRs on film, Calendars of wills in Diocese of Lichfield.

Postal Research: In Calendar of Wills only; charge made.

Facilities: Toilets but no public telephone. No refreshment facilities but cafe/pub two minutes. Shops five minutes including bookshop with local history publications.

Publications: County map, *Handlist of Diocesan Probate and Church Commissioners' Records at the RO.* Free: regulations of the RO.

Other Repositories: Whittington Barracks Museum, Lichfield, Staffs WS14 9PY.

Places of Interest: The RO is in the house of David Garrick; Staffordshire Regimental Museum (Prince of Wales); Dr.Johnson's Birthplace; Lichfield Heritage Exhibition, Treasury and Muniment Room; cathedral.

Tourist Office: Donegal House, Bore Street, Lichfield WS13 6NE. Telephone (0543) 252109.

Remarks: Bags to be left at supervisor's desk. Donations can be made to manuscript purchasing fund. Historical county map on display. New premises due to open in 1990.

STAFFORDSHIRE Record Office
Eastgate Street
Stafford ST16 2LZ
Telephone: (0785) 223121

Opening Hours: Monday to Thursday 9 am to 1 pm and 1.30 pm to 5 pm, Friday 9 am to 1 pm and 1.30 pm to 4.30 pm, Saturdays 9.30 am to 1 pm by appointment only. Annual closure: public holidays plus normally the following Tuesday; complete week at Christmas.

Car Parking: None

Children: 12 years plus.

Disabled: Disabled friendly. Parking by arrangement.

Appointments System: Prior booking for seats: up to eight seats may be reserved and as much notice as possible should be given. Prior booking for viewers is also necessary. Signing in register plus card index and reader's ticket. More than 18 seats and ten dual viewers.

Document Ordering: Prior ordering for Saturdays only; (by letter or telephone). Catalogue numbers preferred. Three at a time. Delivery five to ten minutes, longer if busy. No ordering between 12.45 pm and 2 pm; last orders 4.30 pm (4 pm Fridays). Photocopying at archivist's discretion; by staff and sent by post; no volumes. No facilities for typing or taping. Cameras permitted.

Records: Some Ts of PRs on open shelves, some original PRs, some original PRs on fiche/film.

Postal Research: Professional genealogist; charge made.

Facilities: Toilets. No public telephone. No refreshment facilities but cafe/pub two minutes. Shops five minutes including bookshop with local history publications.

Publications: County map, *List of PRs, sources, Nonconformist Registers,* maps, *Medical Remedies, Civil War, Second World War,* estate maps, manorial records, farm records, local authorities and Poor Law Unions, *Skeletons in the Cupboard.* Free: leaflets on main records, history of your house.

Other Repositories: William Salt Library, Eastgate Street, Stafford ST16 2LZ (local collection).

Places of Interest: Two Norman churches, Stafford Art Gallery and Craft Shop, 16th/5th The Queen's Royal Lancers and Staffordshire Yeomanry (QORR) Museum.

Tourist Office: The Ancient High House, Greengate Street, Stafford. Telephone (0785) 40204.

Remarks: District and County Council records, including some educational, stored elsewhere require 48 hours prior notice. Bags to be left at supervisor's desk. Donations may be made to manuscript purchase fund. Historical county map on display. Diocesan records of Lichfield are to be found at Lichfield Joint RO.

SUFFOLK

**Suffolk Record Office
BURY St EDMUNDS Branch
Raingate Street
Bury St Edmunds IP33 1RX**
Telephone: (0284) 763141 Ext 2522, Saturdays (0284) 756020

Opening Hours: Monday to Thursday 9 am to 5 pm, Friday 9 am to 4 pm, Saturday 9 am to 1 pm and 2 pm to 5 pm. Annual closure: public holidays; Good Friday to Easter Monday; from Saturday closest to Christmas Day until Boxing Day, plus one extra day; New Year's Day.
Car Parking: Limited
Children: At archivist's discretion.
Disabled: Previous notification required as facilities very limited.
Appointments System: Prior booking for seats and viewers unnecessary. Signing in register plus CARN. More than 32 seats. Ten film viewers and seven fiche.
Document Ordering: Prior ordering by letter or telephone. Catalogue numbers preferred. Four at a time, delivery five to fifteen minutes, longer if busy. Last orders Monday to Thursday 4.45 pm; Friday 3.45 pm; documents for Saturdays must be ordered by 1 pm on previous day. Photocopying by staff (to be collected or sent by post); PRs by printout only. Prior permission required for typing/taping. Cameras not allowed.
Records: Ts of PRs and a few BTs on open access film; original PRs only when not on film; original PRs/BTs on fiche/film.
Postal Research: Yes; charge made.
Facilities: Toilets. No public telephone. No refreshment facilities but cafe/pub five minutes. Shops five to ten minutes including bookshop with local history publications.
Publications: *Guide to Genealogical Sources in Suffolk*, county map. Free: notes for searchers on various sources, finding aids etc.
Places of Interest: Abbey ruins, Moyse's Hall Museum, Gersholm Parkington Memorial Collection of Clocks and Watches, The Suffolk Regimental Museum, theatre, Athenaeum, Dickens Hotel, the country's smallest pub.
Tourist Office: 6 Angel Hill, Bury St Edmunds IP31 1UZ. Telephone (0284) 763233, weekends 764667.
Remarks: Bags not allowed, storage facilities available. Historical county map on display.

**Suffolk Record Office
IPSWICH Branch
St Andrew House
County Hall
St Helens Street
Ipswich IP4 2JS**
Telephone: (0473) 230000 Ext 4235, Saturday (0473) 230732

Opening Hours: Monday to Thursday 9 am to 5 pm, Friday 9 am to 4 pm, Saturday 9 am to 1 pm and 2 pm to 5 pm. Annual closure: public holidays; Good Friday to Easter Monday; Saturday closest to Christmas Day until Boxing Day, plus one extra day.
Car Parking: None
Children: At archivist's discretion.
Disabled: Wheelchair access. Parking by arrangement.
Appointments System: Prior booking for seats is helpful and for viewers necessary. Signing in register plus CARN. More than twenty seats. Eight film viewers and eight fiche.
Document Ordering: Prior ordering by letter or telephone. Catalogue numbers preferred. Four at a time; delivery twenty minutes. Ordering half hourly; documents for Saturdays must be ordered by 12 noon on previous day. Photocopying by staff on same day or by post or collection; PRs/BTs by printout only.
Typing/taping by arrangement.
Cameras not allowed.
Records: Ts of PRs/BTs on film; original PRs on film; originals only when not on film.
Postal Research: Yes; charge made.
Facilities: Toilets. Public telephone adjacent. Room for own food, also drink vending machine. Cafe/pub two minutes. Shops five minutes including bookshop with local history publications.
Publications: County map, *Guide to Genealogical Sources in Suffolk (Ipswich)*. Free: notes for searchers on various sources, finding aids etc.
Places of Interest: The Ancient House, Dickens Great White Horse Hotel, docks, Elizabethan mansion in Christchurch Park, Wolsey Art Gallery, Ipswich Museum and High Street Exhibition Gallery. The RO is part of the old Ipswich prison.
Tourist Office: Town Hall, Princes Street, Ipswich IP1 1BZ. Telephone (0473) 258070.
Remarks: Ipswich borough, certain family, solicitors, societies, Coroner and Petty Sessions Division records stored elsewhere require 48 hours prior notice. Bags

not allowed, storage facilities available. Historical county map on display.

This branch will move to premises in Bramford Road/Gatacre Road in spring or early summer 1990 and will probably close at that time for approximately six weeks.

Local Studies collections are divided between the three Suffolk branches.

Suffolk Record Office
LOWESTOFT Branch
Central Library
Clapham Road
Lowestoft NR32 1DR
Telephone: (0502) 566325 Ext 3308

Opening Hours: Monday to Thursday and Saturday 9.15 am to 5 pm; Friday 9.15 am to 6 pm. Annual closure: public holidays; Good Friday to Easter Monday; Saturday closest to Christmas Day until Boxing Day, plus one extra day.
Car Parking: None
Children: At archivist's discretion.
Disabled: Disabled friendly.
Appointments System: Prior booking for seats unnecessary, but preferred for viewers. Signing in register plus CARN. More than 19 seats. Four film viewers and four fiche.
Document Ordering: Prior ordering by letter or telephone. Catalogue numbers preferred. Four at a time; delivery five to ten minutes. Last orders Monday to Thursday 4.45 pm; Friday 5.45 pm; no production Saturday 12 noon to 2 pm; maybe some restrictions during the week between 12 noon and 2 pm. Photocopying by staff on same day, collection or by post; PRs by printout only. No facilities for typing. Prior permission required before taping. Cameras not allowed.
Records: Ts of PRs on open shelves; some original PRs on fiche/film; originals only when not on film.
Postal Research: Yes; charge made.
Facilities: Toilets and public telephone on premises. Refreshments but no room for own food. Cafe/pub two minutes. Shops two minutes including bookshop with local history publications.
Publications: County map, *Guide to Genealogical Sources in Suffolk*. Free: notes for searchers on various sources, finding aids.
Places of Interest: The Ness, St Margaret's Church, Lowestoft Maritime Museum, Fritton (6 miles), Lowestoft Museum (local and domestic history).
Tourist Office: The Esplanade, Lowestoft NR33 0QF. Telephone (0502) 565989.
Remarks: Bags not allowed, no lockers

but area at entrance. Historical county map on display. Parish records of the Deanery of Lothingland (including Lowestoft) are held by Norfolk RO or by incumbent, no film/fiche of these yet held at this branch.

SURREY

CROYDON see LONDON

GUILDFORD Muniment Room
Castle Arch
Guildford
Surrey GU1 3SX
Telephone: (0483) 573942

Opening Hours: Tuesday to Thursday 9.30 am to 12.30 pm and 1.45 pm to 4.45 pm; first and third Saturday in month 9.30 am to 12.30 pm by appointment only; closed Mondays and Fridays. Annual closure: public holidays.
Car Parking: None
Children: Accompanied: at archivist's discretion. Unaccompanied: 10 years plus.
Disabled: Two steps, no special arrangements.
Appointments System: Prior booking for seats essential (at least 24 hours). Appointment system operates. Signing in by register. Approximately seven seats. One film viewer.
Document Ordering: Prior ordering by letter or telephone. Catalogue numbers necessary. Approximately five at a time; delivery approximately five minutes. Photocopying at archivist's discretion; by staff usually on same day or sent by post. Typing/taping permitted only if no annoyance caused to others. Cameras usually permitted.
Records: Ts of PRs and a few BTs on open shelves, records of the Borough of Guildford; Guildford diocesan records. Very few BTs survive for this area.
Postal Research: Limited specific enquiry.
Facilities: Toilets in adjacent museum. No public telephone. No refreshment facilities but cafe/pub two minutes. Shops five minutes including bookshop with local history publications.
Publications: For sale: map. Free: notes for family historians, Surrey RO.
Other Repositories: Local Studies Library, North Street, Guildford; British Red Cross Historical Exhibition and Archives, Barnett Hill, Wonersh (Reference Library and research facilities by appointment only).
Places of Interest: St Mary's (Saxon),

Guildhall, Guildford House Gallery, Castle Museum, ruined castle with keep, Royal Horticultural Society Gardens, Wisley (7 miles), cathedral, The Queen's Royal Surrey Regimental Museum, Clandon Park, The Women's Royal Army Corps Museum.
Tourist Office: The Civic Hall, London Road, Guildford GU2 1AA. Telephone (0483) 575857.
Remarks: Business records stored elsewhere require at least seven days' prior notice. Bags to be left in lobby. Historical county map on display.˙ Donations box.

KEW see LONDON

KINGSTON UPON THAMES see below and LONDON

MITCHAM see LONDON

RICHMOND see LONDON

SUTTON see LONDON

SURREY Record Office
County Hall
Penrhyn Road
Kingston Upon Thames
Surrey KT1 2DN
Telephone: (01) 541 9065, but from May 1990: (081) 541 9065

Opening Hours: Monday to Wednesday, Friday 9.30 am to 4.45 pm; second and fourth Saturday in month 9.30 am to 12.30 pm by appointment only.
Closed Thursdays.
Annual closure: public holidays.
Car Parking: Nearby
Children: Accompanied: not encouraged. Unaccompanied: 10 years plus.
Disabled: Ramp, toilet (ladies only), small wheelchairs only.
Appointments System: Prior booking for seats preferred (one day) and necessary for viewers. Signing in by register (perhaps CARN in future). Fifteen seats, five film viewers and two fiche.
Document Ordering: Prior ordering by letter or telephone. Catalogue numbers preferred where possible. Approximately five at a time; delivery twenty minutes; probably none during lunch period. Photocopying restricted; by staff on same day; if large quantity or busy, sent by post. Typing/taping allowed but only one person at a time. Cameras permitted.
Records: Some Ts of PRs on open shelves; original PRs on fiche/film; County Council archives; parts of Southwark and Guildford diocesan records;

Quarter Sessions.
Postal Research: None
Facilities: Toilets and public telephone on premises. Area for own food, also drink vending machine in County Hall. Cafe/pub five minutes. Shops five to ten minutes including bookshop with local history publications.
Publications: County map, *Guides to PRs, Nonconformist Registers, Brief Introduction to Parish Records.* Free: leaflets on Surrey RO, notes for family historians.
Places of Interest: Hampton Court, Richmond, Ham House, Canbury Gardens.
Tourist Office: Wheatfield Way, Kingston upon Thames KT1 2PS. Telephone (01) 546 5386; from May 1990 (081) 546 5386.
Remarks: Some infrequently used records stored elsewhere require two day's prior notice. Special area for bags. Historical county map on display. Donations box. Records for Spelthorne and surviving BTs are at the Greater London RO. Records for the Peculiar of the Deanery of Croydon are at Lambeth Palace Library, London SE1 7JU.

SUSSEX

EAST SUSSEX Record Office
The Maltings
Castle Precincts
Lewes
East Sussex BN7 1YT
Telephone: (0273) 482349

Opening Hours: Monday to Thursday 8.45 am to 4.45 pm, Friday 8.45 am to 4.15 pm. Annual closure: public holidays.
Car Parking: None
Children: At archivist's discretion.
Disabled: Prior telephone call for parking place and accommodation at ground level (RO on first floor).
Appointments System: Prior booking for seats and viewers unnecessary.
Signing in register plus CARN. 30 seats, six film viewers and one fiche.
Document Ordering: Prior ordering by letter or telephone. Catalogue numbers unnecessary. Three at a time, delivery five minutes; no production between 12.45 pm and 2 pm. Photocopying restricted; by staff and mainly sent by post; PRs by printout only. No facilities for typing or taping. Prior permission required for cameras.
Records: Ts of PRs/BTs on open shelves;some original PRs, some on film.
Postal Research: Limited, charge made.
Facilities: Toilets, but no public telephone. No refreshment facilities but

cafe/pub two minutes. Shops two minutes including bookshop with local history publications.

Publications: *Short Guide to East Sussex RO, East Sussex Sentences of Transportation at Quarter Sessions 1790-1854*, map, catalogues, *How to Trace History of Your Family, How to Trace History of Your House, The History of a Parish*. Free: publications list, sources, PRs list, introductory notes for searchers.

Other Repositories: Sussex Archaeological Society, Barbican House, Lewes, has useful library/reference material.

Places of Interest: Norman Castle and Priory ruins; Barbican House Museum; Folk Museum at Anne of Cleves' House; Bentley Wildfowl and Motor Museum, Halland (6 miles); Lewes History Centre.

Tourist Office: 32 High Street, Lewes BN7 2LX. Telephone (0273) 471600.

Remarks: Some official records, eg local authority, hospital etc stored elsewhere require one day's prior notice. Historical county map on display. Donations box. BTs at Chichester RO. Friends of the RO operate a bookstall in entrance hall.

WEST SUSSEX Record Office
Sherburne House
Orchard Street
Chichester
West Sussex PO19 1RN
Telephone: (0243) 533911

Opening Hours: Monday to Friday 9.15 am to 12.30 pm and 1.30 pm to 5 pm (subject to alteration). Annual closure: public holidays.

Car Parking: None

Children: At archivist's discretion.

Disabled: Access, toilets, parking.

Appointments System: Prior booking for seats and viewers unnecessary. Signing by register (CARN under review). Approximately 50 seats. Twenty film viewers and five fiche.

Document Ordering: Prior ordering by letter or telephone. Last documents produced 4.30 pm. Catalogue numbers necessary. Three at a time, delivery approximately five minutes. Photocopying by staff same day and sent by post. Typing/taping permitted. Cameras by prior arrangement.

Records: Ts of PRs/BTs on open shelves; PRs/BTs on film.

Postal Research: Professional genealogist; charge made.

Facilities: Toilets and public telephone on premises. Room for own food. Cafe/pub two minutes. Shops five minutes including bookshop with local history publications.

Publications: *Genealogist's Guide to the West Sussex RO, Local History in West Sussex: A Guide to Sources*, map.

Places of Interest: Chichester District Museum, Guildhall Museum, Mechanical Music and Doll Collection, Pallant House, Roman Palace at Fishbourne, Weald and Downland Open Air Museum at Singleton.

Tourist Office: St Peter's Market, West Street, Chichester PO19 1AH. Telephone (0243) 775888.

Remarks: Petworth House archives (estate and family - mainly Wyndham) stored elsewhere require two weeks' prior notice. Phillimore's Bookshop (genealogical and local history) at Shopwyke (two miles). Bags not allowed, storage facilities available. Donations box. Historical county map on display.

TYNE AND WEAR

(Also see Northumberland)

Local Studies Department
GATESHEAD Central Library
Prince Consort Road
Gateshead NE8 4LN
Telephone: (091) 477 3478

Opening Hours: Monday, Tuesday, Thursday, Friday 9.30 am to 7.30 pm; Wednesday 9.30 am to 5 pm; Saturday 9.30 am to 1 pm. Annual closure: public holidays.

Car Parking: Approximately 100 places.

Children: No age limit

Disabled: Access ramp, toilet.

Appointments System: Prior booking for seats and viewers unnecessary. Nine seats, four film viewers, one fiche, and one dual viewer.

Document Ordering: Prior ordering by letter or telephone. Catalogue numbers unnecessary. Unlimited number at a time. Delivery five minutes. Photocopying DIY; PRs by printout only; by staff on same day. No facilities for typing and prior permission required for taping. Cameras permitted.

Records: Ts of PRs on open shelves, MIs, rate books, electors' lists, poll books, newspapers, books, PRs on film, directories.

Postal Research: Yes, no charge made.

Facilities: Toilets and public telephone on premises. Refreshments but no room for own food. Cafe/pub two minutes. Shops five minutes.

Publications: Free: *Tracing Your Family Tree.*

Other Repositories: Parks and Recreation Department, Prince Consort Road,

Gateshead (cemetery records).
Places of Interest: Bowes Railway, Springwell Village, Gateshead; Shipley Art Gallery; Tanfield Railway; North East Bus Museum, Bedlington.
Tourist Office: Central Library, Prince Consort Road, Gateshead NE8 4LN. Telephone (091) 477 3478/9.

NEWCASTLE UPON TYNE
City Libraries
Central Library
Princess Square
Newcastle Upon Tyne NE99 1DX

POSTAL ADDRESS:
PO Box 1DX
Newcastle Upon Tyne NE99 1DX
Telephone: (091) 2610691

Opening Hours: Monday to Thursday 9.30 am to 8 pm, Friday 9.30 am to 5 pm, Saturday 9 am to 5 pm. Annual closure: public holidays.
Car Parking: None
Disabled: Access to all floors.
Appointments System: Prior booking for seats and viewers unnecessary. Signing in by register. Forty seats, six film viewers and three fiche.
Document Ordering: Prior ordering by letter or telephone. Catalogue numbers unnecessary. Mostly on open shelves. Photocopying DIY. No facilities for typing or taping. Cameras permitted.
Records: Ts of PRs on open shelves, books, photographs, maps, audio material, newspapers, directories, entertainment programmes.
Postal Research: Yes, charge made.
Facilities: Toilets and public telephone on premises. Refreshments but no room for own food. Cafe/pub two minutes. Shops two minutes including bookshop with local history publications.
Publications: Free: user guides, numbers 1 to 15.
Places of Interest: Museum of Antiquities, Mining Engineering Museum, Hatton Gallery, Bagpipe Museum, Black Friars Priory ruins, Trinity Maritime Centre, John George Joicey Museum.
Tourist Office: Monk Street, Newcastle upon Tyne NE1 4XW. Telephone (091) 261 5367; Central Library, Princess Square, Newcastle upon Tyne NE99 1DX. Telephone (091) 261 0691 Ext 231.
Remarks: Wills and inventories for Diocese of Durham are at the Department of Paleography, University of Durham. Historical county map on display.

Local Studies Centre
Old Central Library
Howard Street
NORTH SHIELDS NE30 1LY
Telephone: (091) 2582811 Ext 140

Opening Hours: Monday, Thursday, Friday 9 am to 1 pm and 2 pm to 5 pm; Tuesday 9 am to 1 pm and 2 pm to 7 pm; Wednesday 9 am to 1 pm. Annual closure: public holidays.
Car Parking: None
Children: No specific ruling.
Disabled: No facilities.
Appointments System: Prior booking for seats unnecessary but for viewers necessary. Sixteen seats, two film viewers and one fiche. Photocopying. Typing permitted but not taping.
Cameras permitted.
Records: Ts of PRs on open shelves, some PRs on film/fiche, no original documents held (transferred to Tyne and Wear Archive Service).
Postal Research: Limited, no charge made.
Facilities: Toilets, but no public telephone. No refreshment facilities but cafe/pub two minutes. Shops two minutes including bookshop with local history publications.

Local History Department
SOUTH TYNESIDE Central Library
Prince Georg Square
South Shields
Tyne and Wear NE33 2PE
Telephone: (091) 427 1818 Ext 2135

Opening Hours: Monday to Thursday 10 am to 7 pm, Friday 10 am to 5 pm, Saturday 10 am to 12 noon and 1 pm to 4 pm. Annual closure: public holidays plus following Tuesday; Saturday after Good Friday.
Car Parking: Nearby
Disabled: Lift and toilet. Staff willing to help visually/hearing impaired but prior notification useful.
Appointments System: Prior booking for seats is unnecessary but is required for viewers. Eighteen seats, four film viewers and one fiche.
Document Ordering: Prior ordering by letter or telephone. Catalogue numbers unnecessary. Reasonable number at a time. Delivery usually immediate. Photocopying DIY. No facilities for typing or taping. Cameras not allowed.
Records: Ts of PRs on open shelves and on film.
Postal Research: Limited, no charge

made.
Facilities: No toilets. Public telephone on premises. No refreshment facilities but cafe/pub two minutes. Shops two minutes including bookshop with local history publications.
Other Repositories: Westoe Road, South Shields, Tyne and Wear, for Roman Catholic records of St Bede's Church.
Places of Interest: Arbeia Roman Fort, Museum and Art Gallery.
Tourist Office: South Shields Museum, Ocean Road, South Shields NE33 2HZ. Telephone (091) 456 612.

TYNE AND WEAR ARCHIVE Service
Blandford House
Blandford Square
Newcastle Upon Tyne NE1 4JA
Telephone: (091) 232 6789 Ext 407

Opening Hours: Monday and Wednesday to Friday 8.45 am to 5.15 pm; Tuesday 8.45 am to 8.30 pm. Annual closure: public holidays plus afternoon of last working day before Christmas and New Year's Day.
Car Parking: Nearby
Children: No specific ruling but dependent on behaviour.
Disabled: Access.
Appointments System: Prior booking for seats unnecessary, except for Tuesday evening when it is essential. Prior booking for viewers essential (a few days to one week). Signing in by register. Eighteen seats, four film viewers and one fiche.
Document Ordering: Prior ordering essential for late evening (by letter or telephone). Catalogue numbers preferred. Three at a time, delivery five minutes. Last orders Monday to Thursday 4.45 pm; Friday 4.15 pm. Photocopying by staff and sent by post. No facilities for typing or taping. Cameras not allowed.
Records: A few Ts of PRs on open shelves, original PRs on fiche/film; original PRs.
Postal Research: Limited specific enquiry, no charge made.
Facilities: Toilets and public telephone on premises. Refreshments but no room for own food. Cafe/pub five minutes. Shops ten minutes including bookshop with local history publications.
Publications: *North Eastern Ancestors, Newcastle Charters, War Lass (Sources for Women's History in North East), Sunderland in the 1850s, Tyneside Chartism.* Free: user guides eg PRs, Nonconformist registers, schools, shipbuilding, maritime, medical, publications list.

Other Repositories: Mining Institute, Neville Hall, Newcastle; University of Newcastle upon Tyne Library.
Places of Interest: Museum of Science and Engineering, the Keep and Black Gate, city walls, Guildhall, Customs House, the chares (narrow lanes) running up from the quayside, cathedral, St Andrew's Church, John G Joicey Museum, Museum of Antiquities, Trinity Maritime Centre.
Remarks: Bags not allowed, storage facilities available. Historical county map on display.

WARWICKSHIRE

SHAKESPEARE
BIRTHPLACE TRUST Record Office
Henley Street
Stratford Upon Avon CV37 6QW
(Public access from Guild Street)
Telephone: (0789) 204016

Opening Hours: Monday to Friday 9.30 am to 1 pm and 2 pm to 5 pm, Saturday 9.30 am to 12.30 pm. Annual closure: public holidays plus preceding Saturday.
Car Parking: None
Children: At archivist's discretion.
Disabled: Lift. Prior arrangement required.
Appointments System: Prior booking for seats and viewers unnecessary. Signing in by register. Twelve seats, one film viewer and one fiche.
Document Ordering: Five at a time, delivery five minutes. Photocopying by staff possibly on same day; PRs/BTs allowed. Typing/taping permitted. Cameras permitted.
Records: Ts of PRs/BT require ordering. Original PRs, original PRs on film/fiche, Nonconformists, canals, railways, manorial courts, business, prints, drawings, photographs, newspapers, Stratford Probate records etc.
Postal Research: Limited, no charge made.
Facilities: Toilets. No public telephone. No refreshment facilities but cafe/pub five minutes. Shops five minutes including bookshop with local history publications.
Publications: Free: *Sources for Genealogists*, PRs, *Photograph Collection*, RO brochure.
Places of Interest: Shakespeare's Birthplace; Anne Hathaway's Cottage; Motor Museum; Shakespeare Centre; Mary Arden's House, Wilmcote; Nash's

House; Hall's Croft; Royal Shakespeare Theatre, Gallery and Museum; The Teddy Bear Museum.
Tourist Office: Judith Shakespeare's House, 1 High Street, Stratford upon Avon CV37 6AU. Telephone (0789) 293127/67522.

WARWICK County Record Office
Priory Park
Cape Road
Warwick CV34 4JS
Telephone: (0926) 412735

Opening Hours: Monday to Thursday 9 am to 1 pm and 2 pm to 5.30 pm, Friday 9 am to 1 pm and 2 pm to 5 pm, Saturday 9 am to 12.30 pm. Annual closure: public holidays.
Car Parking: Approximately twelve places.
Children: At archivist's discretion.
Disabled: Access but prior notification advisable.
Appointments System: Prior booking for seats and viewers unnecessary. Signing by register plus reader's ticket. 33 seats, twelve film viewers and two fiche.
Document Ordering: Three at a time, depending on class of document. Delivery approximately three minutes, if not busy. Photocopying by staff on same day. No facilities for typing or taping. Cameras permitted.
Records: Ts of PRs on open shelves, original PRs and on film.
Postal Research: None
Facilities: Toilets and public telephone on premises. No refreshment facilities but cafe/pub ten minutes. Shops ten minutes including bookshop with local history publications.
Publications: PRs, *Warwick Town Maps Teaching Unit*, volumes in the *Warwick County Record Series*. Free: various local history pamphlets.
Other Repositories: Local History Collection, Warwick Library, Church Street, Warwick.
Places of Interest: Castle, Westgate, Eastgate; Doll Museum at Oken's House; County Museum; Market Hall; St John's House, Coten End; Warwickshire Museum of Rural Life, Moreton Morell; The Queen's Own Hussars Museum; The Royal Warwickshire Regimental Museum; Warwickshire Yeomanry Museum.
Tourist Office: The Court House, Jury Street, Warwick CV34 4EW. Telephone (0926) 492212.
Remarks: Donations box. Bags not allowed, storage facilities available. Historical county map on display.

WIGHT ISLE OF see ISLE OF WIGHT

WEST MIDLANDS

Archives Department
BIRMINGHAM Reference Library
Chamberlain Square
Birmingham B3 3HQ
Telephone: (021) 235 4217

Opening Hours: Monday, Tuesday and Thursday to Saturday 9 am to 5 pm (to be extended when staffing permits). Closed Wednesdays. Annual closure: public holidays plus Tuesday following Spring and late Summer public holidays; Easter Friday to Tuesday; three days at Christmas.
Car Parking: None
Disabled: Arrangements can be made to consult records in Local Studies Department on request.
Appointments System: Prior booking for seats unnecessary. Signing by register plus reader's ticket. Approximately 21 seats.
Document Ordering: Prior ordering by letter or telephone. Catalogue numbers preferred, but not necessary. Generally three at a time (depends on nature of document). Delivery five to ten minutes. Photocopying by staff on same day; marriage entries pre 1837 only. Typing/taping permitted. Cameras permitted but no flash.
Records: Some Ts of PRs require ordering. Some original PRs, some original PRs on fiche/film (in Local Studies Department on 6th floor), wills, coroners, hospitals, Nonconformists including Roman Catholic.
Postal Research: Limited, no charge made.
Facilities: Toilets (second floor). Public telephone on premises. No refreshment facilities but cafe in Museum and Art Gallery. Shops five minutes including bookshop with local history publications.
Publications: Bookshop on first floor. Free: list of PRs, general leaflet, genealogical sources, Local Studies Department, Archives Department, *Sources for West Midlands Genealogy*.
Other Repositories: Birmingham Reference Library has many departments which contain items of interest, eg Local Studies (photographs, maps, census, local books, Birmingham diocesan records), History and Geography (maps, directories, IGI, Civil Registration indexes 1837-1912 on film), Social Science (Army and Navy lists).
Places of Interest: City Museum and Art Gallery, Museum of Science and Industry, Railway Museum, Roman Catholic

Cathedral, St Martin's in the Bull Ring, Old Crown House (14th century inn), National Exhibition Centre (8 miles), Aston Hall, Blakesley Hall, Sarehole Mill, The Patrick Collection (Motor Museum).
Tourist Office: 2 City Arcade, Birmingham B2 4TX. Telephone (021) 643 2514.
Remarks: Modern business records, some Planning Department records and little used collections stored elsewhere require 24 hours prior notice. The Archive Department is on the 7th floor.

COVENTRY City Record Office
Mandela House
Bayley Lane
Coventry CV1 5RG
Telephone: (0203) 832418

Opening Hours: Monday to Thursday 8.45 am to 4.45 pm, Friday 8.45 am to 4.15 pm. Annual closure: public holidays.
Car Parking: Nearby
Children: No specific ruling.
Disabled: Ramp and toilet.
Appointments System: Prior booking for seats unnecessary but helpful. Prior booking for viewers is necessary. Signing in by register. Sixteen seats, one film viewer, and one fiche.
Document Ordering: Prior ordering by letter or telephone. Catalogue numbers unnecessary. Four at a time; delivery fifteen to thirty minutes. Photocopying by staff on same day. Typing/taping permitted. Cameras permitted.
Records: Ts of PRs/BTs on open shelves, some on film; Municipal archives from 12th century to date; Quarter Sessions; Poor Law Unions. Extensive collection of tape recordings and Ts covering most aspects of Coventry's recent history are available for study.
Postal Research: None
Facilities: No toilets or public telephone. No refreshment facilities but cafe/pub two minutes. Shops two minutes including bookshop with local history publications.
Publications: Free: subject related guide to holdings in City RO.
Other Repositories: Local Studies Collection, Central Library, Smithford Way, Coventry CV1 1FY.
Places of Interest: Holy Trinity Church, cathedral, almshouses (Bond's Hospital and Ford's Hospital), Guildhall, Whitefriars Museum, Spon Street has reassembled medieval buildings, Herbert Museum and Art Gallery, Museum of British Road Transport, Midland Air Museum, Lunt Roman Fort.

Tourist Office: Central Library, Smithford Way, Coventry CV1 1FY. Telephone (0203) 832311.
Remarks: Departmental records of City Council from 1836, except minute and school log books, are stored elsewhere and require one day's prior notice. Bags not allowed, storage facilities available.

Archives and Local History Department
DUDLEY Library
St James' Road
Dudley
West Midlands DY1 1HR
Telephone: (0384) 456000 Ext 5554/5566

Opening Hours: Monday, Wednesday, Friday 9 am to 1 pm and 2 pm to 5 pm; Tuesday and Thursday 2 pm to 7 pm; first and third Saturday in each month 9.30 am to 12.30 pm by appointment only. Annual closure: public holidays plus following day.
Car Parking: None
Children: Accompanied: 5 years plus dependent on behaviour. Unaccompanied: approximately 10 years plus.
Disabled: Parking, access, lift.
Appointments System: Prior booking for seats and viewers necessary. Signing in by register plus identification and address. Thirteen seats, one film viewer, one fiche and four dual viewers.
Document Ordering: Prior ordering by letter or telephone. Catalogue numbers unnecessary. Three at a time; delivery five to fifteen minutes. Photocopying restricted; by staff on same day; PRs by printout only. No facilities for typing or taping. Cameras by special arrangement.
Records: Some Ts of PRs require ordering. Original PRs if not on film.
Postal Research: Limited, no charge made.
Facilities: Toilets. No refreshment facilities but cafe/pub two minutes. Shops five minutes.
Publications: List of PRs, Nonconformist registers, sources for genealogical enquirers, principal accessions of records.
Places of Interest: Central Museum and Art Gallery, Castle and Zoo, canal, Black Country Museum, Broadfield House Glass Museum.
Tourist Office: 39 Churchill Precinct, Dudley DY2 7BL. Telephone (0384) 50333.
Remarks: Local authority and court records are among the 75% of material stored elsewhere which require at least

one week's prior notice. Historical county map on display. It is likely that this service will be relocated to an archive centre outside Dudley Library during 1990 when more facilities will be available.

Sandwell Local Studies Service
SMETHWICK Library
High Street
Smethwick
Warley B66 1AB
Telephone: (021) 558 2561

Opening Hours: Phone for details.
Car Parking: None
Children: No specific ruling.
Appointments System: Prior booking for seats and viewers necessary (one day). Signing in by register. Sixteen seats.
Records: Some Ts of PRs on open shelves, some original PRs on fiche/film; original PRs only if not in other forms.
Postal Research: Discouraged.
Facilities: No toilets or public telephone. No refreshment facilities but cafe/pub two minutes. Shops two minutes.
Places of Interest: Avery Historical Museum.
Remarks: The service is very new, so advisable to phone for further details.

Local Studies Collection
Central Library
Homer Road
SOLIHULL
West Midlands B91 3RG
Telephone: (021) 704 6977

Opening Hours: Monday to Wednesday 9.30 am to 5.30 pm, Thursday and Friday 9.30 am to 8 pm, Saturday 9.30 am to 5 pm. Annual closure: public holidays plus Easter Saturday.
Car Parking: Nearby
Children: No specific ruling.
Disabled: Access, lift.
Appointments System: Prior booking for seats and viewers unnecessary. Approximately 50 seats. Two film viewers plus reader/printer and two fiche.
Document Ordering: Prior ordering by letter or telephone. Catalogue numbers unnecessary. Unlimited number at a time. No facilities for typing or taping. Cameras not allowed.
Records: Photographs, maps, directories, Solihull Tithe Map and apportionment, newspapers, business.
Postal Research: Limited specific enquiry, no charge made.
Facilities: Toilets and public telephone on premises. Refreshments but no room

for own food. Cafe/pub two minutes. Shops two minutes including bookshop with local history publications.
Publications: Free: guide with list of publications.
Places of Interest: Grimshaw Hall, Knowle; Malvern Park Hall; Berry Hall; Tudor houses in High Street; St Alphege's Church; National Motorcycle Museum.
Tourist Office: Central Library, Homer Road, Solihull B91 3RG. Telephone (021) 704 6130.
Remarks: Business records relating to BSA factory at Small Heath require prior ordering. Historical county map on display. The search room is part of the Reference Library.

Modern Records Office
UNIVERSITY OF WARWICK Library
Coventry CV4 7AL
Telephone: (0203) 523523 Ext 2014

Opening Hours: Monday to Thursday 9 am to 1 pm and 1.30 pm to 5 pm, Friday 9 am to 1 pm and 1.30 pm to 4 pm. Annual closure: public holidays; ten days at Christmas; one week at Easter.
Car Parking: Yes
Children: Not allowed.
Disabled: Access.
Appointments System: Prior booking for seats is advisable. Signing in register plus card index. Twelve seats.
Document Ordering: Prior ordering by letter or telephone. Catalogue numbers unnecessary. Number at a time variable. Delivery five to ten minutes. Restricted service 12.30 pm to 2 pm. Photocopying by staff, sometimes same day and sometimes sent by post. No facilities for typing. Taping permitted. Cameras restricted.
Records: Industrial relations, industrial politics, motor industry, trade union membership and related records.
Postal Research: Very limited, no charge made.
Facilities: Toilets and public telephone on premises. Refreshments but no room for own food; various facilities on campus (including bookshop). Shops fifteen minutes including bookshop with local history publications.
Publications: Guide, supplement, consolidated guide, *Trade Union and Related Records.*
Places of Interest: Cathedral, Museum of British Road Transport, Lady Godiva's Statue, St Mary's Guildhall, Herbert Art Gallery and Museum.
Tourist Office: Central Library, Smithford Way, Coventry CV1 1FY. Telephone

(0203) 832311.
Remarks: Donations can be made to a Development Fund.

WALSALL Archive Service
Walsall Local History Centre
Essex Street
Walsall
West Midlands WS2 7AS
Telephone: (0922) 721305/6

Opening Hours: Tuesday and Thursday 9.30 am to 5.30 pm, Wednesday 9.30 am to 7 pm, Friday 9.30 am to 5 pm, Saturday 9.30 am to 1 pm (closed Mondays). Annual closure: public holidays.
Car Parking: Fourteen places.
Children: Accompanied: no specific ruling - dependent on behaviour. Unaccompanied: approximately 8 years plus.
Disabled: Disabled friendly.
Appointments System: Prior booking for seats and viewers unnecessary. Signing in by register. 21 seats, four film viewers and five fiche.
Document Ordering: Prior ordering not allowed. Four at a time; delivery five minutes. Photocopying by staff on same day; PRs by printout only. Typing/taping permitted by special arrangement and lap-top computers allowed. Cameras not allowed.
Records: Ts of PRs on open shelves, some original PRs on fiche/film. Nonconformist registers plus film of local pre-1837 ones deposited at PRO London; photographs, pamphlets, catalogues, tape recordings, local studies books.
Postal Research: Limited to thirty minutes; no charge made.
Facilities: Toilets, but no public telephone. Room for own food, also drink vending machine. Cafe/pub five minutes. Shops fifteen minutes.
Publications: *Handlist of Archive Accessions*, extensive range of local history publications at own bookshop. Free: various leaflets including *Tracing Your Ancestors*.
Places of Interest: Garman-Ryan Museum and Art Gallery (local history museum), Lock Museum, Walsall Leather Centre.

WOLVERHAMPTON
Borough Archives
Central Library
Snow Hill
Wolverhampton WV1 3AX
Telephone: (0902) 312025 Ext 137

Opening Hours: Monday to Saturday 10 am to 1 pm and 2 pm to 5 pm. Annual closure: public holidays.
Car Parking: None

Children: No specific ruling.
Disabled: Lift. Other arrangements by appointment.
Appointments System: Prior booking for seats and viewers unnecessary. Signing by register plus identification. Eight seats, four film viewers and two fiche.
Document Ordering: Prior ordering by letter or telephone. Catalogue numbers not always necessary. Four at a time; delivery usually ten minutes. Photocopying DIY. No facilities for typing but taping by special arrangement. Cameras not allowed.
Records: Ts of PRs require ordering; some original PRs on fiche/film.
Postal Research: Limited, no charge made.
Facilities: Toilets but no public telephone. No refreshment facilities but cafe/pub two minutes. Shops two minutes including bookshop with local history publications.
Publications: Local interest books. Free: summary guide to collection, booklets on genealogy, Nonconformist registers etc.
Places of Interest: Central Museum and Art Gallery, Bantock House Museum, Moseley Old Hall (4 miles), Bilston House Museum.
Tourist Office: 18 Queen Square, Wolverhampton WV1 1TQ. Telephone (0902) 312051.
Remarks: Coroners records stored elsewhere require three working days' prior notice. Historical county map on display.

WILTSHIRE

WILTSHIRE Record Office
County Hall
Trowbridge BA14 8JG
Telephone: (0225) 753641 Ext 3502

Opening Hours: Monday, Tuesday, Thursday, Friday 9 am to 5 pm; Wednesday 9 am to 8.30 pm; occasional closure 12.30 pm to 1.30 pm. Annual closure: public holidays; two weeks before Christmas.
Car Parking: Ten places.
Children: School age but dependent on behaviour.
Disabled: Access to documents on ground floor by prior arrangement.
Appointments System: Prior booking for viewers necessary but not for seats. Signing in register plus CARN. 52 seats, five film viewers and ten fiche.
Document Ordering: Reasonable number at a time. Delivery five minutes. Photocopying by staff possibly on same day; if large quantity or busy, sent by post;

PRs by printout only. Prior permission required for typing/taping. Cameras permitted.
Records: Ts of PRs on open shelves, original PRs on fiche/film, BTs, newspapers.
Postal Research: Very limited, no charge made.
Facilities: Toilets and public telephone on premises. Refreshments in County Hall nearby; snack area for own food, also drink vending machine. Cafe/pub five minutes. Shops ten minutes including bookshop with local history publications.
Publications: Guides to Diocesan and Quarter Sessions, list of PRs, BTs. Free: leaflets on family history, history of house, history of parish.
Other Repositories: Wiltshire Archaeological and Natural History Museum and Library, Long Street, Devizes (local history collections).
Places of Interest: Historic woollen town, Avebury and the Great Barn, Marlborough, Devizes, Trowbridge Museum, Great Chalfield Medieval Manor (5 miles), Stonehenge.
Tourist Office: St Stephen's Place, Trowbridge. Telephone (0225) 777054.
Remarks: Donations box. Historical county map on display. Local History Library in same building sells local and genealogical publications and maps. See *Locations of Documents for Wiltshire Parishes* by Barbara J Carter (seven booklets).

WORCESTERSHIRE
see HEREFORD and WORCESTER

NORTH YORKSHIRE

BORTHWICK INSTITUTE
of Historical Research
(UNIVERSITY OF YORK)
St Anthony's Hall
Peasholme Green
York YO1 2PW
Telephone: (0904) 642315

Opening Hours: Monday to Friday 9.30 am to 12.50 pm and 2 pm to 4.50 pm. Annual closure: public holidays; one week following end of Autumn term; Christmas Eve to New Year; Good Friday to following Wednesday.
Car Parking: Nearby
Children: Sixth form only.
Disabled: By special arrangement.
Appointments System: Prior booking for seats and viewers necessary (two months for seats). Signing in by register.

Approximately 16 seats in search room and ten to twelve in library. Six film viewers and one fiche.
Document Ordering: Prior ordering by letter or telephone. Catalogue numbers sometimes necessary. Six at a time. Ordering times: on arrival, 11 am, 12 noon, 2 pm, 3 pm, 3.45 pm. Photocopying by staff and sent by post. Typing/taping permitted by special arrangement. Cameras not allowed.
Records: Ts of PRs/BTs on open shelves, original PRs/BTs on fiche/film; Archbishopric of York from 1215; Archdeaconry of York; Southern Africa archives; Probate records of Prerogative Court of York (PCY).
Postal Research: Yes; charge made.
Facilities: Toilets and public telephone on premises. Room for own food, also drinks provided. Cafe/pub two minutes. Shops two minutes including bookshop with local history publications.
Publications: *Borthwick Papers*, text and calendars, Institute bulletin, guide to archive collections and supplements, guide to genealogical sources. Free: leaflets with details of various sources for family and local historians, publications list.
Other Repositories: York Reference Library, Museum Street, York YO1 2DS.
Places of Interest: See entry for York Minster Archives.
Tourist Office: See entry for York Minster Archives.
Remarks: Bags not allowed, storage facilities available. Historical county map on display.

NORTH YORKSHIRE
County Record Office
County Hall
Northallerton
North Yorkshire DL7 8AD
Telephone: (0609) 780780 Ext 2455

Opening Hours: Monday, Tuesday, Thursday 9 am to 4.50 pm; Wednesday 9 am to 8.50 pm; Friday 9 am to 4.20 pm. Usually closes at lunchtime but researchers may make special arrangements to continue working.
Annual closure: public holidays.
Appointments System: Prior booking for seats and viewers necessary. Signing in by register plus enquirer's card.
Document Ordering: Prior ordering by letter or telephone. Catalogue numbers: exact references, if possible. For photocopying, special leaflet (SR 3) required; PRs by printout only.
Records: Diocesan office for Bradford,

Rippon and York; York archives (York acts as associate office and holds all church records); Registry of Deeds.
Postal Research: Limited; charge made.
Publications: Various guides, eg PRs, maps; Ts; various texts and facsimiles of historical documents; Enclosure Awards; publications list.
Places of Interest: All Saints Church, street market.
Tourist Office: Applegarth Car Park, Northallerton. Telephone (0609) 6864.
Remarks: Further details of this RO have not been completed due to lack of information.

YORK City Archives
Art Gallery Building
Exhibition Square
York YO1 2EW
Telephone: (0904) 651533

Opening Hours: Tuesday to Thursday 9.30 am to 12.30 pm and 2 pm to 5.30 pm; Mondays and Fridays by appointment only. Annual closure: public holidays.
Car Parking: None
Children: Accompanied: five years plus, dependent on behaviour.
Unaccompanied: eleven years plus.
Disabled: Ramp.
Appointments System: Prior booking for seats unnecessary except Monday and Fridays but necessary for viewers.
Signing in by register. Approximately fourteen seats and one film viewer.
Document Ordering: Prior ordering by letter or telephone. Catalogue numbers unnecessary. Approximately five at a time. Delivery one to ten minutes. Ordering times: fifteen minutes before closure. Photocopying by staff usually on same day. Typing/taping possible. Cameras permitted.
Records: No PRs, city records only including Ainsty area.
Postal Research: First 45 minutes free; charge made for further work.
Facilities: Toilets. No public telephone. No refreshment facilities but cafe/pub two minutes. Shops two minutes plus bookshop with local history publications
Publications: *Brief Guide to Records, Richard III and York Wallet.*
Tourist Office: See entry for York Minster.
Remarks: Bags allowed in search room at present: policy under review.

YORK MINSTER Archives
York Minster Library
Dean's Park
York YO1 2JD

Telephone: (0904) 625308

Opening Hours: Monday to Friday 9 am to 5 pm. Annual closure: public holidays and between Christmas and New Year.
Car Parking: None
Children: At archivist's discretion.
Disabled: A few steps, but assistance available to help with wheelchair.
Appointments System: Prior booking for seats necessary but for viewers unnecessary. Signing by register plus proof of identity. Approximately eight seats, one film viewer and one fiche.
Document Ordering: Prior ordering by letter or telephone. Catalogue numbers preferred. Number at a time at archivist's discretion. Delivery five minutes. Photocopying by staff usually on same day; PRs/BTs allowed. No facilities for typing or taping. Cameras permitted.
Records: Some printed PRs on open shelves, original PRs on fiche/film.
Postal Research: Limited specific enquiries; charge made for over one hour's work.
Facilities: Toilets but no public telephone. No refreshment facilities but cafe/pub two minutes. Shops five minutes including bookshop with local history publications.
Publications: Local history publications, postcards.
Places of Interest: York Minster, York Castle Museum, National Railway Museum, Jorvik Viking Centre, The Shambles, Castle Museum, York Story (Heritage Centre), Treasurer's House, The Chocolate Experience (Rowntree), Fairfax House, Bar Convent Museum, 4th/7th Royal Dragoon Guards Museum.
Tourist Office: De Grey Rooms, Exhibition Square, York YO1 2HB. Telephone (0904) 21756/7. York Railway Station, Outer Concourse, Station Road, York YO2 2AY. Telephone (0904) 643700.
Remarks: Dean and Chapter modern records (require special permission for consultation) stored elsewhere require one week's prior notice. Bags not allowed, limited storage facilities available. Donations box.

SOUTH YORKSHIRE

BARNSLEY Archive Service
Central Library
Shambles Street
Barnsley
South Yorkshire S70 2JF
Telephone: (0226) 733241 Ext 23
(Ext 41 for Local Studies Department)

Opening Hours: Monday to Wednesday 9.30 am to 1 pm and 2 pm to 6 pm; Friday 9.30 am to 1 pm and 2 pm to 5 pm; Saturday 9.30 am to 1 pm. Closed Thursdays. Annual closure: public holidays.
Car Parking: None
Children: At archivist's discretion.
Disabled: Access and lift.
Appointments System: Prior booking for seats and viewers unnecessary.
Signing in by register. Six seats, one film viewer and one fiche.
Document Ordering: Prior ordering by letter or telephone (essential for Saturdays). Catalogue numbers unnecessary. Three at a time; delivery ten minutes. Photocopying at archivist's discretion; by staff on same day; if large quantity or busy, sent by post; some DIY; PRs by printout only. No facilities for typing or taping. Cameras not allowed.
Records: A few Ts of PRs, business, societies, registers of miners killed in pits, Urban District Councils, some Nonconformists, photographs, newspapers, Poor relief, deeds, diaries.
Postal Research: Yes, charge made.
Facilities: Toilets and public telephone on premises. Refreshments but no room for own food. Cafe/pub two minutes. Shops five minutes including bookshop with local history publications.
Publications: Free leaflet outlining holdings.
Places of Interest: Cannon Hall Museum, Cooper Gallery, Victoria Jubilee Museum, Worsbrough Mill Museum, Monk Bretton Priory (two miles).
Tourist Office: 56 Eldon Street, Barnsley S70 2JL. Telephone (0226) 206757.
Remarks: Urban District Council and Borough Council records stored elsewhere require two days' prior notice. Local Studies Department in same building holds original PRs/BTs on fiche/film plus Ts (hours: Monday to Friday 9.30 am to 1 pm and 2 pm to 6 pm, Saturday 9.30 am to 1 pm and 2 pm to 5 pm; 12 seats).

DONCASTER Archives Department
King Edward Road
Balby
Doncaster
South Yorkshire DN4 0NA
Telephone: (0302) 859811

Opening Hours: Monday to Friday 9.30 am to 12.30 pm and 2 pm to 5 pm. Annual closure: public holidays plus occasional following day.
Car Parking: Twenty places
Children: Fifteen years plus.
Disabled: Access
Appointments System: Prior booking

for viewers necessary but not for seats. Signing in by register. Twelve seats, one film viewer.
Document Ordering: Prior ordering by letter or telephone. Catalogue numbers unnecessary. Four at a time; delivery within a few minutes. Photocopying by staff on same day. No facilities for typing or taping. Cameras permitted.
Records: Ts of PRs on open shelves, original PRs, diocesan records for Archdeaconry of Doncaster, local public records, Nonconformists, Quarter Sessions.
Postal Research: Limited, specific enquiry.
Facilities: Toilets. No public telephone. Room for own food. Cafe/pub five minutes. Shops five minutes.
Publications: Guide to holdings. Free: leaflets on PRs, Nonconformists.
Places of Interest: Museum and Art Gallery, The Museum of South Yorkshire Life, Cusworth Park (two miles), Mansion House, The King's Own Yorkshire Light Infantry Museum (51st Foot).
Tourist Office: Central Library, Waterdale, Doncaster DN1 3JE. Telephone (0302) 734309.
Remarks: Historical county map on display.

Archives and Local Studies Section
Brian O'Malley Central Library
Walker Place
ROTHERHAM
South Yorkshire S65 1JH
Telephone: (0709) 382121 Ext 3616; evenings and Saturdays (0709) 823616

Opening Hours: Monday, Tuesday, Friday 10 am to five pm; Wednesday 1 pm to 7 pm; Thursday 10 am to 7 pm; Saturday 9 am to 5 pm. Annual closure: public holidays plus two extra days at each; between Christmas and New Year.
Car Parking: Nearby
Children: Accompanied: no specific ruling - dependent on behaviour. Unaccompanied: school age.
Disabled: Access, lift to first floor.
Appointments System: Prior booking for viewers necessary but not for seats. Signing in by register. 25 seats, three film viewers and two fiche.
Document Ordering: Prior ordering by letter or telephone. Catalogue numbers unnecessary. Number at a time at archivist's discretion. Delivery five to ten minutes, longer at lunchtimes especially Saturdays. Photocopying by staff on same day; if large quantity or busy, sent by post. Typing/taping permitted by special arrangement. Cameras by special arrangement.

Records: Ts of PRs on open shelves, original PRs on fiche/film, business, Police Force, Poor Law Unions, hospitals, Nonconformists, cemeteries. Original PRs for Rotherham area are either at Sheffield RO or Doncaster Archives.
Postal Research: Limited, no charge made.
Facilities: Toilets and public telephone on premises. Refreshments but no room for own food. Cafe/pub five minutes. Shops five minutes including bookshop with local history publications.
Publications: Free: brief guide, *Sources for Family History*, PRs, Nonconformists, county map.
Places of Interest: Clifton Park Museum, All Saints Church, Art Gallery, York and Lancaster Regimental Museum, Roman Fort (two miles).
Tourist Office: Brian O'Malley Central Library and Art Centre, Walker Place, Rotherham, Telephone (0709) 382121 Ext 3611/2, evenings and Saturdays telephone (0709) 823611/2.
Remarks: Original newspapers (if not on fiche) stored elsewhere require at least one week's prior notice. Historical county map on display.

SHEFFIELD Record Office
Central Library
Surrey Street
Sheffield S1 1XZ
Telephone: (0742) 734756

Opening Hours: Monday to Friday 9.30 am to 5.30 pm; Saturday 9 am to 1 pm and 2 pm to 4.30 pm; second Monday in month open until 8.30 am (appointment only). Annual closure: public holidays.
Car Parking: None
Children: No specific ruling.
Disabled: Lift at rear of building, RO on first floor.
Appointments System: Prior booking for seats is advisable; essential for late night and Saturday. Prior booking is necessary for viewers. Signing in by card index plus reader's ticket. Fifteen seats, six film viewers and three fiche.
Document Ordering: Prior ordering by letter or telephone; for Saturdays, by noon on previous Friday. Catalogue numbers necessary. Number at a time at archivist's discretion. Delivery on the hour between 10 am and 12 noon, and 2 pm and 4 pm; all documents must be returned thirty minutes before closure. Photocopying by staff on same day; if large quantity or busy, sent by post. No facilities for typing or taping. Cameras not allowed.
Records: Ts of PRs/BTs require orde-

ring. Original PRs/BTs on fiche/film, original PRs/BTs, MIs, Nonconformists, indexes of PRs held at Sheffield Cathedral, registers of cemeteries etc. Records cover some areas in South Yorks and North Derbyshire.
Postal Research: Limited, no charge made.
Facilities: Toilets and public telephone on premises. Refreshments but no room for own food. Cafe/pub two minutes. Shops two minutes including bookshop with local history publications.
Publications: Family history guides (8), local history guides (3).
Places of Interest: Cathedral, Cutler's Hall (founded 1624), museum, Ruskin Gallery, Bishop's House, Kelham Island Industrial Museum, Abbeydale Industrial Hamlet (4 miles).
Tourist Office: Town Hall Extension, Union Street, Sheffield S1 2HH.
Telephone (0742) 734671/2.
Remarks: Some records stored elsewhere require one week's prior notice.

WEST YORKSHIRE

West Yorkshire Archive Service
YORKSHIRE ARCHAEOLOGICAL SOCIETY
Claremont
23 Clarendon Road
Leeds
West Yorkshire LS2 9NZ
Telephone: (0532) 456362

Opening Hours: Monday (except for Monday following Saturday opening), Thursday, Friday 9.30 am to 5 pm; Tuesday, Wednesday 2 pm to 8.30 pm; first and third Saturday in month 9.30 am to 5 pm. Annual closure: public holidays plus following day.
Car Parking: Approximately six places
Children: No specific ruling.
Disabled: Access. One step to main area.
Appointments System: Prior booking for viewers necessary but not for seats. Signing in by register. Eight seats, one film viewer and two or three fiche.
Document Ordering: Prior ordering by letter or telephone. Catalogue numbers necessary. Four at a time; delivery approximately five minutes. Photocopying by staff on same day; if large quantity or busy, sent by post. No facilities for typing or taping. Cameras permitted (copyright undertaking to be signed).
Records: Ts of PRs/BTs require ordering except those in published form. Original PRs on fiche/film.

Postal Research: None

Facilities: Toilets. Visitors may use ROs telephone for cost. Refreshments, also room for own food and kettle for drinks. Cafe/pub five minutes.

Publications: Various guides and catalogues. Free leaflets.

Other Repositories: Leeds City Library, Calverley Street, Leeds LS1 3AB; Leeds University, Brotherton Library, Leeds LS2 9JT.

Places of Interest: See entry for Leeds RO.

Tourist Office: See entry for Leeds RO.

Remarks: Donations box. Historical county map on display.

West Yorkshire Archive Service (BRADFORD)
15 Canal Road
Bradford
West Yorkshire BD1 4AT
Telephone: (0274) 731931

Opening Hours: Monday to Wednesday 9.30 am to 1 pm and 2 pm to 5 pm; Thursday 9.30 am to 1 pm and 2 pm to 8 pm; Friday 9.30 am to 1 pm. Annual closure: public holidays and one week in February.

Car Parking: Four places

Children: By prior arrangement.

Disabled: By prior arrangement.

Appointments System: Prior booking for seats and viewers necessary (at least one day). Signing in by register. 21 seats, five fiche viewers.

Document Ordering: Prior ordering by letter or telephone. Catalogue numbers necessary. Four at a time; delivery approximately five minutes. Photocopying by staff on same day; if large quantity or busy, sent by post. No facilities for typing or taping. Cameras permitted.

Records: Ts of PRs require ordering. Original PRs, original PRs on fiche/film.

Postal Research: Very limited, no charge made.

Facilities: Toilets, but no public telephone. No refreshment facilities but cafe/pub two minutes. Shops two minutes including bookshop with local history publications.

Publications: List of parish, Nonconformist and educational records, maps. Free: information leaflets on the Archive Service in West Yorkshire.

Other Repositories: Bradford Central Library, Princes Way, Bradford BD1 1NN; Keighley Library, Reference Department, North Street, Keighley BD21 3SX.

Places of Interest: National Museum of Photography, Film and TV; City Hall; Wool Exchange; Bolling Hall; Industrial Museum; Saltaire (model industrial village); Bracken Hall Countryside Centre; Colour Museum; Manor House Museum.

Tourist Office: City Hall, Hall Ings, Channing Way, Bradford BD1 1HY. Telephone (0274) 753678.

Remarks: Bags not allowed, storage facilities available. Historical county map on display, computer terminal link with Wakefield RO providing information on archives throughout the West Riding Archive Service.

West Yorkshire Archive Service (CALDERDALE)
Central Library
Northgate House
Northgate
Halifax
West Yorkshire HX1 1UN
Telephone: (0422) 57257 Ext 2636

Opening Hours: Monday, Tuesday, Thursday, Friday 10 am to 5.30 pm; Wednesday 10 am to 12 noon. Annual closure: public holidays.

Car Parking: None

Children: Accompanied: no specific ruling. Unaccompanied: 16 years plus.

Disabled: Lift and toilet.

Appointments System: Prior booking for seats necessary (at least 24 hours) and advisable for viewers. Signing in by register. 22 seats, ten film viewers, two printers and two fiche.

Document Ordering: Prior ordering essential; by letter or telephone. Catalogue numbers necessary. Unlimited number at a time; but only one issued. Photocopying by staff and sent by post or collected; PRs/BTs by printout only. Typing/taping permitted. Cameras permitted.

Records: Some Ts of PRs on open shelves, original PRs/BTs on fiche/film.

Postal Research: None

Facilities: Toilets and public telephone on premises. No refreshment facilities but cafe/pub two minutes. Shops two minutes including bookshop with local history publications.

Publications: Free: information leaflets, county map.

Other Repositories: Calderdale MBC Libraries, Reference Library, Central Library, Northgate House, Halifax.

Places of Interest: Piece Hall; Wainhouse Tower; Bankfield Museum; West Yorkshire Folk Museum, Shibden Hall; Halifax Gibbet; Calderdale Industrial Museum; The Duke of Wellington's Regimental Museum.

Tourist Office: Piece Hall, Halifax HX1 1RE. Telephone (0422) 68725.

Remarks: Historical county map on display. Computer terminal link with Wakefield RO providing information on archives throughout the West Riding Archive Service.

West Yorkshire Archive Service (KIRKLEES)
Central Library
Princess Alexandra Walk
Huddersfield
West Yorkshire HD1 2SU
Telephone: (0484) 513808 Ext 207

Opening Hours: Monday to Thursday 9 am to 8 pm; Friday 9 am to 4 pm; Saturday by appointment only. Annual closure: public holidays.
Car Parking: None
Children: Accompanied: No specific ruling. Unaccompanied 16 years plus.
Disabled: Ramp and lift access.
Appointments System: Prior booking for seats necessary (two days) but not for viewers. Signing in by register. Approximately ten seats. Three film viewers and five fiche.
Document Ordering: Prior ordering by letter or telephone. Catalogue numbers necessary. Four at a time; delivery five minutes. Photocopying by staff on same day; PRs by printout only. No facilities for typing or taping. Cameras permitted.
Records: Ts of PRs on open shelves, original PRs on fiche/film.
Postal Research: Limited, no charge made.
Facilities: Toilets but no public telephone. No refreshment facilities but cafe/pub two minutes. Shops two minutes including bookshop with local history publications.
Publications: Various for sale. Free leaflets.
Places of Interest: Art Gallery, Tolson Memorial Museum, Cloth Hall, railway station, St Peter's Church, Colne Valley Museum, Golcar.
Tourist Office: 3-5 Albion Street, Huddersfield HD1 2NW. Telephone (0484) 22133, evenings and weekends (0484) 23877.
Remarks: Local authority records (except minutes), large business collections (mainly relating to textile industry) stored elsewhere require two weeks' prior notice. Computer terminal link with Wakefield RO providing information on archives throughout the West Riding Archive Service.

West Yorkshire Archive Service (LEEDS)
Chapeltown Road

Sheepscar
Leeds LS7 3AP
Telephone: (0532) 628339
Opening Hours: Monday to Friday 9.30 am to 5 pm. Annual closure: public holidays; one week for stocktaking.
Car Parking: None
Children: Permitted if accompanied. Unaccompanied: 12 years plus.
Disabled: No facilities.
Appointments System: Prior booking for seats and viewers necessary (2 days). Signing in by register. Fifteen seats, one film viewer and one fiche.
Document Ordering: Prior ordering by letter or telephone. Catalogue numbers preferred. Four at a time; delivery ten minutes. No ordering between 12.15 pm and 2 pm; last orders 4 pm. Photocopying by staff and sent by post. No facilities for typing or taping. Cameras permitted.
Records: Ts of PRs on open shelves, original PRs, original PRs on fiche/film, BTs.
Postal Research: None
Facilities: Toilets but no public telephone. Refreshments and room for own food. Cafe/pub two minutes.
Publications: *Guide (Leeds Archives 1938-88)*, plus others. Free: leaflets on RO, probate records, parish records, BTs plus others.
Places of Interest: Brontë country, St John's Church, Roman Catholic Cathedral, Kirkstall Abbey and Museum, Museum of Leeds, Armley Mills, Harewood House (8 miles), Middleton Colliery Railway (two miles).
Tourist Office: 19 Wellington Place, Leeds LS1 4DG. Telephone (0532) 462454/5.
Remarks: Local authority, family and estate, business and voluntary bodies' records stored elsewhere require two weeks' prior notice. Bags not allowed, storage facilities available. Historical county map on display. Computer terminal link with Wakefield RO providing information on archives throughout the West Riding Archive Service.

West Yorkshire Archive Service (Headquarters)
Registry of Deeds
Newstead Road
WAKEFIELD
West Yorkshire WF1 2DE
Telephone: (0924) 367111 Ext 2352

Opening Hours: Monday 9 am to 8 pm, Tuesday to Thursday 9 am to 5 pm, Friday 9 am to 1 pm. Annual closure: public holidays; council holidays; one week in February.

Car Parking: Approximately ten places
Children: No specific ruling but dependent on behaviour.
Disabled: Stairs but staff will assist with wheelchairs.
Appointments System: Prior booking for seats and viewers unnecessary. Signing in by register. 36 seats, two film viewers and fourteen fiche.
Document Ordering: Prior ordering by letter or telephone. Catalogue numbers unnecessary. Four at a time; delivery five minutes. Photocopying by staff usually on same day. Typing/taping permitted. Cameras permitted.
Records: Ts of PRs require ordering. Original PRs on fiche/film, original PRs, former West Riding Registry of Deeds 1704-1970, British Waterways Board, diocesan records for Wakefield.
Postal Research: None
Facilities: Toilets. No public telephone. Refreshments and room for own food. Cafe/pub five minutes. Shops five minutes including bookshop with local history publications.
Publications: *Guide to Sources for Family History, Guide to West Riding Quarter Sessions.* Free: leaflets on holdings, addresses of RO in West Yorkshire Archive Service.
Other Repositories: Local Studies Section, Wakefield District Library Headquarters, Balne Lane, Wakefield WF1 0DQ.
Places of Interest: Chantry Chapel; Art Gallery; museum; Pontefract Castle; the old streets of Warrengate, Northgate, Westgate and Kirkgate; Elizabethan Gallery, Nostill Priory (6 miles).
Tourist Office: Town Hall, Wood Street, Wakefield WF1 2HQ. Telephone (0924) 370211 Ext 7021/2.
Remarks: Bags not allowed, storage facilities available. Historical county map on display. The computer central database at Wakefield provides information on archive collections throughout the West Yorkshire Service.

NORTHERN IRELAND

BELFAST

GENERAL REGISTER OFFICE
Oxford House
49-55 Chichester Street
Belfast BT1 4HL.
Telephone: (0232) 235211

Opening Hours: Monday to Friday.
Records: Indexes on film. Records of births and deaths relate mainly to those registered since 1 January 1864 in that part of Ireland which is now Northern Ireland. Civil Registration of Marriages from 1922 only (other than Roman Catholic Marriages which are from 1 April 1845).
Publications: Leaflet GRO43.
Remarks: General searches are not undertaken by office staff. Information on a marriage which occurred subsequent to civil registration and prior to 1922 can be obtained on application to the Registrar General at the above address.

LINEN HALL LIBRARY
17 Donegall Square North
Belfast BT1 5GD
Telephone: (0232) 321707

Opening Hours: Monday to Wednesday, Friday 9.30 am to 6 pm; Thursday 9.30 am to 8.30 pm; Saturday 9.30 am to 4 pm. Annual closure: public holidays and two weeks in summer.
Car Parking: None.
Children: Accompanied: at archivist's discretion. Unaccompanied: 12 years plus.
Disabled: No facilities.
Appointments System: Prior booking unnecessary. Signing in by register plus reader's ticket. 26 seats, two film viewers and one fiche.
Document Ordering: Prior ordering by letter or telephone. Four at a time; delivery five minutes. Photocopying by staff on same day; DIY. No facilities for typing or taping. Cameras not allowed.
Records: Ts of PRs require ordering. Newspapers.
Facilities: Toilets and public telephone on premises. No refreshment facilities but cafe/pub two minutes. Shops two minutes plus bookshop with local history publications.
Remarks: Mss of family histories; Belfast and Ulster street directories 1819 onwards; printed MIs; printed Church Registers and Transcripts; printed family histories and pedigrees; printed English Marriage Licences and Musgrave Obituaries; printed Irish Wills, Indexes and Marriage Licences; printed Emigrant Lists; peerage and gentry reference books; Belfast poll books and electoral registers; Army and Navy Lists; university and school lists; Church fasti all require one week's prior notice. Donations box.

PUBLIC RECORD OFFICE OF NORTHERN IRELAND (PRONI)
66 Balmoral Avenue

Belfast BT9 6NY.
Telephone: (0232) 661621

Opening Hours: Monday to Friday 9.15 am to 4.45 pm. Annual closure: public holidays and first two weeks in December.
Car Parking: Twelve places.
Children: At archivist's discretion.
Disabled: Access, ramp, access to restaurant.
Appointments System: No prior booking. Signing in by register plus form plus identification; reader's ticket. 42 seats in reading room, twenty in search room. Eleven film viewers and one fiche.
Document Ordering: No prior ordering. Three at a time, delivery 45 minutes. Ordering times 9.15 am to 4.15 pm (4 pm July and August). Photocopying restricted; by staff and sent by post. No facilities for typing or taping. Cameras not allowed.
Records: Photocopies of PRs require ordering. Some original PRs, family and family histories, manor rolls on film, militia and army lists, government departments, courts, local authorities, public bodies, business etc.
Postal Research: None
Facilities: Toilets and public telephone on premises. Refreshments and restaurant. Pub/cafe ten minutes.
Publications: Free: *A Guide to the PRONI,* information leaflet for readers, GRO43 (services and fees of GRO), *Tracing Your Ancestry in Ulster,* list of record agents in Northern Ireland, publications list.
Other Repositories: Ulster Museum, Stranmillis Road, Belfast; Ulster Folk and Transport Museum, 153 Bangor Road, Hollywood; Belfast City Hall, Donegall Square, Belfast; Belfast Central Library, Royal Avenue, Belfast.
Places of Interest: Ulster Museum.
Tourist Office: 52 High Street, Belfast BT1 2DS, Telephone (0232) 246609.
Remarks: Three days prior notice required for primarily official records which are stored elsewhere. Bags not allowed, storage facilities available. Further reading: see *How to Trace Your Family History in Northern Ireland* by Kathleen Neill and *Handbook on Irish Genealogy* (Heraldic Artists).

REPUBLIC OF IRELAND

DUBLIN

CHURCH OF IRELAND
Representative Church Body Library
Braemor Park
Rathgar

Dublin 14.
Telephone: (01) 979979 (within Ireland); or (0001) 979979 (from Great Britain)
Opening Hours: Monday to Friday 9.30 am to 1 pm and 1.45 pm to 5 pm. Annual closure: public holidays and two weeks in August.
Car Parking: Ten places.
Children: Not allowed.
Disabled: No facilities.
Appointments System: No prior booking. Signing in by register plus identification. Ten seats, one film viewer, one fiche.
Document Ordering: Prior ordering by letter or telephone. Number at a time at archivist's discretion. Delivery ten minutes. Photocopying by staff on same day or by post. No facilities for typing or taping. Cameras not allowed.
Records: Some Ts of PRs on open shelves, some require ordering, some original PRs on fiche/film. Religious Census of 1766, will abstracts, Hearth Tax, subsidy rolls, Dissenters lists, estate papers, list of Scottish Freeholders: notes on Plantation of Ulster, newspapers etc.
Postal Research: None.
Facilities: Toilets but no public telephone. No refreshment facilities but cafe/pub five minutes. Shops five minutes.
Publications: Introductory leaflet (other leaflets in preparation).
Remarks: Permission may be granted, free of charge, to those wishing to read in the library during normal opening hours (application in advance not required). Membership (which confers borrowing rights) may be granted on the recommendation of a clergyman (on payment of subscription). The library is the principal theological and reference library of the Church of Ireland and the major repository for church archives and manuscripts. Bags not allowed, storage facilities available.

DUBLIN CORPORATION Archives
City Hall
Dame Street
Dublin 2
Telephone: (01) 796111 Ext 2818 (within Ireland); or (0001) 796111 Ext 2818 (from Great Britain)

Opening Hours: Monday to Friday 10 am to 1 pm and 2.15 pm to 5 pm, by appointment only. Annual closure is variable - check in advance.
Car Parking: None
Children: Accompanied: 7 years plus. Unaccompanied: 13 years plus.
Disabled: Lift

Appointments System: Prior booking for seats essential (24 hours) but unnecessary for viewers.

Signing in by register. Four seats, one film viewer.

Document Ordering: Prior ordering by letter or telephone. Three at a time; delivery approximately thirty minutes. Photocopying by staff on same day or by post. No facilities for typing or taping. Cameras not allowed.

Records: City, council and committee minutes, court, charity petitions, title deeds, maps and plans, photographs, Urban District Councils. Free Citizens of Dublin 1468-1918, Mansion House Fund for Relief of Distress.

Postal Research: None

Facilities: Toilets, but no public telephone. No refreshment facilities but cafe/pub two minutes. Shops five minutes including bookshop with local history publications.

Publications: Map catalogue, *Graveyards Index. Free: Dublin Archives, Free Citizens of Dublin.*

Other Repositories: Dublin Civic Museum, South William Street, Dublin 2 (photographs).

Remarks: Some records stored elsewhere require three days' prior notice. Bags not allowed, storage facilities available. Further reading: *Calendar of Ancient Records of Dublin.*

NATIONAL ARCHIVES
FOUR COURTS
Dublin 7

Telephone: (01) 733833 (within Ireland); or (0001) 733833 (from Great Britain)

Opening Hours: Monday to Friday 10 am to 5 pm. Annual closure: public holidays.

Car Parking: None.

Children: No specific ruling but dependent on behaviour.

Disabled: By prior arrangement only

Appointments System: No prior booking. Signing in by register plus reader's ticket. 38 seats, four or five dual viewers.

Document Ordering: Prior ordering by special arrangement only. Three at a time; delivery ten to fifteen minutes, maybe longer when busy. No ordering between 12.45 pm and 2 pm. Photocopying restricted; by staff and sent by post. Typing/taping permitted (including computers) provided no disturbance to others. Cameras by prior arrangement.

Records: A few Ts of PRs, a few original PRs (no BTs), some Church of Ireland diocesan records on microfilm, family papers, Poll Tax, Hearth Tax, subsidy rolls, Irish Civil List, army and militia,

card index to probate records etc.

Postal Research: None; photocopies supplied if precise details given.

Facilities: No toilets or public telephone. Refreshments across Four Courts Yard. Cafe/pub five minutes. Shops ten minutes plus bookshop with local history publications.

Publications: *The Public Record - Sources for Local History in the National Archives, short guide to photocopies, Directory of Irish Archives, Sources for Genealogy* (free leaflet).

Remarks: This office was the PRO of Ireland. The State Paper Office is now a sub-office. Apply for a reader's ticket in advance. New accessions and less frequently used records require prior notice. Further reading: see the new *Directory of Irish Archives* and *Irish History from 1700: A Guide to Sources in the Public Record Office* by Alice Prochaska (British Records Association - Archives and the User No 6).

NATIONAL ARCHIVES
STATE PAPER OFFICE
Dublin Castle
Dublin 2

Telephone: (01) 792777 Ext 2518 (within Ireland); or (0001) 792777 Ext 2518 (from Great Britain)

Opening Hours: Monday to Friday 10 am to 5 pm. Annual closure: public holidays.

Car Parking: None.

Children: Accompanied: ten years plus. Unaccompanied: 15 years plus.

Disabled: No specific arrangements.

Appointments System: No prior booking. Signing in by register plus reader's ticket. Eight seats.

Document Ordering: Prior ordering by letter or telephone. Catalogue numbers necessary. Number at a time at archivist's discretion. Delivery ten to fifteen minutes. Ordering times restricted between 1 pm and 2 pm. Photocopying by staff on same day, if large quantity or busy, sent by post. Typing/taping restricted. Cameras not allowed.

Records: See entry for National Archives, Four Courts.

Postal Research: Limited; no charge made.

Facilities: Toilets, but no public telephone. No refreshment facilities but cafe/pub two minutes. Shops ten minutes plus bookshop with local history publications.

Publications: Free: summary list of holdings. For sale: *The Public Record Office - Sources For Local Studies in the Archives,*

The Rebellion of 1798: Facsimile Documents, The Famine of 1845-51: Facsimile Documents.
Remarks: Reading room open during lunchtime. Bags not allowed in search rooms.

NATIONAL LIBRARY OF IRELAND
Kildare Street
Dublin 2.
Telephone: (01) 618811 (within Ireland); or (0001) 618811 (from Great Britain)

Opening Hours: Monday and Tuesday 10 am to 5.15 pm, Wednesday and Thursday 10 am to 9 pm, Friday 10 am to 5 pm, Saturday 10 am to 1 pm. Annual closure: public holidays plus one week at Christmas.
Car Parking: None.
Children: 11 years plus but dependent on behaviour.
Disabled: Ramp; lift (doormen will assist); toilet
Appointments System: No prior booking. Signing in register plus identification. 77 seats, nineteen film viewers, two fiche.
Document Ordering: No prior ordering. Three books or one microfilm at a time. Delivery ten to fifteen minutes. Photocopying by staff on same day; DIY except PRs. No facilities for typing or taping. Cameras by prior arrangement.
Records: PRs on microfilm, wills and administrations, 19th century convict register, Dublin voters' list, extensive collection of printed pedigrees, estate maps, assize etc.
Postal Research: Very limited; no charge made.
Facilities: Toilets and public telephone on premises. No refreshment facilities but cafe/pub two minutes. Shops two minutes plus bookshop with local history publications.
Publications: Free leaflets
Remarks: A relatively small selection of non-Irish books require 24 hours prior notice. Bags are allowed in search rooms (under review).

REGISTRAR GENERAL
Joyce House
8-11 Lombard Street East
Dublin 2

Opening Hours: Monday to Friday.
Records: Protestant marriages 1845-1921; Roman Catholic marriages and births 1864-1922 (all Ireland); British Consul records: births of children of Irish parents, deaths of Irish born people

(abroad); births and deaths at sea; Army births, deaths and marriages.

Remarks: For further information apply to the Registrar General at above address.

REGISTRY OF DEEDS
Henrietta Street
Dublin 1
Telephone: (01) 733300 (within Ireland); or (0001) 733300 (from Great Britain)

Opening Hours: Monday to Friday 10 am to 4.30 pm. Annual closure: New Year's Day, St Patrick's Day, Good Friday, Easter Monday, first Monday in June and August, last Thursday in October, Christmas Day.
Car Parking: None.
Children: No specific ruling but dependent on behaviour.
Disabled: No arrangements (building more than 200 years old, with many stairs-no lift).
Appointments System: Prior booking unnecessary. Signing in by register plus entrance fee.
Document Ordering: Prior ordering by letter. Catalogue numbers necessary. Number at a time: no specific ruling. Delivery depends on circumstances. Photocopying by staff and sent by post. No facilities for typing or taping. Cameras not allowed.
Records: Memorial of deeds from 1708, records of wills 1708-1835.
Postal Research: Limited; no charge.
Facilities: Toilets and public telephone on premises. No refreshments but drink vending machine. Cafe/pub two minutes. Shops five minutes including bookshop with local history publications.
Publications: Leaflet: *A Guide to the Registry of Deeds.*
Other Repositories: The Genealogical Office, Kildare Street, Dublin 2; Land Registry, Chancery Street, Dublin 7; Valuation Office, 6 Ely Place, Dublin 2; The Library of Trinity College, Dublin; Society of Friends Library, Dublin; The Royal Irish Academy.
Places of Interest: Dublin Civic Museum, Guinness Museum, National Gallery of Ireland, National Museum of Ireland.
Tourist Office: British Tourist Authority, 123 Lower Baggot Street, Dublin 2. Telephone (01) 614188.
Remarks: Deeds are not contained in the registry, only the memorial retained after registration. No maps are retained in support of registration: has index of Grantors and denominations affected (pre-1947).

SCOTLAND

BORDERS

**BORDERS REGION Archive
and Local History Centre
Regional Library Headquarters
St Mary's Mill
Selkirk TD7 5EW.**
Telephone: (0750) 20842

Opening Hours: Monday to Thursday 8.45 am to 1 pm and 2 pm to 5 pm, Friday 8.45 am to 1 pm and 2 pm to 4 pm. Annual closure: January 1 and 2; December 25 and 26; Good Friday; May Day.
Car Parking: Approximately five places.
Children: No specific ruling.
Disabled: No facilities (under review).
Appointments System: Prior booking essential (at least one day). Signing in by register. Six seats, one film viewer, and one fiche.
Document Ordering: Prior ordering by letter or telephone. Six at a time. Delivery five to ten minutes. Photocopying by staff on same day. No facilities for typing or taping. Cameras permitted.
Records: PRs on fiche/film. Pre 1974 counties: Berwickshire, Peeblesshire, Roxburghshire and Selkirkshire.
Postal Research: Limited; no charge made.
Facilities: Toilets, but no public telephone. No refreshment facilities but cafe/pub two minutes.
Publications: Lists supplied on request.
Other Repositories: Ettrick and Lauderdale District Council, Council Chambers, Paton Street, Galashiels.
Places of Interest: Halliwell's House Museum.
Tourist Office: Halliwell's House, Selkirk TD7. Telephone (0750) 20054 (not open all year).
Remarks: Aimers and McLean Waverley Ironworks (Galashiels) firm's records (D/30) require two weeks' prior notice.

CENTRAL REGION

**CENTRAL REGION Council Archives
Department
Unit 6
Burghmuir Industrial Estate
Stirling FK7 7PY**
(This address is on a "medium-term" temporary basis)
Telephone: (0786) 73111

Opening Hours: Monday to Friday 9 am to 5 pm. Annual closure: Scottish public holidays and between Christmas and New Year.

Car Parking: Yes.
Children: No specific ruling.
Disabled: Access
Appointments System: No prior booking. Signing in: identification required. Approximately five seats. One film viewer, one fiche.
Document Ordering: Prior ordering by letter or telephone. Approximately three at a time. Delivery three to four minutes. Photocopying by staff on same day. No facilities for typing or taping. Cameras permitted.
Records: A few Ts of PRs, some PRs on film/fiche (baptisms and marriages pre 1837); local authority.
Facilities: Toilets, but no public telephone. No refreshment facilities but cafe/pub five minutes. Shops five minutes plus bookshop with local history publications.
Other Repositories: Falkirk Museum, Orchard Street, Falkirk.
Places of Interest: Smith Art Gallery and Museum, Argyll and Sutherland Highlanders Museum.
Tourist Office: Dumbarton Road, Stirling, FK8 2LQ
Telephone (0786) 75019.

DUMFRIES AND GALLOWAY

**DUMFRIES Archive Centre
33 Burns Street
Dumfries DG11 1QW.**
Telephone: (0387) 69254

Opening Hours: Tuesday to Friday 11 am to 1 pm and 2 pm to 5 pm (under review). Closed Mondays. Annual closure: Scottish public holidays; two days at Christmas; New Year; occasional additional closures.
Car Parking: Nearby.
Children: Accompanied: at archivist's discretion. Unaccompanied: eleven years plus.
Disabled: Access but no specific arrangements and space strictly limited.
Appointments System: Prior booking essential (maximum notice possible). Signing in by register. Six seats, one film viewer (additional viewers soon).
Document Ordering: No prior ordering. Three to four at a time. Delivery within a few minutes. Photocopying by staff usually on same day. Typing/taping not usually allowed. Cameras not allowed.
Records: PRs on film/fiche.
Postal Research: Very limited; charge for photocopying.
Facilities: Toilets, but no public telephone. No refreshment facilities but cafe/pub five minutes. Shops two

minutes plus bookshop with local history publications.

Publications: Outline holdings list and short articles about the centre can be photocopied (charge made).

Remarks: No bags in search rooms. Donations box. Historical county map available on request. Search room space very limited so only room for those actually researching.

EWART LIBRARY
Catherine Street
Dumfries DG1 1JB.
Telephone: (0387) 53820

Opening Hours: Monday to Wednesday, Friday 10 am to 7.30 pm; Thursday and Saturday 10 am to 5 pm. Annual closure: Christmas; two days at New Year; Easter (Friday to Monday); May Day.

Car Parking: 22 places.

Children: No specific ruling but dependent on behaviour.

Disabled: Ramp and toilets. Viewers accessible and staff will assist if required.

Appointments System: No prior booking for seats. Viewers essential for film. Twenty seats, one film viewer and four fiche.

Document Ordering: Prior ordering by letter or telephone (as much notice as possible). Reasonable number at a time. Delivery one to fifteen minutes. No ordering on Saturdays. Photocopying DIY. No facilities for typing or taping. Cameras permitted.

Records: No PRs nor Ts. Local authority, local history, newspapers on fiche.

Postal Research: Limited specific enquiry, charge made.

Facilities: Toilets and public telephone on premises. No refreshment facilities but cafe/pub five minutes. Shops five minutes plus bookshop with local history publications.

Other Repositories: Nithsdale District Archive Centre, 22 Burns Street, Dumfries.

Places of Interest: Dumfries Museum, Old Bridge House Museum, Burns House, Robert Burns Centre, Sanquhar Museum, Savings Bank Museum.

Tourist Office: Whitesands, Dumfries DG1 2SB. Telephone (0387) 53862 (not open all year).

Remarks: Original newspapers stored elsewhere require prior notice. Historical county map on display. Information held elsewhere nationally (eg Register House) is not duplicated here.

FIFE

DUNFERMLINE Central Library
Abbot Street
Dunfermline
Fife KY12 7NW.
Telephone: (0383) 723661

Opening Hours: Mondays, Tuesdays, Thursdays and Fridays 10 am to 1 pm and 2 pm to 7 pm. Closed Wednesdays. Annual closure: Scottish public holidays and local holidays.

Appointments System: Prior booking by letter or telephone preferred. Some microfilm/fiche viewers. Photocopying by staff.

Records: MI notes, local history collection, Nonconformists, roads.

Other Repositories: Dunfermline District Council, City Chambers, Dunfermline, holds town clerk's and borough chamberlain's records.

Places of Interest: Andrew Carnegie's Birthplace Museum, Dunfermline Museum, Pittencrieff House Museum.

Tourist Office: Glen Bridge Car Park, Dunfermline, Fife. Telephone (0383) 720999 (not open all year).

KIRCALDY Central Library
War Memorial Grounds
Kircaldy, Fife KY1 1YG.
Telephone: (0592) 260707

Opening Hours: Monday to Thursday 10 am to 7 pm; Fridays and Saturdays 10 am to 5 pm. Annual closure: Scottish public holidays.

Appointments System: Prior booking by letter or telephone preferred. Microfilm/fiche viewers. Photocopying by staff.

Records: Local collection, photographs, old PRs for district, newspapers, census.

Other Repositories: Kircaldy Museum and Art Gallery, War Memorial Gardens, Kircaldy KY1 1YG, holds records of trade, business, local government, trade unions and guilds.

Places of Interest: Burntisland Edwardian Fair, McDougall Stuart Museum.

Tourist Office: Esplanade, Kircaldy, Fife KY1. Telephone (0592) 267775.

The Hay Fleming Reference Library
ST ANDREWS Branch Library
Church Square
St Andrews
Fife
Telephone: (0334) 73381, Enquiries (0334) 53722.

Opening Hours: Monday to Wednesday and Friday 10 am to 7 pm, Thursdays and Saturdays 10 am to 5 pm. Annual closure: Scottish public holidays.
Appointments System: No prior booking necessary. Photocopying allowed.
Records: Deeds, Nonconformist, ecclesiastical, trade, business.
Publications: Guide to library.
Other Repositories: St Andrews University (Muniments Department), North Street, St Andrews KY16 9TR, holds records of North East fife area burghs and the parishes of St Andrews and Cupar Hospital (appointment necessary).
Places of Interest: Crawford Arts Centre.
Tourist Office: South Street, St Andrews KY16 9TE. Telephone (0334) 72021.

GRAMPIAN

ABERDEEN CITY ARCHIVES
City of Aberdeen
Town Clerk's Department
Town House
Aberdeen AB9 1FY.
Telephone: (0224) 642121 Ext 513

Opening Hours: Monday 10.15 am to 12.30 pm and 2 pm to 4.30 pm, Tuesday to Friday 9.30 am to 12.30 pm and 2 pm to 4.30 pm. Annual closure: Scottish public holidays.
Car Parking: None.
Children: Accompanied: school age. Unaccompanied: at archivist's discretion.
Disabled: No facilities
Appointments System: Prior booking essential. Six seats.
Document Ordering: Prior ordering essential. Document ordering: only produced before each morning and afternoon session.
Records: Former Town Councils of Aberdeen and Old Aberdeen, private deposits, registers of burial grounds, Poor records, school and university.
Publications: *Family History Research in Aberdeen.*
Other Repositories: Aberdeen City Libraries, Central Library, Rosemount Viaduct AB9 1GU: microfilm of established church baptisms, proclamations and burials for the area, fiche index of old parish registers for the area (baptisms and marriages), film of some census returns.
Remarks: Access to the old printed catalogue (published 1890) *Charters and Other Documents Illustrative of the History of Aberdeen* edited by P J Anderson, is limited. Essential reading: *North-East*

Roots: A Guide to Sources by Lesley Diack (published by Aberdeen and North-East Scotland Family History Society).

GRAMPIAN REGIONAL ARCHIVES
Old Aberdeen House
Dunbar Street
Aberdeen AB2 1UE
Telephone: (0224) 481775

Opening Hours: Monday to Friday 9 am to 12 noon and 1 pm to 5 pm. Annual closure: Scottish public holidays.
Car Parking: Six places.
Disabled: No special arrangements, one step.
Appointments System: Prior booking essential (one week). Signing in by register. Eight seats.
Document Ordering: Prior ordering by letter or telephone. Three at a time, delivery approximately fifteen minutes. Photocopying by staff on same day or by post. No facilities for typing or taping. Cameras permitted.
Records: No PRs. Minutes and registers of parochial boards and parish councils; admission registers and school log books; valuation rolls; local government records for the counties of Aberdeen, Banff, Kincardine and Moray, Aberdeen City (schools and registers of electors only).
Postal Research: Very limited, no charge made.
Facilities: Toilets, but no public telephone. No refreshment facilities, but cafe/pub two minutes. Shops two minutes plus bookshop with local history publications.
Publications: Free leaflet on sources for family history.
Other Repositories: Aberdeen University Archives, University Library, King's College, Aberdeen AB8 2UB; The Central Library, Aberdeen.
Places of Interest: Aberdeen Maritime Museum, James Dun's House, Provost Skene's House, Provost Ross's House, The Gordon Highlanders Museum.
Tourist Office: St Nicholas House, Broad Street, Aberdeen AB9 1DE. Telephone (0224) 632727/637353.
Remarks: Limited staffing. Office situated off St Machar's Drive between King Street and Chanonry.

MORAY District Record Office
The Tolbooth
High Street
Forres
Moray IV36 0AB
Telephone: (0309) 73617

Opening Hours: Monday to Friday 9 am to 12.30 pm and 1.30 pm to 4.30 pm.
Annual closure: Scottish public holidays.
Car Parking: None.
Children: No specific ruling but dependent on behaviour.
Disabled: Disabled friendly
Appointments System: No prior booking. Signing by register plus identification. Three seats.
Document Ordering: Prior ordering by letter or telephone. Three at a time, delivery ten minutes. Photocopying by staff.
No facilities for typing or taping.
Cameras permitted.
Records: Established Church Kirk Sessions, Presbytery, maps and plans, family, local government, photographs.
Postal Research: None.
Facilities: Toilets, but no public telephone. No refreshment facilities but cafe/pub two minutes. Shops two minutes.
Publications: Leaflet which lists official archives.
Places of Interest: Falconer Museum.
Tourist Office: Falconer Museum, Tolbooth Street, Forres, Moray IV36 0PH. Telephone (0309) 72938 (not open all year).
Remarks: Bags not allowed, storage facilities available. Historical county map on display. Donations box. Reference library has directories, year books etc. Extensive card indexes and descriptive catalogues of RO collections.

HIGHLAND REGION

HIGHLAND REGION Archives
c/o Public Library
Farraline Park
Inverness IV1 1LS
Telephone: (0463) 236463

Opening Hours: Monday and Friday 9 am to 7.30 pm, Tuesday and Thursday 9 am to 6.30 pm, Wednesday and Saturday 9 am to 5 pm. **Annual closure:** Public holidays, two days at Christmas and Easter, three days at New Year, May Day.
Car Parking: None.
Children: No specific ruling.
Disabled: Access, ramp.
Appointments System: No prior booking. Four film viewers, four fiche.
Document Ordering: Prior ordering by letter or telephone. Reasonable number at a time, delivery variable. Photocopying by staff, normally on same day, PRs from film. Typing/taping permitted. Cameras

permitted.
Records: Mainly public records relating to former counties in the Highlands and Inverness Burgh, some private and estate papers, PRs on microfilm.
Postal Research: Yes, charge made (send for details).
Facilities: No toilets or public telephone. No refreshment facilities but cafe/pub two minutes. Shops five minutes plus bookshop with local history publications.
Other Repositories: Queen's Own Highlanders Regimental Headquarters, Cameron Barracks, Inverness (appointment only): museum at Fort George.
Places of Interest: Inverness Museum and Art Gallery.
Tourist Office: 23 Church Street, Inverness IV1 1EZ. Telephone (0463) 234353.
Remarks: Holding Lists and Catalogues available for inspection on premises. Highland Region archives are housed in Inverness Public Library; access to archives is dependent on availability of library staff with relevant experience; a full-time archivist should be appointed shortly who will report directly to the Director of Libraries and Leisure Services, not to the Regional Librarian.

LOTHIAN

CITY OF EDINBURGH DISTRICT
Council Archives
Department of Administration
City Chambers
High Street
Edinburgh EH1 1YJ.
Telephone: (031) 225 2424 Ext 5196

Opening Hours: Monday to Thursday 9 am to 5 pm, Friday 9 am to 3.45 pm.
Annual closure: Scottish public holidays.
Car Parking: None.
Children: Accompanied: ten years plus. Unaccompanied: 16 years plus.
Disabled: No facilities.
Appointments System: Prior booking essential (24 hours). Signing in by register. Six seats.
Document Ordering: No prior ordering. Three at a time, delivery approximately ten minutes. Last orders Monday to Thursday 4.30 pm, Friday 3 pm. Photocopying by staff usually on same day. No facilities for typing or taping. Cameras not allowed.
Records: Local authority.
Postal Research: Limited
Facilities: Toilets but no public telephone. No refreshment facilities but

cafe/pub two minutes. Shops two minutes plus bookshop with local history publications.
Other Repositories: Heriot-Watt University Library, Riccarton, Edinburgh EH14 4AS.
Remarks: Donations box.

GENERAL REGISTER OFFICE FOR SCOTLAND
New Register House
Edinburgh EH1 3YT
(Access is from West Register Street, opposite the North British Hotel)
Telephone: (031) 556 3952

Opening Hours: Monday to Thursday 9.30 am to 4.30 pm, Friday 9.30 am to 4 pm. Annual closure: Scottish public holidays.
Car Parking: None
Disabled: By prior arrangement.
Records: Most PRs on film: 1553-1854 births, baptisms, marriages, proclamations of banns, deaths, burials. Registers of neglected entries 1801-1854, stillbirths, adoptions, divorces, miscellaneous registers, census records 1841-1891, statutory civil registers 1855 on: births, marriages and deaths.
Postal Research: Specific enquiry, statutory fee.
Publications: Free: leaflet on main records, search procedures and issue of extracts, details of fees.
Places of Interest: Canongate Tollbooth, No 7 Charlotte Square, Edinburgh Wax Museum, Huntly House, John Knox House Museum, Lady Stair's House, Museum of Childhood, Museum of Communication, National Galleries of Scotland, Scotch Whisky Heritage Centre, Scottish Agricultural Museum, The Royal Scots Dragoon Guards Museum, The Royal Scots Regimental Museum, Scottish United Services Museum.
Tourist Office: Waverley Market, Princes Street, Edinburgh EH2 2QP. Telephone (031) 557 1700.

Department of Manuscripts
NATIONAL LIBRARY OF SCOTLAND
George IV Bridge
Edinburgh EH1 1EW.
Telephone: (031) 226 4531

Opening Hours: Monday to Friday 9.30 am to 8.15 pm, Saturday 9.20 am to 12.45 pm. Annual closure: Scottish public holidays, first full week in October (subject to possible alteration).
Car Parking: None.
Children: Accompanied: no specific rul-

ing. Unaccompanied: long-term tickets issued to third year plus students, others at archivist's discretion.
Disabled: Lifts, toilets.
Appointments System: No prior booking. Signing by register plus identification plus reader's ticket (entry through main library Reading Room). Seventeen seats. No viewers (main library has film and fiche viewers).
Document Ordering: Prior ordering by letter or telephone. Catalogue numbers helpful but not essential. Reasonable number at a time, only three issued. Delivery five to ten minutes, last delivery 4.45 pm, last orders 4.30 pm. Photocopying by staff and sent by post. Typing/taping permitted. Cameras not allowed.
Records: Family, political, business, trade unions, oral history etc.
Postal Research: Limited, no charge made.
Facilities: Toilets and public telephone on premises. No refreshment facilities but cafe/pub two minutes. Shops two minutes plus bookshop with local history publications.
Publications: Publications list.
Other Repositories: Edinburgh University Library, George Square, Edinburgh.
Remarks: Free Church account books require 24 hours prior notice. Bags not allowed, storage facilities available. Donations box. Map room at Causewayside Building, 33 Salisbury Place, Edinburgh EH9 1SL.

SCOTTISH CATHOLIC ARCHIVES
Columba House
16 Drummond Place
Edinburgh EH3 6PL.

Remarks: Catholic PRs are not kept here but have remained in each locality with the parish priest. PRs containing entries before 1855 have been photocopied by the Scottish Record Office, Old Register House, Princes Street, Edinburgh. Enquiries may be addressed to Scots Ancestry Research Society, 3 Albany Street, Edinburgh EH1 3PY.

SCOTTISH RECORD OFFICE (HISTORICAL SEARCH ROOM)
HM General Register House
Princes Street
Edinburgh EH1 3YY.
Telephone: (031) 556 6585

Opening Hours: Monday to Friday 9 am to 4.45 pm. Annual closure: Scottish public holidays; two days at, or after, New Year; Good Friday; Edinburgh Spring

Monday (April); last Monday in May; two days at, or after, Christmas; Edinburgh Autumn Monday (September); first fortnight in November.
Car Parking: None.
Children: Accompanied: no specific ruling. Unaccompanied: senior school pupils.
Disabled: Access, lifts.
Appointments System: No prior booking (early attendance recommended at holiday periods). Signing in by reader's ticket plus identification. 27 seats, two film viewers and one fiche.
Document Ordering: Prior ordering by letter. Catalogue numbers necessary. Three at a time, delivery approximately twenty minutes depending where stored, restricted between 11.30 am and 2.30 pm. Photocopying by staff on same day or sent by post. Battery operated silent computers allowed. Cameras not allowed.
Records: Kirk session PRs, valuation rolls, wills, Court of Session, Court of Judiciary (criminal), Burgh.
Postal Research: Limited to single specific enquiry.
Facilities: Toilets and public telephone on premises. No refreshment facilities but cafe/pub two minutes. Shops two minutes and bookshop with local history publications five to ten minutes.
Publications: For sale and free: *Facilities for Historical Research, Short Guide to the Records, Family History, Early Family History, Indexes to Deeds, Sasines and Testamentary Records etc.*
Remarks: Various records, including sheriff court records, require three clear working days' prior notice. Bags not allowed, storage facilities. Series of county maps available. *Guide to the Public Records of Scotland* (1905) by M Livingstone: a new guide is in preparation. Particulars of accessions are in the *Annual Report of the Keeper of the Records of Scotland.*

SCOTTISH RECORD OFFICE (WEST SEARCH ROOM)
West Register House
Charlotte Square
Edinburgh EH2 4DF.
Telephone: (031) 556 6585

Opening Hours: Monday to Friday 9 am to 4.45 pm. Annual closure: Scottish public holidays, third week in November.
Car Parking: None.
Children: Accompanied: at archivist's discretion. Unaccompanied: school age.
Disabled: Access, lifts.
Appointments System: No prior booking. Signing in by reader's ticket plus identification. Sixteen seats, four film viewers and one fiche.
Document Ordering: Prior ordering by letter only. Catalogue numbers necessary. Three at a time, delivery approximately twenty minutes. Photocopying by staff on same day or if large quantity or busy, sent by post. Three sound-proof cubicles for typing/taping. Cameras not allowed.
Records: Public archives of Scotland.
Postal Research: Specific enquiry, no charge made.
Facilities: Toilets but no public telephone. No refreshment facilities but cafe/pub five minutes. Shops five minutes plus bookshop with local history publications.
Publications: Relevant publications. Free: SRO leaflets.
Remarks: Some court records, railway staff records from BR Scottish archives, maps and plans accessioned in recent years all require three clear working days' prior notice. Bags not allowed, storage facilities available. Historical map on display.

ORKNEY ISLES

ORKNEY Archives Office
The Orkney Library
Laing Street
Kirkwall
Orkney KW15 1NW.
Telephone: (0856) 3166/5260 Ext 25

Opening Hours: Monday to Friday 9 am to 1 pm and 2 pm to 5 pm. Annual closure: Scottish public holidays, Christmas to New Year.
Car Parking: None.
Children: By prior arrangement.
Disabled: By prior arrangement. Access and toilet in library
Appointments System: Prior booking essential (at least 24 hours). Six seats, two film viewers, one fiche.
Document Ordering: Prior ordering by letter or telephone. Catalogue numbers necessary. Maximum of five at a time. Delivery five minutes. Photocopying by staff on same day, or if large quantity or busy, sent by post, PRs allowed. Cameras by prior arrangement.
Records: PRs on fiche/film, local authority, family, business, photographs, sound archive.
Postal Research: Extremely limited
Facilities: Toilets but no public telephone. No refreshment facilities but cafe/pub two minutes. Shops two minutes plus bookshop with local history publications.

Publications: Lists available through the National Register of Archives (Scotland) at the Scottish RO, Edinburgh.

Other Repositories: Orkney Library (adjacent): apply to local Registrars for birth, marriages and death certificates from 1855 onwards.

Places of Interest: Tankerness House Museum.

Tourist Office: Broad Street, Kirkwall, Orkney Islands KW15 1DH. Telephone (0856) 2856.

Remarks: Records of the Established and Free Churches in Orkney require at least 48 hours prior notice.

SHETLAND ISLANDS

SHETLAND Archives
King Harald Street
Lerwick
Shetland ZE1 0EQ.
Telephone: (0595) 3535 Ext 269

Opening Hours: Monday to Thursday 9 am to 1 pm and 2 pm to 5 pm, Friday 9 am to 1 pm and 2 pm to 4 pm. Annual closure: Scottish public holidays and local authority holidays.

Car Parking: Yes.

Children: No specific ruling.

Disabled: Access, toilet proposed in near future.

Appointments System: Prior booking for seats unnecessary, but necessary for viewers. Nine seats, two film viewers one fiche.

Document Ordering: Prior ordering by letter or telephone. Number at a time at archivist's discretion. Immediate delivery. Photocopying by staff on same day. No facilities for typing or taping. Cameras permitted.

Records: Ts of PRs require ordering. PRs on film/fiche, local authority, oral history.

Postal Research: Very limited, no charge made.

Facilities: Toilets but no public telephone. No refreshment facilities but cafe/pub two minutes. Shops five minutes plus bookshop with local history publications.

Publications: Handlists, catalogues.

Other Repositories: Shetland Museum and Library, Lower Hillhead, Lerwick, Shetland ZE1 0EL.

Places of Interest: Böd of Gremista, Shetland Croft House Museum.

Tourist Office: Lerwick, Shetland Isles, ZE1 0LU. Telephone (0595) 3434.

Remarks: Historical map on display.

STRATHCLYDE

ARGYLL AND BUTE District Archives
Kilmory
Lochgilphead
Argyll PA31 8RT.
Telephone: (0546) 2127 Ext 120

Opening Hours: Monday to Thursday 9 am to 1 pm and 2 pm to 5.15 pm, Friday 9 am to 1 pm and 2 pm to 4 pm. Annual closure: Scottish public holidays.

Car Parking: Ample

Children: Accompanied: at archivist's discretion. Unaccompanied: twelve years plus.

Disabled: Ramp

Appointments System: Prior booking essential (as much as possible). Six seats.

Document Ordering: Prior ordering by letter or telephone. Three at a time, delivery two minutes. Photocopying by staff usually on same day or by post. No facilities for typing or taping. Cameras permitted.

Records: No PRs. Local authority.

Postal Research: Limited to specific enquiry.

Facilities: Toilets but no public telephone. No refreshment facilities but cafe/pub two minutes. Shops five minutes plus bookshop with local history publications.

Publications: None, but archivist willing to copy sections of own lists (charge made).

Tourist Office: Lochgilphead, Argyll. Telephone (0546) 2344 (not open all year).

Remarks: Records of Rothesay Town Council stored elsewhere require two weeks' prior notice. Historical county map on display.

Strathclyde Regional Archives
(AYR Sub-Region Office)
Regional Offices
Wellington Square
Ayr KA7 1DR.
Telephone: Wednesdays only (0292) 266922, other days (041) 227 2405

Opening Hours: Wednesday 10 am to 1 pm and 2 pm to 4.30 pm. Other times by arrangement with archivist.

Car Parking: None.

Children: Accompanied: at archivist's discretion. Unaccompanied: 11 years plus.

Disabled: By prior arrangement.

Appointments System: Prior booking essential (one week). Signing in by register. Six seats.

Document Ordering: Prior ordering by letter or telephone. Three at a time, delivery five to fifteen minutes. Photocopying by staff and sent by post. No facilities for typing or taping. Cameras not allowed.

Records: All those relating to Ayrshire.

Postal Research: Yes, charge made.

Facilities: Toilets and public telephone on premises. No refreshment facilities but cafe/pub two minutes. Shops five minutes plus bookshop with local history publications.

Publications: Free: *Genealogical Sources Available at Ayr Sub Regional Archives, Guide to Records at Ayr Sub Regional Archives, Tracing Your Ancestors (Guide to Sources at Regional Archives and Mitchell Library, Glasgow).*

Other Repositories: Reference Library, Kyle and Carrick District Libraries, Main Street, Ayr KA8 8EB.

Places of Interest: Ayr Carnegie Library, Maclaurin Gallery and Rozelle House, Tam O'Shanter Museum, Ayrshire (ECO) Yeomanry Museum, Alloway by Ayr.

Tourist Office: 39 Sandgate, Ayr KA7 1BG. Telephone (0292) 284196.

Remarks: Historical county map on display. Modifications to the building to allow disabled access are in progress. Catalogues to the collections are available at Strathclyde Regional HQ, Mitchell Library, Glasgow and at the Reference Library, Main Street, Ayr.

CUMNOCK AND DOON VALLEY District Reference Library
Library Headquarters
Council Offices
Lugar
Ayrshire KA18 3JQ
Telephone: (0290) 22111

Opening Hours: Monday to Friday 9 am to 4.30 pm. Annual closure: Scottish public holidays.

Car Parking: Approximately 100 places.

Children: No specific ruling.

Disabled: No facilities.

Appointments System: No prior booking. Ten seats.

Document Ordering: No prior ordering. Six at a time. Photocopying by staff, usually on same day. No facilities for typing or taping.

Records: Local authority.

Postal Research: Limited, no charge made.

Facilities: Toilets but no public telephone.

Publications: Free: brief list of archives available for each parish within the district.

Remarks: Some local government

archives and minute books require a few days' prior notice.

Strathclyde Regional Archives (incorporating GLASGOW CITY Archives)
Mitchell Library
North Street
Glasgow G3 7DN.
(The Archive Office is in the Jeffrey Room)
Telephone: (041) 227 2401

Opening Hours: Monday to Thursday 9.30 am to 4.45 pm, Friday 9.30 am to 4 pm, evening opening by prior arrangement. Annual closure: Scottish public holidays.

Car Parking: None.

Children: No specific ruling.

Disabled: Access, prior arrangement necessary.

Appointments System: No prior booking. Signing in by register. One film viewer, two fiche.

Document Ordering: Prior ordering by letter or telephone. Three at a time, delivery ten minutes. No ordering between one pm and 2 pm. Photocopying by staff and sent by post, PRs allowed. No facilities for typing or taping. Cameras permitted.

Records: Ts of PRs require ordering. Original PRs, PRs on film/fiche, Kirk session records of Church of Scotland within Presbytery of Glasgow. Censuses from 1841 on. Former county councils and parish authorities within Strathclyde region, Poor Laws, school records, voters' rolls, valuation rolls, retours, sasines, register of deeds, cemetery registers.

Postal Research: Yes, charge made.

Facilities: Toilets and public telephone on premises. Refreshments and restaurant/canteen. Cafe/pub two minutes. Shops five minutes plus bookshop with local history publications.

Publications: Free: leaflet *Tracing Your Ancestors: Mitchell Library and Archives Sources.*

Other Repositories: Glasgow University Archive, The University, Glasgow; Glasgow District Council, Parks Department, Cemeteries and Crematoria Section, 302 Buchanan Street, Glasgow (cemetery registers and more recent records not yet deposited); Charles Rennie Mackintosh Society, Queen's Cross, 870 Garscube Road, Glasgow G20 7EL.

Places of Interest: Art Gallery and Museum, Collins Gallery, Haggs Castle, The Hunterian Museum and Art Gallery, Museum of Transport, People's Palace, Pollok House, Provand's Lordship, Provanhall House, Rutherglen Museum,

Springburn Museum and Exhibition Centre, The Tenement House, The Royal Highland Fusiliers Museum.
Tourist Office: 35-39 St Vincent Place, Glasgow G2 1ES. Telephone (041) 227 4880.
Remarks: Some business records stored elsewhere require 24 hours prior notice. Argyll records are at Inveraray. The Rare Books and Manuscripts Department and the Glasgow Room, in the Mitchell Library, have local records.

RENFREW District Council
Central Library
High Street
Paisley PA1 2BB
Telephone: (041) 887 3672 or 889 2360

Opening Hours: Monday to Friday 9 am to 8 pm, Saturday 9 am to 5 pm. Annual closure: Scottish public holidays.
Car Parking: None.
Children: Accompanied: at librarian's discretion. Unaccompanied: ten years plus.
Disabled: No facilities - stairs
Appointments System: Prior booking for seats unnecessary but necessary for viewers. 24 seats, jointly with general reference library. Two film viewers and two fiche.
Document Ordering: Prior ordering by letter or telephone. Catalogue numbers helpful. Number at a time: no specific ruling. Delivery within a few minutes. Photocopying by staff on same day. No facilities for typing or taping. Cameras permitted.
Postal Research: Limited, no charge made.
Facilities: No toilets or public telephone. No refreshment facilities but cafe/pub nearby. Shops five minutes plus bookshop with local history publications.
Publications: Leaflets.
Places of Interest: Paisley Museum and Art Galleries (some local archives).
Tourist Office: Paisley Town Hall, Abbey Close, Paisley, PA1 1JS. Telephone (041) 889 0711.
Remarks: Renfrew Library, Collier Street, Johnstone, Renfrew, is closed and most items are now stored in the joint library/museum building so one to two days' notice is required for these records; it is anticipated that this library will merge with the museum.

TAYSIDE

Archive and Record Centre
City of DUNDEE District Council

21 City Square
Dundee DD1 3BY.
(Callers use 1 Shore Terrace)
Telephone: (0382) 23141 Ext 4494

Opening Hours: Monday to Friday 9 am to 1 pm and 2 pm to 5 pm. Annual closure: Scottish public holidays.
Car Parking: None.
Children: No specific ruling.
Disabled: No facilities - stairs, staff prepared to assist, by prior arrangement.
Appointments System: Prior booking essential (three days). Signing in by register. Eight seats, one film viewer, two fiche.
Document Ordering: Prior ordering by letter or telephone. Three at a time, delivery fifteen minutes. Photocopying restricted, by staff on same day, or if large quantity or busy, sent by post. Typing/taping for disabled only, by prior arrangement. Cameras at archivist's discretion.
Records: City of Dundee District Council and the former Corporation of Dundee 1518-1985, Dundee Presbytery and JP, Sasines, family, business, shipping. The centre administers the official records of the Tayside Regional Council including those relating to the former County Councils of Angus, Perth and Kinross.
Postal Research: None.
Facilities: No toilets or public telephone. No refreshment facilities but cafe/pub two minutes. Shops two minutes plus bookshop with local history publications.
Publications: Free: *Dundee District Archive and Record Centre List of Holdings*, local research agents.
Other Repositories: Local History Department, Dundee Central Library, Wellgate, Dundee; Dundee University Archives, The University, Perth Road, Dundee.
Places of Interest: Barrack Street Museum, Broughty Castle Museum, McManus Galleries, Mills Observatory, Royal Research Ship *Discovery*.
Tourist Office: 4 City Square, Dundee DD1 3BA. Telephone (0382) 27723.
Remarks: Historical county map on display. Donations box for Friends Organisation.

PERTH AND KINROSS District Archive
Sandeman Library
16 Kinnoull Street
Perth PH1 5ET
Telephone: (0738) 23329

Opening Hours: Monday to Friday 9.30 am to 1 pm and 2 pm to 5 pm. Annual closure: eleven Scottish public holidays.
Car Parking: None.
Children: No specific ruling.
Disabled: Limited access, ramp at side. No access to Local Studies Department.
Appointments System: Prior booking for seats and viewers essential (one week). Signing in by card index. Six seats, three film viewers and one fiche (all in Local Studies Department).
Document Ordering: Prior ordering by letter or telephone. Number at a time: no specific ruling. Delivery five minutes. Photocopying by staff on same day or, if large quantity or busy, sent by post. No facilities for typing or taping. Cameras permitted.
Records: PRs on film/fiche; official records of the City and Royal Burgh of Perth and district; former County Councils of Perth, Kinross, Perth and Kinross; series of records from the Keeper of the Records of Scotland, etc.
Facilities: No toilets or public telephone. No refreshment facilities but cafe/pub five minutes. Shops five minutes plus bookshop with local history publications.
Publications: Various local history publications. Free: summary list of archives.
Other Repositories: Perth Museum and Art Gallery, George Street, Perth. Its Local Studies Department holds microfilms of old parochial records for parishes presently within Perth and Kinross District, some census returns 1841-1881, volumes of MIs of Perthshire and Kinrosshire pre-1855, local maps and plans from 1795, school log-books and admission registers from 1863, voters' lists from 1832, valuation rolls and cess books from 1650, cemetery records from 1794.
Places of Interest: The Scottish Tartans Museum, Drummond St, Comrie, Perthshire. Telephone (0764) 70779; The Black Watch (RHR) Museum, Balhousie Castle.

WALES

CLWYD

Clwyd Record Office
The Old Rectory
Hawarden
DEESIDE
Clwyd CH5 3NR
Telephone: (0244) 532364

Opening Hours: Monday to Thursday 9 am to 4.45 pm, Friday 9 am to 4.15 pm.

Annual closure: public holidays.
Car Parking: Limited
Children: No specific ruling.
Disabled: Access
Appointments System: Prior booking for seats unnecessary but two days necessary for viewers. Signing in by register (CARN to be introduced shortly). Ten seats, five film viewers, one fiche.
Document Ordering: Prior ordering advisable, by letter or telephone. Three at a time, delivery within a few minutes. No documents may be ordered between 12 noon and 1.30 pm. Photocopying by staff on same day or if large quantity or busy, sent by post, small quantity of PRs and BTs allowed (larger orders require special permission). Typing/taping permitted. Cameras not allowed.
Records: A few Ts of PRs/BTs on open shelves. PRs/BTs on fiche/film: not complete, particularly before 1813 (no originals produced unless film is illegible). Printed local history sources, Diocese of St Asaph on film. Denbighshire PRs held by the Ruthin office and a few parishes where registers are in the NLW are on film. Local authority, family, old county of Flintshire.
Postal Research: Limited to specific enquiry, no charge made.
Facilities: Toilets but no public telephone. No refreshment facilities but cafe/pub two minutes. Shops two minutes.
Publications: Publications list, guides, lists and calendars, record agents, *Guide to the PRs of Clwyd, Parish Registers of Wales, Sources for the Genealogist, County ROs in Wales, List of PRs,* historical county map.
Other Repositories: St Deniol's Library, Hawarden (manuscript collections); Clwyd Library Service, Headquarters Library, Civic Centre, Mold (local history collection).
Remarks: Records from St Deniol's Library require two days prior notice. Bags not allowed, storage facilities available. Historical county map on display.

Clwyd Record Office
46 Clwyd Street
RUTHIN
Clwyd LL15 1HP.
Telephone: (08242) 3077

Opening Hours: Monday to Thursday 9 am to 4.45 pm, Friday 9 am to 4.15 pm.
Annual closure: public holidays.
Car Parking: Very limited.
Children: No specific ruling.
Disabled: Access through rear entrance and via a lift, prior arrangements preferred.

Appointments System: Prior booking for seats and viewers necessary (two days for viewers). Signing in by register (CARN to be introduced). Ten seats, five film viewers. one fiche.

Document Ordering: Prior ordering by letter or telephone. Three at a time, delivery within a few minutes. No ordering between 12.30 pm and 1.30 pm. Photocopying by staff on same day, or if large quantity or busy, sent by post, printout takes seven to ten days and can either be collected or posted. No facilities for typing or taping. Cameras not allowed.

Records: A few Ts of PRs on open shelves, PRs/BTs on fiche/film, Diocese of St Asaph on film, local authority, old county of Denbighshire.

Postal Research: Twenty minutes only, no charge.

Facilities: Toilets but no public telephone. No refreshment facilities but cafe/pub two minutes. Shops two minutes plus bookshop with local history publications.

Publications: Publications list - see Hawarden, *Sources for the Genealogist*, lists available records.

Places of Interest: Ruthin Craft Centre, St Peter's Church, historic market town.

Tourist Office: Craft Centre, Ruthin LL15 1BB. Telephone (08242) 3992.

Remarks: Bags not allowed, storage facilities available. Historical county map on display. Branch library is next door on ground floor.

DYFED

Dyfed Archive Service
CARDIGANSHIRE Record Office
Swyddfa'r Sir
Marine Terrace
Aberystwyth SY23 2DE
Telephone: (0970) 617581 Ext 2120

Opening Hours: Tuesday and Thursday only 9 am to 4.45 pm. Annual closure: public holidays.

Car Parking: None.

Children: At any age if undertaking a school project.

Disabled: Access

Appointments System: Prior booking for seats unnecessary but for viewers, necessary, especially in the summer. Signing in by register. Twelve to fourteen seats, two film viewers, one fiche.

Document Ordering: Prior ordering by letter or telephone. Number at a time at archivist's discretion. Delivery approximately five minutes. Photocopying restricted; by staff on same day or if large

quantity or busy, sent by post. No facilities for typing or taping. Cameras by special arrangement.

Records: Some Ts of PRs on open shelves, some require ordering (St Michael's Aberystwyth and St Padam, Llanbandam Fawr). PRs of Henfynyw and Llanddewi, Aberarth and some Cardiganshire Nonconformist registers on film. Census returns, electoral registers, newspapers, Petty Sessions, coroners, schools, shipping registers, crew agreements and log books, some parish, urban and rural district councils, old county of Cardiganshire.

Postal Research: Limited to specific enquiry: no charge made; longer searches: charge made.

Facilities: Toilets and public telephone on premises. No refreshment facilities but cafe/pub five minutes. Shops five minutes plus bookshop with local history publications.

Publications: *A Guide to PRs in St David's Diocese, Guide to Local Newspapers in Dyfed, An Introduction to Local Maps in Dyfed.* Free: notes for searchers, *Tracing Your Ancestors, Cardiganshire RO, Education in Cardiganshire, Records of the Borough of Cardigan, Cardiganshire Shipping and Harbour Records, Railways in Cardiganshire.*

Remarks: Historical county map on display.

Dyfed Archives
CARMARTHENSHIRE Record Office
County Hall
Carmarthen
Dyfed SA31 1JP.
Telephone: (0267) 233333 Ext 4182

Opening Hours: Monday to Thursday 9 am to 4.45 pm, Friday 9 am to 4.15 pm, first and third Saturday in month 9.30 am to 12.30 pm (by prior arrangement). Annual closure: public holidays; Christmas until day after New Year.

Car Parking: None.

Children: No specific ruling.

Disabled: Access; by prior arrangement.

Appointments System: No prior booking. Signing in by register. Ten to twelve seats, one film viewer, three fiche.

Document Ordering: Prior ordering by letter or telephone. Catalogue numbers necessary. Number at a time at archivist's discretion. Delivery five to ten minutes. Photocopying by staff on same day; PRs allowed. No facilities for typing or taping. Cameras permitted.

Records: Some Ts of PRs on open shelves, original PRs, local authority, pedigrees, old county of Carmarthenshire.

Postal Research: None.
Facilities: Toilets and public telephone on premises. Refreshments and restaurant/canteen, also room for own food. Cafe/pub five minutes. Shops two minutes.
Publications: *Carmarthenshire RO - A Survey of Archive Holdings, Guide to Local Newspapers in Dyfed, An Introduction to Local Maps in Dyfed.* Free: *Tracing Your Ancestors,* notes for searchers, publications list, Carmarthenshire RO etc.
Other Repositories: Carmarthen Library, St Peter's Street, Carmarthen, holds census returns and newspapers on film which are not available at the RO.
Places of Interest: Carmarthen Museum.
Tourist Office: Lammas Street, Carmarthen SA31 1HY. Telephone (0267) 231557.
Remarks: Some local authority records, vehicle licensing registers, Poor Law, hospital records and some estate agents' records require three working days prior notice. Historical county map on display.

NATIONAL LIBRARY OF WALES
Aberystwyth
Dyfed SY23 3BU.
Telephone: (0970) 623816

Opening Hours: Monday to Friday 9.30 am to 6 pm; Saturday 9.30 am to 5 pm. Annual closure: public holidays and first full week in October.
Car Parking: 100 places.
Children: Under 18 years by special arrangement.
Disabled: Disabled friendly.
Appointments System: Prior booking for seats unnecessary but necessary for viewers. Signing in by register plus identification and reader's ticket. 30 seats, eleven film viewers, two fiche.
Document Ordering: Prior ordering essential for Saturdays (by letter or telephone). Catalogue numbers necessary. Six at a time. Delivery twenty minutes. Last orders normally 4 pm; very restricted on Saturdays. Photocopying by staff and sent by post; PRs only with written permission of the incumbent. Typing/taping by prior arrangement. Cameras not allowed.
Records: Ts of PRs/BTs for some parishes require ordering. Original PRs/BTs (issued until more readers available), Nonconformists, Great Sessions, family, estate, Powys county.
Postal Research: Yes; charge made.
Facilities: Toilets and public telephone

on premises. Canteen/restaurant and room for own food, also drink vending machine. Cafe/pub ten minutes. Shops ten minutes plus bookshop with local history publications.
Publications: *A Guide to Genealogical Sources at the NLW.* Free: search fees, publications list.
Other Repositories: University of Wales, Penglais, Aberystwyth; National Monuments Record, Queens Road, Aberystwyth.
Places of Interest: Vale of Rheidol Narrow Gauge Steam Railway, Ceredigion Folk Museum, Arts Centre, Catherine Lewis Gallery and Print Room, Llywernog Silver-Lead Mine Museum.
Tourist Office: Eastgate, Aberystwyth SY23 2AR. Telephone (0970) 612125/611955.
Remarks: The NLW contains Bishop's Transcripts for Welsh parishes, these are not usually held at CROs unless on microfilm. Bags not allowed, storage facilities available. Maps showing Welsh Ecclesiastical parishes are on display. Donations box.

PEMBROKESHIRE Record Office
The Castle
Haverfordwest
Pembrokeshire
Dyfed SA61 2EF
Telephone: (0437) 3707

Opening Hours: Monday to Thursday 9 am to 4.45 pm, Friday 9 am to 4.15 pm, first and third Saturday in month 9.30 am to 12.30 pm (bank holiday weekends excepted). Annual closure: public holidays.
Car Parking: Limited
Children: No specific ruling.
Disabled: Access; toilet.
Appointments System: No prior booking. Signing in by register. Fifteen seats, two film viewers and two dual.
Document Ordering: No prior ordering. Number at a time at archivist's discretion. Delivery approximately five minutes. Last orders Monday to Thursday 4.30 pm, Friday 4 pm. Photocopying restricted; by staff on same day or if large quantity or busy, sent by post; DIY; PRs/BTs allowed. No facilities for typing or taping. Cameras permitted.
Records: A few Ts of PRs require ordering, PRs/BTs on fiche/film, local authority, family, old county of Pembrokeshire.
Postal Research: Limited to specific enquiry.
Facilities: Toilets but no public telephone. No refreshment facilities but cafe/pub five minutes. Shops five

minutes plus bookshop with local history publications.

Publications: *Guide to Local Newspapers in Dyfed, An Introduction to Local Maps in Dyfed.* Free: notes for searchers, *Tracing Your Ancestors*, Pembrokeshire RO (summary of main collections), *Shipping Records, Coal Mining in Pembrokeshire, Rebecca Riots.*

Other Repositories: The Public Library, Dew Street, Haverfordwest, Dyfed.

Places of Interest: Castle Museum and Art Gallery; Penrhos Cottage, Llanycefn; Scolton Manor Museum, Spittal; Pembroke Yeomanry Historical Trust, The Castle.

Tourist Office: 40 High Street, Haverfordwest SA62 6SD. Telephone (0437) 820144.

Remarks: Historical county map on display.

GLAMORGAN

GLAMORGAN Record Office
County Hall
Cathays Park
Cardiff CF1 3NE.
Telephone: (0222) 820284

Opening Hours: Tuesday to Thursday 9 am to 5 pm, Friday 9 am to 4.30 pm (closed Mondays). Annual closure: public holidays.

Car Parking: Nearby.

Children: Accompanied: ten years plus. Unaccompanied: twelve years plus when on school project.

Disabled: Access by prior arrangement.

Appointments System: Prior booking for seats not necessary, but necessary for viewers. Signing by register (CARN to be introduced). Seventeen seats, three film viewers, one fiche.

Document Ordering: No prior ordering. Three at a time; delivery five to ten minutes. Limited production between 12 noon and 2 pm. Last orders thirty minutes before closure. Photocopying by staff on same day or, if large quantity or busy, sent by post; PRs/BTs allowed to 1837 only. No facilities for typing or taping. Cameras not allowed.

Records: A few Ts of PRs/BTs on film, photocopied original PRs on open shelves, local authority, Nonconformists, business, family, old county of Glamorgan.

Postal Research: Yes; charge made.

Facilities: Toilets and public telephone on premises. Canteen; room for own food, also drink vending machine. Cafe/pub five minutes. Shops ten minutes plus bookshop with local history

publications.

Publications: Publications list.

Other Repositories: Cardiff Library, South Glamorgan Library HQ, St David's Link, Cardiff (local history plus newspaper collections); University College Library, Cardiff CF1 1XL; Welsh Folk Museum, St Fagan's, Cardiff CF5 6XB; Welsh Industrial and Maritime Museum, Cardiff.

Places of Interest: Llandaff Cathedral, Roman Catholic Cathedral, The Welch Regimental Museum, 1st Queen's Dragoon Guards Museum, National Museum of Wales.

Tourist Office: 8-14 Bridge Street, Cardiff CF5 2EJ. Telephone (0222) 227281.

Remarks: District Council, National Coal Board, Crew Agreements and many other collections require one week's prior notice. Limited storage facilities for bags. Historical county map on display. Donations box. Space in office is extremely limited.

WEST GLAMORGAN

WEST GLAMORGAN Area Record Office
County Hall
Oystermouth Road
Swansea.
Telephone: (0792) 471589

Opening Hours: Monday to Wednesday 9 am to 12.45 pm and 2 pm to 4.45 pm; Monday evening by appointment 5.30 pm to 7.30 pm. Closed Thursdays and Fridays. Annual closure: public holidays.

Car Parking: Yes.

Children: Accompanied: ten years plus. Unaccompanied: twelve years plus when on school project.

Disabled: Access; ramps.

Appointments System: Prior booking for seats unnecessary, but for viewers necessary. Signing by register (CARN to be introduced). Fifteen seats, four film viewers, and one fiche.

Document Ordering: Prior ordering essential for evening opening (by letter or telephone); advisable to check on documents held. Three at a time; delivery five to fifteen minutes. Photocopying by staff on same day or if large quantity or busy, sent by post; PRs/BTs allowed. No facilities for typing or taping. Cameras not allowed.

Records: Photocopies of original PRs on open shelves, BTs on film to 1837 only, local authority, West Glamorgan area.

Postal Research: Yes; charge made.

Facilities: Toilets and public telephone on premises. Canteen/restaurant and room for own food, also drink vending machine. Cafe/pub two minutes. Shops ten minutes plus bookshop with local history publications.

Publications: Publications list from West Glamorgan RO HQ, Cardiff.

Other Repositories: Swansea Central Library, Alexander Road, Swansea (local history collection); University College Library, Swansea SA2 8PP.

Places of Interest: Glynn Vivian Art Gallery and Museum, Maritime and Industrial Museum, University College of Swansea and Royal Institution of South Wales Museum.

Tourist Office: Singleton Street, Swansea SA1 3QN. Telephone (0792) 468321; Ty Croeso, Gloucester Place, Swansea SA1 1TY. Telephone (0792) 465204.

Remarks: Historical county map on display. Donations box. Bags not allowed, storage facilities available. Space in office extremely limited.

GWENT

GWENT County Record Office
County Hall
Cwmbran NP44 2XH.
Telephone: (0633) 838838

Opening Hours: Tuesday to Thursday 9.30 am to 5 pm, Friday 9.30 am to 4 pm (closed Mondays). Annual closure: public holidays plus following day.

Car Parking: 150 places.

Children: Accompanied: young children discouraged. Unaccompanied: by special arrangement with the school.

Disabled: Access

Appointments System: Prior booking necessary (24 hours). Signing in by register plus CARN. Ten seats, one film viewer, one dual.

Document Ordering: Prior ordering by letter or telephone. Three or one bundle at a time. Delivery five to ten minutes. Photocopying by staff on same day or, if large quantity or busy, sent by post; PRs allowed. No facilities for typing or taping. Cameras by special arrangement.

Records: Original PRs; parish; local authority; diocesan records for Brecon, Swansea and Monmouth.

Postal Research: Yes; charge made.

Facilities: Toilets and public telephone on premises. Canteen/restaurant and area for own food, also drink vending machine. Shops 25 minutes plus bookshop with local history publications.

Publications: County map for sale, publications list, guides to research, leaflet on Gwent CRO and ROs of Wales.

Other Repositories: Central Library, John Frost Square, Newport (local history collection).

Places of Interest: Llanyrafon Farm; Royal Monmouthshire Royal Engineers Museum, Monmouth; Vale of Usk.

Remarks: Historical county map on display. Bags not allowed, storage facilities available at duty officer's desk.

GWYNEDD

ANGLESEY Area Record Office
Shirehall
Llangefni
Anglesey
Gwynedd LL77 7TW.
Telephone: (0248) 750262 Ext 269

Opening Hours: Monday to Friday 9 am to 1 pm and 2 pm to 5 pm. Annual closure: public holidays and first full week in November.

Car Parking: Limited.

Children: Not allowed.

Disabled: Arrangements can be made to study documents on ground floor.

Appointments System: Prior booking unnecessary for seats but necessary for viewers. Signing in by register. Eight seats, two film viewers, one fiche.

Document Ordering: Prior ordering by letter or telephone. Catalogue numbers necessary. Two at a time; delivery two to four minutes. Photocopying by staff on same day. Typing/taping permitted. Cameras not allowed.

Records: Ts of some PRs on open shelves, original PRs, local authority, family, business, old county of Anglesey.

Postal Research: None.

Facilities: Toilets and public telephone on premises. No refreshment facilities but cafe/pub five minutes. Shops five minutes plus bookshop with local history publications.

Publications: Lists of holdings for inspection.

Places of Interest: Museum of Childhood; Beaumaris Gaol; Plas Newydd, Llanfairpwll; Menai Suspension Bridge.

Tourist Office: Penyrorsedd, Llangefni. Telephone (0248) 724666.

Remarks: Bags not allowed, storage facilities available. Historical county map on display.

Gwynedd Archives and Museums Service
CAERNARVON Area Record Office
Victoria Dock
Caernarvon.

Correspondence to:
County Offices

Shire Hall Street
Caernarvon LL55 1SH.
Telephone: (0286) 4121

Opening Hours: Monday, Tuesday, Thursday, Friday 9.30 am to 12.30 pm and 1.30 pm to 5 pm; Wednesday 9.30 am to 12.30 pm and 1.30 pm to 7 pm. Annual closure: public holidays, Christmas to New Year and second full week in October.
Car Parking: Nearby
Children: No specific ruling.
Disabled: Access; ramps; wide doors
Appointments System: Prior booking unnecessary for seats, but necessary for viewers. Signing in by register plus CARN. 24 seats, four film viewers, one fiche.
Document Ordering: No prior ordering. Three documents or one volume of newspapers at a time. Delivery five minutes. Photocopying by staff on same day. No facilities for typing or taping. Cameras not allowed.
Records: Original PRs, some PRs on fiche/film, local authority, business, shipping, photographs and prints, old counties of Anglesey and Merioneth.
Postal Research: Specific limited enquiry; no charge made.
Facilities: Toilets but no public telephone. No refreshment facilities but cafe/pub five minutes. Shops five minutes plus bookshop with local history publications.
Publications: Office has active book/pamphlet publishing policy. Free leaflets: *List of Caernarvon PRs, Family History, History of Houses.*
Other Repositories: University College of North Wales Library, Bangor; Royal Welch Fusiliers Museum, Caernarvon Castle, Caernarvon (regimental records).
Places of Interest: Caernarvon Castle, *Seiont II* Maritime Museum, Segontium Roman Fort Museum.
Tourist Office: Oriel Pendeitsh, Caernarvon LL55 2BP. Telephone (0286) 2232.
Remarks: Some modern council records, rate books etc require 48 hours prior notice. Bags not allowed, storage facilities available. Historical county map on display.

Gwynedd Archives and Museum Service
Area Record Office
Cae Penarlag
DOLGELLAU
Gwynedd LL40 2YB.
Telephone: (0341) 422341 Ext 260

Opening Hours: Monday, Tuesday, Thursday, Friday 9 am to 1 pm and 1.55 pm to 4.45 pm; Wednesday 9 am to 1 pm and 1.55 pm to 7 pm. Annual closure: public holidays and first full week in November.
Car Parking: Limited
Children: Accompanied: no specific ruling. Unaccompanied: school age.
Disabled: Ramp; toilet.
Appointments System: Prior booking for seats unnecessary, but for viewers necessary. Signing in by register. Fourteen seats, two film viewers, one fiche.
Document Ordering: Prior ordering by letter or telephone. Catalogue numbers necessary. Three at a time. Last orders Monday, Tuesday, Thursday, Friday 12.25 pm and 4.25 pm; Wednesday 12.25 pm and 6.25 pm. Photocopying by staff on same day or, if large quantity or busy, sent by post; PRs with written consent of incumbent. No facilities for typing or taping. Cameras not allowed.
Records: Original PRs and Nonconformist registers on fiche/film, Quarter Sessions, family, estate, business, local authority, old county of Merioneth.
Postal Research: Very limited; no charge made.
Facilities: Toilets but no public telephone. No refreshment facilities but cafe/pub five minutes. Shops five minutes plus bookshop with local history publications.
Publications: Various
Places of Interest: Snowdonia National Park, Mawddach Estuary, Cymmen Abbey.
Tourist Office: The Bridge, Dolgellau LL40 1LF. Telephone (0341) 422888.
Remarks: Some public, official and private records require 24 hours prior notice. Bags not allowed, storage facilities available. Historical county map on display.

POWYS

POWYS Archives
Library Headquarters
Cefnllys Road
Llandrindod Wells
Powys LD1 5LD.
Telephone: (0597) 2212

Opening Hours: Monday to Thursday 9 am to 12.30 pm and 1.30 pm to 5 pm, Friday 9 am to 12.30 pm and 1.30 pm to 4 pm. Annual closure: public holidays.
Car Parking: Nearby.

Children: Twelve years plus and only those on examination projects if unaccompanied.

Disabled: Access by rear entrance; by prior arrangement.

Appointments System: Prior booking essential (at least two weeks notice: leave telephone number for contact). Signing in by register. Five seats. Viewing facilities shared with library.

Document Ordering: Prior ordering by letter or telephone. Catalogue numbers generally unnecessary. Generally one at a time. Delivery ten minutes. Photocopying by staff on same day, or if large quantity or busy, sent by post. No facilities for typing or taping. Cameras by special arrangement.

Records: No PRs/BTs. Local history material, old county of Powys.

Postal Research: None

Facilities: Toilets but no public telephone. No refreshment facilities but cafe/pub five minutes. Shops five minutes plus bookshop with local history publications.

Publications: Free: *Powys Archives, County ROs in Wales.*

Places of Interest: Llandrindod Museum.

Tourist Office: Town Hall, Llandrindod Wells LD1 6AA. Telephone (0597) 2600.

Remarks: Mainly modern (20th century) local authority records (for District and former County Councils) stored elsewhere require two weeks' prior notice. Directories, local histories, journals and census are at Area Libraries in Newtown (0686 26934), Brecon (0874 3346) and at library HQ (0597 2212). Facilities for bags in search room. The Local History Collection, in the same building, contains printed material including newspapers and census on film: visits by arrangement. Many of the official and non-official records are held by the NLW. Archive Service is under review.

CHANNEL ISLANDS

GUERNSEY

The Greffe
Royal Court House
St Peter Port
GUERNSEY
Channel Islands
Telephone: (0481) 25277

Opening Hours: Monday to Friday. Enquiries in writing in first instance.

Records: Civil registration of births, marriages and deaths; wills and administrations; family; deeds; judicial records for Guernsey; World War II German archives.

Other Repositories: Priaulx Library, Candie, St Peter Port (local and family records); La Societe Guernesiase, St Sauveur, Guernsey.

Places of Interest: Candie Gardens, Castle Cornet, Fort Grey, German Occupation Museum, Hauteville House.

Tourist Office: Crown Pier, St Peter Port. Telephone (0481) 23552 (enquiries) 23555 (accommodation).

Remarks: For Roman Catholic records apply to the Bishop of Portsmouth, Hampshire, England. Further reading *How to Trace Your Ancestors in Guernsey* by D W Le Poidevin (Taunton 1978).

JERSEY

Judicial Greffe
States Building
Royal Square
St Helier
JERSEY
Channel Islands
Telephone: (0534) 77111

Opening Hours: Monday to Friday enquiries in writing in first instance Signing in Fee charged

Records: Civil Registration of births, marriages and deaths; wills and administrations; Royal Court; deeds.

Other Repositories: Societe Jersiase, The Library, The Museum, 9 Pier Road, Jersey (Channel Islands' history).

Places of Interest: St Peter's Bunker Museum, Elizabeth Castle, Jersey Museum, La Hougue Museum, Sir Francis Cook Gallery.

Tourist Office: Weighbridge, St Helier. Telephone (0534) 78000/31958 (accommodation), 24779 (local information).

Remarks: Original records of baptisms, marriages and burials held by local incumbents. For Roman Catholic records apply to the Bishop of Portsmouth, Hampshire, England. Census returns for the Channel Islands from 1841 are in the PRO Census Search Room, London. Further reading: *Genealogical Research in the Channel Islands (Society of Genealogists' Magazine* Vol 19 No 5, March 1978).

INDEX TO PLACES

Middlesbrough 9
Mitcham 39
Moray 86
Morden 39
Newcastle upon Tyne 59 68 69
Newham 40
Newport (IOW) 23
North Gosforth 59
North Shields 68
Northallerton 74
Northampton 58
Norwich 58
Nottingham 60
Oldham 56
Oxford 61
Paisley 92
Perth 92
Plymouth 13
Portsmouth 17
Preston 26
Ramsgate 25
Reading 6
Richmond 41
Rochdale 56
Romford 35
Rotherham 76
Ruthin 93
Sale 56
Salford 54
Selkirk 84
Sevenoaks 26
Sheepscar 79
Sheffield 77
Shrewsbury 61
Smethwick 72
Solihull 72
South Shields 68

Southampton 18
Southend on Sea 16
Southwark 41
St Andrews 85
St Helens (Merseyside) 56
St Helens (Worcester) 19
St Helier 99
St Peter Port 99
Stafford 63
Stalybridge 55
Stirling 84
Stockport 54
Stratford 40
Stratford upon Avon 69
Strood 25
Sutton (Surrey) 42
Swansea 96
Swiss Cottage 30
Tameside 55
Taunton 62
Tower Hamlets 42
Trowbridge 73
Truro 9
Twickenham 42
Uxbridge 35
Wakefield 79
Walsall 73
Walthamstow 43
Wandsworth 43
Warwick 70
Westminster 44 45
Wigan 55
Winchester 17
Wolverhampton 73
Worcester 19
York 74 75

LONDON BOROUGHS OF:

Barking 28
Barnet 28
Bexley 29
Brent 29
Bromley 29
Camden 30
Chelsea 37
Chiswick 31
Croydon 31
Dagenham 28
Ealing 31
Enfield 32
Finsbury 32
Fulham 34
Greenwich 33
Hackney 33
Hammersmith 34
Haringey 34
Harrow 35
Havering 35
Hillingdon 35

Holborn 30
Hounslow 36
Islington 36
Kensington 37
Kew 40
Kingston upon Thames 37
Lambeth 38
Lewisham 38
Marylebone 39
Merton 39
Mitcham 39
Morden 39
Newham 40
Richmond 41
Southwark 41
Sutton 42
Tower Hamlets 42
Twickenham 42
Walthamstow 43
Wandsworth 43
Westminster 44

REPOSITORIES IN:

British Library, Newspaper Library, Colindale 46
British Library, Department of Manuscripts 46
British Library, India Office Library and Records 46
Corporation of London Record Office 47
Dr Williams's Library 51
General Register Office, St Catherine's House 48
Greater London Record Office 48
Guildhall Library, Department of Manuscripts 49
House of Lords Record Office 45
Huguenot Society of Great Britain and Ireland 49
Imperial War Museum, Department of Documents 49

National Army Museum 45
National Maritime Museum, Greenwich 33
Principal Registry of the Family Division, Somerset House 50
Public Record Office -
  Chancery Lane 50
  Kew 40
Society of Genealogists 47
United Reform Church History Society 50
United Synagogue, Office of the Chief Rabbi 43
Westminster Abbey Muniment Room and Library 44
Westminster Diocesan Archives 44
Westminster, House of Lords 45

INDEX TO COUNTIES

NOTES

NOTES